THE SAVVY COOK

@IzyHossack

An Hachette UK Company
www.hachette.co.uk

First published in Great Britain in 2017
by Mitchell Beazley, a division of
Octopus Publishing Group Ltd
Carmelite House, 50 Victoria Embankment
London EC4Y 0DZ
www.octopusbooksusa.com

This edition published in North America in 2017.

Text and photographs copyright © Izy Hossack 2017
Design and layout copyright © Octopus Publishing
Group Ltd 2017

Distributed in the US by Hachette Book Group
1290 Avenue of the Americas, 4th and 5th Floors
New York, NY 10020

Distributed in Canada by Canadian Manda Group
664 Annette St., Toronto, Ontario, Canada M6S 2C8

ISBN 978-1-78472-270-8
Printed and bound in China
10 9 8 7 6 5 4 3 2 1

Publisher: Alison Starling
Art Director: Juliette Norsworthy
Design: Isabel de Cordova
Assistant Editor: Ella Parsons
Senior Production Controller: Allison Gonsalves

Author portrait on page 7 by Portia Hunt

RECIPE NOTES

Standard level spoon measurements are used in all recipes.
1 tablespoon = one 15ml spoon
1 teaspoon = one 5ml spoon

When reading an ingredients list, if an action comes
after the ingredient, do that action after measuring the
ingredient. If the action is before the ingredient, do the
action and then measure. For example:
½ cup dates, pitted: measure out 1 cup dates with
their pits inside and THEN remove the pits
½ cup pitted dates: remove and discard the pits
from the dates first and THEN measure out 1 cup dates.

When storing dishes in the freezer, it's best to put on a label
saying what's in it and when you made it.

When a recipe states: "bring to a boil, then reduce the heat
to a simmer," place a pan of liquid over high heat until large
bubbles appear in the liquid (this is usually done for water
in which you are cooking grains). Once those large bubbles
appear, reduce the heat to low or medium-low so that the
liquid is only gently bubbling.

Eggs should be large unless otherwise stated. The USDA
advises that no one should eat foods containing raw eggs.
This book contains dishes made with raw or lightly cooked
eggs. High-risk persons such as infants, young children,
older adults, pregnant women, and people with weakened
immune systems should avoid uncooked or lightly cooked
dishes made with eggs. Once prepared, these dishes should
be kept refrigerated and used promptly.

To measure out dry ingredients such as flour, ground nuts
and oats consistently, it is important to use the same
method each time. The best way to do this is the "fluff,
spoon, and sweep method": first fluff up the dry ingredient
in its container, then use a spoon to gently scoop it into the
cup measure (don't tap or shake the cup), and fill it so the
cup is piled high. Lastly, use the back of a knife to sweep
the excess dry ingredient off so that it is level in the cup.

THE SAVVY COOK

@IzyHossack

MITCHELL BEAZLEY

CONTENTS

Key:

V Vegetarian

VG Vegan

DF Dairy Free

GF Gluten Free

EF Egg Free

LS Low Added Sugar

NS No Added Sugar

> ## "You stand in the kitchen at 7 p.m. peering into the fridge wondering what to make..."

Lots of my friends find the idea of cooking a bit daunting. It's not that they don't have the ability to make themselves a meal, but they are lacking in the confidence that they can make something delicious and inexpensive. As someone starting university this year, I wasn't sure how to tackle the new challenges I'd face. Cooking in a small, basic kitchen is a challenge in itself—many of us don't have a lot of equipment, fridge/freezer, or general storage space. Along with that, budgeting a paycheck or weekly stipend of loan money, which barely covers your rent, is a scary prospect. On top of all that, you'd like to be healthy! But you don't have the cash to splash on daily avocado toast and the idea of having to cook kale freaks you out. You stand in the kitchen at 7 p.m. peering into the fridge wondering what to make with the random head of cauliflower you bought on a whim because it was on offer. Another challenge: You have no damn idea what to cook.

That's where this book comes in— helping overcome the idea that healthy, cheap cooking is arduous and tasteless, for a new cook operating on a tight budget and a busy schedule. With things like menu plans, clever alternatives to meat (although I include omnivore options, all my recipes are vegetarian), dishes that can be prepped ahead of time, and ideas for giving last-night's leftovers a makeover, these recipes will be kind to your body, wallet, and free time. They'll also give a little help to the earth. Consuming fewer animal products and more local, seasonal food in general is a simple way to reduce your environmental impact, boost your health, and leave you with some extra moolah. It's not about health fads, "antioxidants," or obscure ingredients. Just honest, nourishing, and delicious cooking that will make you glow inside and out!

THE BASICS

Must-have Kitchen Tools

Essential

CHEF'S KNIFE—a good chef's knife saves time and is also safer to use. Get one about 8 inches long from the tip of the blade to the end of the handle. I like French Sabatier knives, as they are good-quality and not too expensive. Remember, an unsharp knife is more likely to slip on food, leading to accidents.

PARING KNIFE—a smaller knife, for small, precise slicing jobs like removing the tops from strawberries.

WOODEN CUTTING BOARD—wood is better than plastic for hygiene, your knives, and the environment.

BAKING SHEET—use a flat one with a slight rim.

WOODEN SPOON—use for baking, sautéing, and stirring sauces and grains.

SILICONE SPATULA—flexible and good for scraping sauces out of pans, stirring oatmeal, risotto, or bread dough, sautéing, and scraping cake batter from bowls.

METAL SPATULA (OR PANCAKE TURNER)—use for flipping pancakes or flatbreads, roasted vegetables, and removing food from skillets.

MEASURING SPOONS AND CUPS—you can use a regular teaspoon for adding spices when you are cooking, but when baking, you do need a set of measuring spoons, as well as a set of measuring cups.

DIGITAL KITCHEN SCALES—use for weighing out ingredients that are not appropriate for measuring by volume in cups.

VEGETABLE PEELER—use for peeling butternut squash, or sweet/regular potatoes and peeling vegetables into ribbons. Create shavings of cheese (especially Parmesan) or chocolate for decorating cakes.

HANDHELD (IMMERSION) BLENDER—these often come with an attachment to turn it into a mini food processor. Good for making pesto, pastes, purees, soups, and flours.

BOX GRATER—this is indispensable for shredding cheese, apples, carrots, and zucchini.

CASSEROLE DISH OR DEEP ROASTING PAN—needed for any casserole-type dish, such as pasta bakes, pies, or bread pudding. At a pinch, it can be used for baking simple cakes or roasting vegetables.

GOOD-QUALITY NONSTICK SKILLET—you need a medium or large skillet depending on the number of people you are cooking for. Check that the handle is heat-resistant (Bakelite handles can be placed under high heat) if you are making skillet pizzas (see page 158).

LARGE, MEDIUM, AND SMALL SAUCEPANS/POTS—always useful to have a range of sizes! Especially good if they all have lids, but sometimes you can just use a plate or baking sheet as a makeshift lid anyway.

MIXING BOWLS—These are super-useful for baking, but even if you don't like to bake, mixing bowls are always helpful. Toss together a salad in one, or mix ingredients for making fritters, frittatas, and quiches.

Useful equipment

GARLIC PRESS (GARLIC CRUSHER)—I love these because I hate having garlicky hands. And you don't even have to peel the cloves before putting them into a garlic press.

MICROPLANE GRATER—for grating the zest of citrus fruits, chocolate, cheese, or even garlic (instead of using a garlic press or mincing garlic by hand).

BAMBOO GINGER GRATER—amazing! You can grate ginger root without peeling it first. Find them online.

COUNTERTOP BLENDER OR FOOD PROCESSOR—this can take on more heavy-duty kitchen tasks than a handheld blender, such as making cake batter, blending soup, and making bread crumbs (which you can only do with a handheld blender if you have the attachment to turn it into a mini food processor).

BAKING PANS—I like to have a standard 2-pound loaf pan, an 8-inch round cake pan, and an 8-inch square brownie pan. Also include a small, 1-pound loaf pan, an 8-inch bundt pan, and a 12-cup muffin pan if you like baking.

MEASURING BEAKER—useful both for measuring liquids and other ingredients and for blending ingredients with a handheld (immersion) blender.

Ingredients

Eggs

I use large, free-range eggs. When baking, always let the eggs come to room temperature first—place in a bowl of warm (not hot) water and let sit for 5 to 10 minutes.

Butter

You can freeze butter for up to 3 months and use frozen butter right away by shredding it. Buy unsalted for baking.

Oils

Buy light, refined olive oil, as it has very little flavor and is perfect for cooking and baking.

CANOLA OIL—another favorite of mine. It is neutral in flavor and has a vibrant yellow color. I buy cold pressed.

COCONUT OIL—makes a good substitute for butter in vegan baking, as it is a saturated fat, so is solid at room temperature. "Virgin" coconut oil has a coconut flavor and "refined" coconut oil (which is cheaper) has no flavor.

EXTRA VIRGIN OLIVE OIL—keep this for salad dressings and other uses (such as for pesto, drizzling over soup, or dipping bread into).

Seeds

Seeds are packed with healthy mono—and polyunsaturated fats, fiber, and protein.

GROUND FLAX SEED—in many of my baking recipes, eggs are either not used or can be substituted with ground flax seed mixed with water, a vegan egg replacement suitable for baking.

CHIA SEEDS—I use these occasionally and sometimes slip them into overnight oats for a fiber boost, or use them as a vegan egg substitute in baking.

SUNFLOWER AND PUMPKIN SEEDS—these are cheap and cheerful! I especially like pumpkin seeds in salads because of their color. Sunflower seeds are delicious raw, but even tastier when toasted in a skillet until crisp.

SESAME SEEDS—these are packed with flavor. They can be used for both sweet and savory recipes.

Oats

I love oats, as they are high in fiber and protein. Some "gluten-free" or "gluten-free option" recipes may contain oats. I have suggested using oats that are certified gluten free, but some celiacs are not able to eat oats due to cross-contamination. If you aren't able to tolerate oats, I have given suitable alternatives wherever possible.

REGULAR ROLLED OATS—also called porridge or quick-cooking oats, these oats are milled quite finely.

OLD-FASHIONED ROLLED OATS—these are chunkier and take longer to cook.

Nuts

I keep a range of nuts in the pantry for baking and store them in the refrigerator or freezer to stop them from going rancid. I use almonds or ground almonds, almond butter, or, occasionally, almond milk.

Milk and nondairy milk

I generally use nondairy milk. For savory recipes, make sure it doesn't contain any added sugar. If you're relying on nondairy milk for your calcium intake, check the label to ensure it has added calcium, as the "organic" varieties usually don't. Cow's milk with 1% or low fat, 2% or reduced fat, and whole will also work in my recipes.

Yogurt and cheese

I often use Parmesan for topping my pasta dishes—although technically it isn't vegetarian, as the rennet (an enzyme) used in it is extracted from cows' stomachs. One of the many vegetarian cheeses available will be fine—just check the label to make sure it's suitable.

I love using plain whole milk yogurt for both savory and sweet dishes. If using soy yogurt for savory dishes, make sure it's unsweetened and unflavored.

Coconut products

CREAMED COCONUT—to use, microwave the package on high in short bursts, kneading until liquid. Alternatively, place the package in a bowl, cover with hot water, and let stand for 20 minutes to soften, then knead. Once liquid, open the package and pour it into a clean, lidded glass jar, which can be kept in the cupboard at room temperature for a few months. In warmer weather, store in the refrigerator. When ready to use, microwave the jar of creamed coconut (without the lid on) until liquid OR place it in a bowl of just-boiled water and leave it to soften.

1 (7oz) package (when mixed with hot water) will be equal to 2 (14oz) cans of coconut milk.

COCONUT CREAM—can be bought in small cartons, but it's usually more expensive than simply buying a can of coconut milk, chilling the can overnight, then scooping off the soft, creamy stuff that accumulates on the top.

COCONUT MILK—if you have excess canned coconut milk, freeze it in ice cubes, then pop each cube into a small plastic bag and freeze for use another day.

DRY (DESICCATED) UNSWEETENED SHREDDED COCONUT—toat the coconut in a dry skillet over medium heat, stirring continuously. Watch it carefully (it burns very easily); as soon as it turns golden, immediately remove.

Aromatics and herbs

RED ONIONS—to prepare, remove the pointy tip and root base of the onion. Cut straight down the middle, from top to base, then peel off the papery skin and discard it. If you only need half, wrap the other half in plastic wrap or place in a lidded container and chill for up to 2 weeks.

GARLIC—a "clove" is the little segment that you separate out from the head of garlic. One clove of finely chopped garlic is about a scant teaspoon. Always peel garlic before using unless you have a garlic press. Store in a cool place.

GINGER ROOT—keep ginger root in a small pot of soil with the cut/broken edge just nestling slightly in the soil. Water it when the soil feels dry. This will keep the ginger fresh for months! Rinse it before cutting off a chunk to use.

CHILES—finely chop and freeze in a plastic bag.

CILANTRO—store by placing in a jar with just enough water to cover the end of the stems by ¾ inch. Cover with a plastic bag and chill for 1 to 2 weeks (you may need to change the water after 1 week).

BASIL—never refrigerate the leaves, as they will turn into a dark mush. Buy a plant to use for garnishes and to make pesto, or blend a large bunch of basil and freeze in ice-cube trays.

THYME—good as a potted plant. If you buy loose thyme, roll it up in a few layers of slightly damp paper towels and enclose it in a small plastic bag to store in the refrigerator.

SAGE—good as a potted plant. It's pretty hardy!

DRIED HERBS—in my view the only ones worth buying are thyme, oregano (or marjoram), and rosemary. I buy a dried herb mix called "herbes de Provence," but mixed dried herbs will work just as well.

Food	Amount at start	Amount when cooked	Cook Method	Storage
Green lentils	½ cup	⅔ cup	Rinse. Cover with water, add a pinch of salt and 1 teaspoon vinegar, and bring to a boil. Turn down to simmer for 20 to 30 minutes. Drain.	Keep in a container in the refrigerator for 5 days.
Short-grain brown rice	½ cup	1½ cups	Rinse, cover with water in a saucepan, and bring to a boil. Turn down to simmer for 30 minutes. Drain, return to the pan, and cover with a lid or large plate for 5 minutes.	COOL QUICKLY (rinse with cold water or spread out on plate). Store in the refrigerator for 1 day or flat-pack and freeze for 2 months.
Long-grain brown rice	½ cup	1½ cups	Rinse, cover with water in a saucepan, and bring to a boil. Turn down to simmer for 20 minutes. Drain, return to the pan, and cover with lid or large plate for 5 minutes.	COOL QUICKLY (see above). Refrigerate for 1 day or flat-pack and freeze for 2 months.
Quinoa	½ cup	1⅔ cups	Rinse. Cover with water and bring to a boil. Turn down to simmer for 10 minutes. Drain, return to the pan, and cover for 5 minutes.	Keep in a container in the refrigerator for 5 days.
Pearl barley	½ cup	1¾ cups	Rinse, cover with water, and bring to a boil. Turn down to simmer for 25 to 30 minutes. Drain and rinse, return to the pan, and cover for 5 minutes.	Keep in a container in the refrigerator for 5 days.
Short-cut pasta	½ cup	1 cup	Cover with boiling, salted water in a saucepan. Bring to a boil and then simmer according to the package directions. Drain.	Keep in a container in the refrigerator for 5 days.
Chick peas (garbanzo beans)	½ cup	1½ cups	Soak overnight. Drain. Cover with water in a saucepan and bring to a boil. Turn down to simmer for 1 to 1½ hours.	Cover with cooking liquid ideally or water. Keep in the refrigerator for 3 days or freeze for 2 months.
Cannellini beans	½ cup	1½ cups	Soak overnight. Drain. Cover with water in a saucepan and bring to a boil. Turn down to simmer for 30 to 45 minutes.	Cover with cooking liquid ideally or water. Keep in the refrigerator for 3 days or freeze for 2 months.
Black beans	½ cup	1½ cups	Soak overnight. Drain. Cover with water in a saucepan and bring to a boil. Turn down to simmer for 45 to 60 minutes.	Cover with cooking liquid ideally or water. Keep in the refrigerator for 3 days or freeze for 2 months.
Red kidney beans	½ cup	1½ cups	Soak overnight. Drain. Cover with water in a saucepan and bring to a boil. Turn down to simmer for 1 to 1¼ hours.	Cover with cooking liquid ideally or water. Keep in the refrigerator for 3 days or freeze for 2 months.
Puy lentils	½ cup	1¼ cups	Rinse. Cover with water, add a pinch of salt and 1 teaspoon vinegar, and bring to a boil. Turn down to simmer for 30 to 45 minutes. Drain.	Keep in a container in the refrigerator for 5 days.
Sweet potato	3½oz	2½oz	Peel or keep skin on. Cut into 1¼-inch cubes. Toss with olive oil to coat and sprinkle with salt. Roast in the oven at 350°F for 30 minutes.	Keep in a container in the refrigerator for 3 days.
White potato	3½oz	2½oz	Prep as for sweet potato. Cook in very salty boiling water for 5 minutes. Toss with olive oil to coat and sprinkle with salt. Roast in the oven at 350°F for 40 to 50 minutes.	Keep in a container in the refrigerator for 3 days.

Spices

BASICS—ground cumin, coriander, cinnamon, (sweet) smoked paprika, cayenne pepper, or crushed red pepper.

EXTRAS—garam masala, Chinese five spice, turmeric, star anise, cardamom, fennel seed. Buy packages of spices in supermarket world foods sections, online, or in Middle Eastern and Indian grocery stores.

Miso

Miso is a paste made from fermented soy beans and salt (similar to soy sauce). It has a rich, salty, umami (savory) taste, which adds a unique depth of flavor to dishes. I buy miso from Chinese, Thai, or Japanese markets or online through specialty retailers. Always check the label on the package—you don't want "miso soup paste" or "miso glaze," which will contain other ingredients. The ingredients of miso should be soy beans, salt, water, and rice (plus possibly "koji," which is used to ferment the soy beans). It keeps well in the refrigerator for a few months.

There are a few types of miso—white (shiro), yellow (shinshu), or red (aka). The darker the color, the stronger the flavor. I suggest trying white miso first, then when you are used to the flavor, move on to a darker miso. Miso is also made from other ingredients such as barley or chick peas (garbanzo beans), but is usually more expensive.

Vegetables

TOMATOES—store tomatoes at room temperature. If they are starting to go wrinkly, roast them, whole or cut up, with a drizzle of olive oil in an oven preheated to 400°F for 30 minutes. Use in a salad or sandwich, or freeze for later.

BAGGED SALAD GREENS—arugula, spinach, pea shoots, and mixed salad greens. If the bag doesn't say that they're ready to eat, always rinse, drain, and dry the salad greens before eating. To dry without a salad spinner, twist the washed greens up in a clean kitchen towel, then swing the bundle around outside to remove excess water.

BUTTERNUT SQUASH—this can be stored at room temperature for a month or two.

FROZEN PEAS, SHELLED EDAMAME, AND CORN KERNELS—so useful and make a pantry meal less sad!

CANNED CORN KERNELS—check that they have no added sugar or salt.

REGULAR AND SWEET POTATOES—keep in a cool, dark place. You shouldn't refrigerate regular potatoes, but you can refrigerate sweet potatoes. If green patches appear on regular potatoes, throw them away, as the green parts are poisonous. You can simply snap off any "eyes" and still use the potato. I usually leave the skins for the enhanced nutrition and texture—just give them a good scrub.

Flours

When mixing a gluten-containing flour (such as wheat/rye/spelt flour) into wet ingredients, DO NOT overmix if you are baking muffins, cakes, or scones, otherwise you will get tough, dense results due to an overdeveloped gluten network. This matters less for brownies and cookies, but still avoid overmixing the batter. For recipes that contain yeast, you usually mix and knead the dough as much as possible to develop the gluten network.

WHOLE-WHEAT FLOUR—whole-wheat flour contains more gluten and is useful for baking bread; otherwise use whole-wheat pastry flour, which has less gluten and is better for baking cakes and cookies.

ALL-PURPOSE FLOUR—even when I use whole-wheat flour, I often mix it with some all-purpose flour for a better texture.

BREAD FLOUR—this contains more gluten than all-purpose flour, so use for bread baking.

CHICK PEA (GARBANZO BEAN) FLOUR—a.k.a. besan flour. Find it in the world foods section of the supermarket or Indian or Middle Eastern grocery stores. It is gluten free and high in protein.

BUCKWHEAT FLOUR—a gluten-free flour that is sometimes used in baking recipes.

OAT FLOUR—wheat free but only gluten free if you use certified gluten-free oats. Even if certified gluten free, celiacs may still not be able to consume it safely.

Grains

QUINOA—choose premium-quality organic whole-grain quinoa and rinse it before use.

PEARL BARLEY—a chewy, nubbly little grain, pearl barley is good in stews and salads. It contains gluten.

COUSCOUS—this is quick to cook, so it's perfect for lunch. It contains gluten.

PASTA—there are many different shapes of pasta and pastas made with different flours. You can also get brown rice pasta for gluten-free dishes.

BROWN RICE—I like short-grain brown rice for its incredible flavor and texture. You need to be very careful when cooking and cooling rice, as the bacteria that live in rice can produce toxic, heat-resistant spores that may cause food poisoning or, scarily, even kill you. If you are planning on keeping rice in the refrigerator, it's vitally important to cool it down as quickly as possible after cooking it. Either rinse it under cold running water or spread it out on a plate or baking sheet. Once cooled, place in a lidded container in the refrigerator or flat-pack it in individual portions in zipper sandwich bags, then freeze. Store in the refrigerator for 1 day or in the freezer for 2 months—label and date the bag. When reheating, make sure the rice is piping hot.

Sweeteners

All sugars are sugar, and in my opinion there's nothing special about the unrefined sugars that you can buy nowadays, except for their flavor. Just use granulated sugar when appropriate. Some granulated sugars may not be considered vegan, so just check the brand you're using is vegan-friendly, if needed.

Liquid sweeteners can be useful for salad dressings or drizzling on pancakes, so I tend to keep honey and real maple syrup (without any added flavorings) in the refrigerator. Some brands of maple syrup may not be considered vegan, so check the syrup before using, if needed.

LEFTOVERS

Refer to pages 228–233 to help you plan meals and use up leftovers. The most efficient way to spend your time in the kitchen is to batch-prep individual ingredients for the week—boiling grains to keep in the refrigerator or freezer, roasting or steaming different vegetables, blending a pesto, and making salad dressings.

Below each recipe there is a box of "leftover" ingredients (see example box below). These are perishable (cheeses, vegetables, open cans of beans) or niche ingredients (miso, creamed coconut). Referring to the "leftovers table" on pages 228–233, use these boxes to find out how to use any leftover ingredients.

Whenever I cook grains, beans and other legumes, or roast vegetables for a recipe, I double or triple the batch, then store them in the refrigerator or freezer to use through the week. It's a good habit to get into and will save you money and time, plus it's a more eco-friendly way to cook (especially the roasted veggies).

LEFTOVERS: see pp. 228–233

- Butternut squash
- Creamed coconut
- Potatoes
- Scallions

FOOD WASTE

Food waste is a big issue for first-world countries. We all get outraged when we see supermarkets dumping expired food (due to legal obligations), but it's the food waste in our homes that we can most easily tackle. Food gets lost at the back of the refrigerator and forgotten about until it's gone moldy. Here are some pointers on how to tackle your cooking and shopping habits:

● Start food planning so that you don't stray from your shopping list.

● Stop falling for the "3 for the price of 2" offers if you know you will never eat it all.

● Start cooking grains and beans from scratch and freezing them rather than relying on cans or packages of ready-cooked food.

● Use food more efficiently, such as trying to buy local and seasonal food as much as possible.

● Try to look at where your food is coming from the next time you go food shopping; it can make a difference to the environment if it has been flown in from far away.

● Go to farmers' markets, as the produce is more likely to be local and you can ask about their farming practices.

● Buying produce at farmers' markets also helps the environment, as it's not usually covered in plastic packaging.

ORGANIC FOOD

Don't feel obligated to buy organic fruit and vegetables, and here is why I don't always buy organic:

● Organic fruit and vegetables are not necessarily pesticide free, so they still require rinsing before eating, and as farmers use livestock manure to fertilize organic crops, you should wash the produce before using.

● Organic fruit and vegetables are not always more environmentally friendly, as organic-approved pesticides may have been used to grow them.

● More water is often used in growing organic crops.

● Organic produce is often smaller than nonorganic.

● However, when it comes to meat, choose products labeled "USDA-certified organic" to be sure they are free of any artificial hormones, or purchase from local, sustainable farms that don't administer hormones to their animals.

WHAT IS GLUTEN?

Gluten is a protein found in certain grains, including wheat, spelt, rye, and barley. It is made up of two sub-units called "glutenin" and "gliadin." Glutenin molecules look like little strands and gliadin molecules look like small spheres. When gluten comes into contact with water, for example when wheat flour is added to water, the water starts to form links ("bonds") between the glutenin and gliadin molecules inside. By mixing or kneading the mixture, those bonds are repeatedly formed and broken, which starts to build up a strong network of linked glutenin strands and gliadin molecules. This strong network is the reason why we knead bread—it allows CO_2 produced by yeast in the dough to become trapped, which causes the bread to rise and creates a light, airy texture.

● About 1 percent of the U.S. population suffers from celiac disease, a condition in which gluten causes an immune response in a person's body and their digestive systems become damaged, leading to malnutrition.

● Some people have a type of wheat intolerance.

● FODMAPs (fermentable oligosaccharides, disaccharides, monosaccharides, and polyols) are short-chain carbohydrates found in certain foods and are digested by the bacteria living in our guts, which make by-products, such as gases. FODMAPS may make you feel bloated and unwell.

● If you suspect that wheat makes you feel bloated, it's possible that you need to decrease your intake of certain FODMAP-containing foods in your diet (see final point).

● Oats do not contain gluten, but as they are often grown or processed near gluten-containing crops, they can become contaminated.

● Some of the recipes in this book use oats or oat flour and have been labeled "gluten free," but if you are cooking for a celiac, check that they can consume (gluten-free) oats, as they may be sensitive to them.

● Always consult your doctor or nutritionist or dietitian before making a drastic change to your diet.

Breakfast & Grab-and-go Snacks

Breakfast really is the most important meal of my day. It sets me up to be alert and able to pay attention in lectures without being distracted by a grumbling stomach. I always have a sweet tooth, but especially in the morning when I crave soul-warming bowls of oatmeal or stacks of fluffy pancakes. I always find it important to strike the right balance, though, so I incorporate whole grains, healthy fats, and a portion of fruits or vegetables into my breakfast to keep me full and happy. I do occasionally foray into savory breakfasts, but in truth, I think the best savory option of all is poached eggs with spinach and toast, which I wouldn't bother writing a recipe for anyway!

For those rushed breaks between lectures or those times when you get back from work/university/college and you're desperate for some food, turn to these snack recipes. Dips, crackers, roasted chick peas (garbanzo beans), and small, sweet bites for satisfying yet light meals to fill that gap.

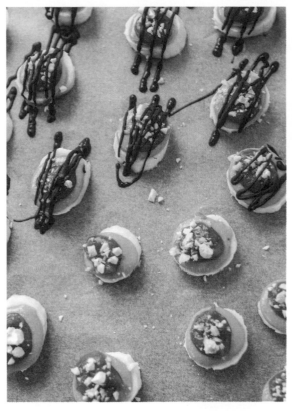

OVERNIGHT OATS

When hot weather finally rolls around, overnight oats become my calling card breakfast. Make a large batch and divide it into jars, and it will last a few days. It travels extremely well and is a super-healthy, but still delicious, breakfast on the go (just don't forget to pack a spoon!).

PEACH & RASPBERRY CRUNCH

Serves 2

1 peach, pitted and cut into small cubes
handful of fresh or frozen raspberries
1 apple, shredded
¾ cup plus 2 tablespoons/3oz/80g old-fashioned rolled oats
1 cup milk or nondairy milk
2 tablespoons dried cranberries or raisins
1 tablespoon chia seeds or ground flax seed
  mixed with 3 tablespoons water (optional)
2 tablespoons pumpkin seeds
1 teaspoon sugar, any kind
1 teaspoon water
¼ teaspoon ground cinnamon

1 In a medium bowl, combine the peach, raspberries, apple, oats, milk, and dried cranberries or raisins, then mix in the chia seeds or flax seed, if using. Divide between 2 (9oz) jars and chill in the refrigerator overnight.

2 In a small skillet, toast the pumpkin seeds, sugar, and water over medium heat until the sugar starts to melt and the seeds clump together. Stir in the cinnamon, then remove from the heat and set aside.

3 In the morning, sprinkle the crispy pumpkin seeds over the granola and eat immediately or pop a lid on the jar and you are good to go! The other jar can be left in the refrigerator for up to 3 days.

Vegan Use nondairy milk.

Gluten Free If you can tolerate oats, use gluten-free certified oats.

CARROT CAKE

Serves 2

2 tablespoons dry unsweetened shredded coconut
¾ cup plus 2 tablespoons/3oz/80g old-fashioned rolled oats
1¼ cups milk or nondairy milk
1 medium carrot, shredded
½ teaspoon ground cinnamon
1 teaspoon grated orange zest
1 apple, shredded
2 tablespoons raisins
¼ cup plain yogurt or soy yogurt (optional)

1 In a dry skillet, toast the coconut over medium heat, stirring continuously. Watch carefully, and once it starts to turn golden, immediately transfer it to a bowl. Set aside for the morning.

2 In a medium bowl, combine the oats, milk, shredded carrot, cinnamon, orange zest, shredded apple, and raisins. Divide the mixture between 2 (9oz/250g) jars and chill overnight in the refrigerator.

3 In the morning, top the oat mixture with the coconut and yogurt (if using) and eat immediately or place a lid on the jar and you are good to go! The other jar can be kept in the refrigerator for up to 3 days.

Vegan Use nondairy milk and soy yogurt.

Gluten Free If you can tolerate oats, use gluten-free certified oats.

CARROT CAKE

PEACH & RASPBERRY CRUNCH

LEFTOVERS: see pp. 228–233

- Apple
- Raspberries (fresh or frozen)
- Peach

- Carrots
- Yogurt, if using
- Apple

TIPS & SWAPS

Buy strawberries or other fruit in
season and freeze it to enjoy all year round.
Or use frozen fruits, such as blueberries
and raspberries.

If you have extra fruit, double up on the compote
and keep in a lidded jar in the refrigerator to swirl
into yogurt or drizzle over pancakes.

Use chopped pecans or hazelnuts instead of the coconut.

Substitute muesli for the same weight of oats
for a different flavor and texture.

Instead of creamed coconut, try stirring
peanut butter into hot water.

VG option

OAT SQUARES WITH STRAWBERRY COMPOTE & COCONUT

Makes 9 squares

COMPOTE
5½oz/150g fresh or frozen strawberries
1 tablespoon water
1 tablespoon sugar, honey,
    or Date Paste (see page 221)

OATS
oil, for greasing
¼ cup/1oz/25g dry unsweetened
    shredded coconut
¾ cup water
1¼ cups milk or nondairy milk
1 egg
½ cup coconut milk or 2 tablespoons
    creamed coconut mixed with
    ½ cup hot water
2 cups/7oz/200g old-fashioned rolled
oats
1 teaspoon baking powder
¼ teaspoon salt
1 tablespoon granulated sugar
    or honey, or 2 tablespoons
    Date Paste (see page 221)

TO SERVE (OPTIONAL)
milk
plain yogurt
fresh fruit
honey

This is a cross between a muffin and a thick, cooked oatmeal. If you enjoy eating the same breakfast for a week, then try this recipe. Just leave a square in a warm oven for 10 minutes while you make your coffee in the morning, then douse it in fridge-cold milk and top with fresh fruit, and some honey if desired. The compote, which is swirled into the oats before baking, can be changed up as you wish, or just top the oats with a handful of blueberries or sliced apple.

1 Preheat the oven to 350°F. Grease an 8-inch square brownie pan or deep cake pan with a little oil.

2 In a dry skillet, toast the coconut over medium heat, stirring continuously. Watch carefully, and once it starts to turn golden, immediately transfer it to a bowl and set aside.

3 Return the skillet to the heat and add all the compote ingredients. Bring to a boil, then reduce the heat to a simmer and cook until the strawberries soften and the juice thickens, 10 minutes.

4 Meanwhile, in a large bowl, mix together the water, milk, egg, and coconut milk or creamed coconut for the oats. Add the oats, baking powder, salt, and sugar and stir until combined. Pour into the prepared pan. Once the compote is ready, spoon it over the surface of the oatmeal, then sprinkle over the toasted coconut.

5 Bake in the oven for 20 to 25 minutes, until it looks dry on top. Remove from the oven, then cut into 9 squares and eat warm. Keep any leftovers wrapped in plastic wrap in the refrigerator. Reheat a square by placing it in a heatproof bowl or on a baking sheet and warming in an oven preheated to 350°F for 10 minutes.

6 Serve with milk, yogurt, fresh fruit, and honey, if desired.

Vegan Use 1 tablespoon ground flax seed mixed with 3 tablespoons water instead of the egg. Use nondairy milk and sugar or Date Paste, and use sugar or Date Paste in the compote.

Gluten Free If you can tolerate oats, use gluten-free certified oats.

LEFTOVERS: see pp. 228–233

● Strawberries (fresh or frozen)
● Coconut milk or creamed
   coconut

TIPS & SWAPS

*The water should be just slightly warm to the touch. Too hot will kill the yeast and the bread won't rise!

**In the winter, set the oven to the lowest heat for 5 minutes, then switch it off and let the dough sit in the oven with the door closed.

CARROT BREAKFAST BREAD

Makes 1 loaf

2¼ teaspoons instant dry yeast
¾ cup plus 4 teaspoons
  lukewarm water*
3 tablespoons honey or granulated sugar
2 tablespoons olive oil, plus extra
  for greasing
grated zest of 1 orange
2 teaspoons ground cinnamon
1 teaspoon ground ginger
2¼ cups/7oz/200g shredded carrot
3¼ cups/14oz/400g whole-wheat
  flour, plus extra for dusting
½ teaspoon salt
½ cup raisins

Baking bread can seem daunting if you have never done it before, but once you have made it a few times, you will get the hang of it! If you don't know how to knead bread dough, a quick Internet search for a video will help you out. Essentially, kneading is just the process of stretching and folding the dough with your hands until it is smooth and stretchy. This helps develop the gluten network (gluten is a protein found in certain grains such as wheat), which makes the dough elastic. One golden rule: Never let the yeast come into contact with a super-high temperature until you are ready to bake. So be sure to use lukewarm liquids in the dough and let the dough rise in a warm, not hot, place. As yeasts are living organisms they like warmth, but will die in high heat conditions!

1 In a large bowl, stir together the yeast, lukewarm water, and honey or sugar until combined. Set aside for 5 minutes. Stir in the olive oil, orange zest, cinnamon, ginger, and carrot. Add the flour and salt and stir until the mixture forms a coarse dough. Transfer the dough to a lightly floured work surface and knead for 10 minutes, dusting lightly with more flour as needed to stop the dough sticking to the surface.

2 Pour a little extra olive oil into the bowl you were mixing the dough in, add the dough, and turn until the dough and bowl are coated in oil. Cover loosely with plastic wrap or paper towels and let rise in a warm place** for 1 hour or until doubled in size.

3 Using paper towels, your hands, or a pastry brush, grease a 2lb loaf pan with a little olive oil. Transfer the risen dough to a clean work surface and pat it out into a rectangle as long as the loaf pan and about ¾ inch thick. Scatter the raisins over the surface of the dough, press them down, and roll the dough up, then place the dough in the prepared loaf pan, seam side down. Cover loosely with oiled plastic wrap and let rise in a warm place for 30 minutes.

4 Meanwhile, preheat the oven to 350°F.

5 Once the dough has risen for 30 minutes, remove the plastic wrap and bake the bread in the oven for 40 minutes or until golden on top. Remove from the oven and let cool for 10 minutes before unmolding onto a wire rack. Let cool completely before slicing.

Vegan Use sugar instead of honey.

LEFTOVERS: see pp. 228–233

● Carrots

NO-KNEAD LOAF

Makes 1 loaf

¼ teaspoon instant dry yeast
1¼ cups plus 2 tablespoons/12fl
   oz/350ml lukewarm water*
2½ cups/10½oz/300g whole-wheat
   flour
1½ cups/7oz/200g bread flour, plus
   extra for dusting
1 teaspoon salt
handful of mixed seeds, such as
   pumpkin, sunflower, sesame,
   flax, poppy, etc. (optional)

This internet-famous bread-baking technique is known as Jim Lahey's no-knead bread and it is very simple. I have changed the method slightly and used a slightly lower percentage of water, but one thing stays the same and that is baking the bread in a heavy, cast-iron casserole dish with a lid. The pan holds the heat in and traps steam around the loaf while it bakes, leading to a better rise and crust. You can bake it on a sheet, but you won't get the same gorgeous, crispy crust.

1   In a large bowl, combine the yeast and lukewarm water, then set aside for 5 minutes. Add the flours, salt, and seeds, if using, and stir together until all the flour is incorporated. Cover the bowl with plastic wrap and set aside for 8 to 12 hours at room temperature.

2   Cut a strip of nonstick parchment paper about 6 inches wide and dust it lightly with flour. Punch the dough down in the bowl and transfer to a lightly floured work surface. Dust your hands with flour and shape the dough into a tight ball. Lift the dough up and place it in the center of the floured parchment paper. Dust with flour, then turn the bowl you were using upside down and place it over the dough. Let rise for 30 minutes.

3   Meanwhile, preheat the oven to 425°F. If you have a large, lidded, cast-iron casserole dish, heat it in the oven for 30 minutes while the dough is rising.

4   Uncover the dough and slash a cross in the top of the bread with the tip of a sharp knife.

5   If you are using a cast-iron casserole dish, remove it from the oven and place on a heatproof surface. Lift the lid of the dish. Take hold of the edges of the parchment paper on which the dough is sitting and carefully lift it into the hot dish. Replace the lid and bake in the oven for 30 minutes, then remove the lid and bake for another 15 minutes, until the loaf is dark brown. Alternatively, if you are using a baking sheet, grasp the edges of the parchment paper on which the dough is sitting and carefully lift the dough onto the sheet. Bake for 40 to 45 minutes, until dark brown.

6   Let the bread cool, uncovered, in the casserole dish or on a wire rack before slicing. I usually slice the whole loaf and freeze half of it.

TIPS & SWAPS
*See Tip, p. 22

The dough will keep in the refrigerator for up to 3 days, so you could just bake half of it (takes 30 minutes) and store half. Let the dough come to room temperature for about an hour before using.

For bread rolls, divide the dough into 16 pieces after it has been left for 8 to 12 hours, then roll into balls and let rise in a warm place for 30 minutes. Bake in the oven for 18 to 20 minutes or until golden.

MICROWAVE BLUEBERRY OAT "MUFFIN"

Serves 1

5 tablespoons regular rolled oats
⅛ teaspoon baking powder
¼ teaspoon ground cinnamon
1 egg
¼ cup milk or nondairy milk
1 heaping tablespoon fresh or frozen blueberries
1 to 2 teaspoons preferred sweetener such as honey, maple syrup, or Date Paste (see page 221)

EXTRA TOPPINGS
plain yogurt
nut butter
fresh fruit
chopped nuts

This is my go-to winter breakfast on mornings when I only have 15 minutes to get dressed and eat before going to class (hello, 9 a.m. lectures). If you know you'll be really pressed for time, mix the oats, baking powder, and cinnamon in the mug the night before, and in the morning just mix in the wet ingredients and microwave away! Please note that these oats seem to absorb the taste of sugar when you mix it in—it's far better to drizzle most of the sweetener over the cooked oats and/or top with a handful of ripe, fresh fruit.

1 In a tall microwave-safe mug, mix together the oats, baking powder, cinnamon, egg, and milk until well combined. Briefly stir in the blueberries.

2 Microwave for 2 minutes on high. It will rise to the top of the mug and sink back a bit once it is removed from the microwave. I like to transfer the muffin to a bowl (more room for toppings!), but you can eat it directly out of the mug. Just let the muffin cool briefly before drizzling with your preferred sweetener and adding on extra toppings of choice.

3 Eat while still warm, as this gets weirdly rubbery when cold.

Gluten Free If you can tolerate oats, use gluten-free certified oats.

Dairy Free Use nondairy milk.

LEFTOVERS: see pp. 228–233

- Blueberries (fresh or frozen)
- Yogurt (if using)
- Nut butter (if using)

TIPS & SWAPS

Use fresh or frozen raspberries or strawberries instead of the blueberries.

For a chocolaty treat, add 2 tablespoons chopped dark chocolate to the mixture before microwaving.

A TRIO OF OATMEAL

TIPS & SWAPS

Try the Banana Bread Oatmeal as a dessert: Omit the dates and sprinkle a handful of chopped dark chocolate over your oatmeal!

Oatmeal is my go-to breakfast and snack during the winter. I used to think that whenever you mix something into it such as sugar, jam, or nut butter, the flavor just disappears, but I have now perfected my formula for the best oatmeal. Pick mix-ins that provide flavor, salt, or sweetness but that won't dissolve into the oats. Dried fruits are always good for a sweet hit, and if you gently swirl in nut butter, you get some in each bite. Toasting sunflower seeds in soy sauce makes them salty and crunchy, which is a great topping for sweet oatmeal. I also like savory oatmeal for a quick and easy lunch—cook it the night before and just microwave until hot.

Serves 1

1 banana or ½ frozen sliced banana
⅔ cup just-boiled water
scant ½ cup/1½oz/40g old-fashioned rolled oats
pinch of salt
¼ teaspoon ground cinnamon
1 heaping teaspoon peanut or cashew butter
milk or nondairy milk, for thinning
2 to 3 dried dates, pitted and roughly chopped

LEFTOVERS: see pp. 228–233

- Bananas
- Dates
- Nut butter

- Raspberries (fresh or frozen)
- Miso

- Miso
- Mushrooms

BANANA BREAD OATMEAL

1 If using a fresh banana, mash half of it and slice the other half (for the topping). If using a frozen, sliced banana, set it aside for now.

2 Pour the water into a small saucepan and bring to a boil. Add the oats, salt, cinnamon, and all the mashed fresh banana or all the frozen sliced banana. Bring to a boil, then reduce the heat to low and simmer gently for 5 minutes. Turn the heat off, cover with a lid or plate, and let stand for another 5 minutes.

3 Meanwhile, scoop up the heaping teaspoon of nut butter on the spoon you want to eat with and place the spoon in a cereal bowl.

4 Uncover the oats and check the texture, adding milk as desired, then stir in the chopped dates. Pour the oatmeal over the spoonful of nut butter in the bowl and let stand for 30 seconds, until the heat of the oatmeal melts the nut butter, then gently swirl the spoon through the oatmeal. The idea is that you are not mixing the nut butter but rippling it through, so that you get a bite of pure flavor in each mouthful.

5 Top with the remaining sliced, fresh banana (if you weren't using frozen) and enjoy!

Vegan Use nondairy milk.

Gluten Free If you can tolerate oats, use gluten-free certified oats.

DONUT OATMEAL

Serves 1

⅔ just-boiled water
scant ½ cup/1½oz/40g old-fashioned rolled oats
pinch of salt
milk or nondairy milk, for thinning
1 teaspoon vanilla extract
handful of fresh or frozen raspberries
2 teaspoons packed light brown sugar
½ teaspoon ground cinnamon

1 Pour the water into a small saucepan and bring to a boil. Pour in the oats and salt, then bring to a boil. Reduce the heat to low and simmer gently for 5 minutes. Turn the heat off, cover with a lid or plate, and let stand for another 5 minutes.

2 Once the oats have sat for 5 minutes, uncover and check the texture, adding milk to thin it out as desired, then stir in the vanilla extract and gently fold in the raspberries. Pour the oatmeal into a cereal bowl.

3 Mix together the sugar and cinnamon and sprinkle in an even layer over the surface of the oatmeal. DON'T mix it in! You want each scoop of oatmeal to have a nice layer of cinnamon–sugar on it. Enjoy!

Vegan Use nondairy milk.

Gluten Free If you can tolerate oats, use gluten-free certified oats.

ARUGULA, MUSHROOM & FRIED EGG OATMEAL

Serves 1

2 teaspoons olive oil or canola oil
1 cup/2¼oz/60g sliced mushrooms
1 teaspoon miso, any kind (optional)
⅔ cup just-boiled water or hot vegetable stock
scant ½ cup/1½oz/40g old-fashioned rolled oats
milk or nondairy milk, for thinning
1 egg
handful of arugula
salt and freshly ground black pepper

1 In a small, nonstick skillet, heat half the oil over medium heat. Add the mushrooms and sauté, stirring frequently, until darkened and soft. Stir in the miso with a bit of water and cook until the water has evaporated. Remove the skillet from the heat and set aside.

2 Pour the water or stock into a small saucepan and bring to a boil. Add the oats and a pinch of salt and bring to a boil. Reduce the heat to low and simmer gently for 5 minutes. Turn the heat off, cover with a lid or plate, and let stand for another 5 minutes.

3 Once the oats have sat for 5 minutes, uncover and check the texture, adding milk to thin it out as desired. Add the mushrooms to the oatmeal, then return the empty skillet to medium-low heat and pour in the remaining oil. Crack in the egg and cook it until the white is set.

4 Pour the oatmeal and mushrooms into a serving bowl, top with the arugula and the fried egg, then season with salt and pepper and serve.

Gluten Free If you can tolerate oats, use gluten-free certified oats.

Dairy Free Use nondairy milk.

TIPS & SWAPS

Make the Argula, Mushroom & Fried Egg Oatmeal lunchbox-friendly by using a peeled soft-boiled egg.

Add leftover roasted veg such as roasted squash with sautéed leeks.

Try using miso, peas, thyme, and Parmesan.

TIPS & SWAPS

Replace the peach and tomatoes
with a diced apple.

If you're halving the recipe, store the chick
peas in water in a lidded container in
the refrigerator for up to 3 days (or freeze
them like that for up to 3 months).

Make all the salsa and keep it for dinner
tonight (more tacos anyone?!) or
for breakfast the next day.

GF option

SCRAMBLED CHICK PEA TACOS WITH PEACH SALSA

Serves 2 to 3
(makes extra salsa)

SALSA
1 peach, pitted and coarsely chopped
5 to 6 cherry tomatoes, finely chopped
juice of ½ lime
handful of cilantro, coarsely
   chopped (leaves and stems)
½ large red onion, finely chopped
pinch of salt

CHICK PEA SCRAMBLE
2 tablespoons olive oil
½ large red onion, roughly chopped
2 teaspoons smoked paprika
1 teaspoon ground cumin
¼ teaspoon ground cinnamon
¼ teaspoon ground coriander
pinch of crushed red pepper
1½ cups/8½oz/240g cooked chick peas
   (garbanzo beans), drained and rinsed
1 teaspoon miso, any kind
¼ cup milk or nondairy milk
4 to 6 tortillas, (see page 214)
   or store-bought, warmed
2 tablespoons plain yogurt or
   nondairy yogurt, or Avocado Cream
   (see page 219)

Most of the time I try to eat plant-based meals for breakfast and lunch, but the one thing that's difficult to try and replace for me is scrambled eggs. They are such a quick, savory meal and always taste good. However, I have found that these scrambled chick peas fill that gap. If you get into eating these for breakfast, brunch, or lunch, just multiply the quantities of spices by eight, mix in a jar, and use about 3½ teaspoons of the mixture when needed.

1 Prepare all the ingredients for the salsa, then stir them together in a bowl and set aside. You can do this the night before, cover with plastic wrap, and let the salsa chill in the refrigerator overnight, if desired.

2 In a medium skillet, heat the olive oil over medium heat. Add the onion and sauté, stirring frequently, until translucent. Add the spices and crushed red pepper and cook for 1 minute, then add the chick peas and stir to coat. Reduce the heat to medium-low and mash the chick peas with the wooden spoon or the back of a fork in the pan. You want some chick peas to remain a bit chunky.

3 In a small bowl, mix together the miso and milk. Add to the pan and cook, stirring, until it has mostly evaporated.

4 Divide the chick pea scramble among the tortillas and top with some salsa and yogurt, if desired. Serve immediately! Store any excess salsa in a bowl covered in plastic wrap in the refrigerator.

Vegan Use nondairy milk and nondairy yogurt or Avocado Cream.

Gluten Free Use gluten-free corn tortillas.

> **LEFTOVERS:** see pp. 228–233
>
> ● Peach
> ● Cherry tomatoes
> ● Red onion
> ● Cilantro
> ● Lime
> ● Cooked chick peas
> ● Avocado Cream or yogurt
> ● Miso

MULTIGRAIN PANCAKES

**Makes 6 to 8
(serves 2)**

DRY MIX (ENOUGH FOR 3 BATCHES)
1½ cups/5½oz/150g Oat Flour (see page 216)
1 scant cup/3¼oz/90g old-fashioned rolled oats
2 cups/8½oz/240g all-purpose or whole-wheat pastry flour
3 teaspoons baking powder
¾ teaspoon baking soda
¾ teaspoon salt
3 tablespoons granulated sugar
3 tablespoons ground flax seed (for the vegan version only)

FOR VEGAN VERSION
1½ cups/7oz/190g cups Dry Mix
¾ cup plus 1½ tablespoons nondairy milk
1 teaspoon apple cider vinegar or lemon juice
2 tablespoons olive oil or rapeseed oil, plus extra for frying

FOR NONVEGAN VERSION
1¼ cups plus 2 tablespoons/6½oz/185g Dry Mix less 2 teaspoons
1 egg
⅔ cup dairy or nondairy milk
1 teaspoon apple cider vinegar or lemon juice
2 tablespoons olive oil or canola oil, plus extra for frying

TO SERVE (OPTIONAL)
maple syrup
plain yogurt
fruit
chopped nuts

If you find yourself lying in bed on a Saturday morning, wishing someone else would get up and make pancakes but knowing that won't happen, this pancake mix could help you out. When it's not a weekend morning, mix up the "dry mix" to keep in a jar in the pantry. That way, when your brunch longings hit, you know you are just a scoop of pancake mix plus a few ingredients away from tasty homemade pancakes.

1 Put all the dry mix ingredients in a medium bowl and stir until well combined. Transfer to a labeled airtight container or a large, labeled sandwich bag. Store in the pantry until needed. (It will last for up to 3 months.)

2 When ready to make pancakes, measure out your dry mix into a medium bowl according to the version you are making. Add the wet ingredients to the bowl and stir with a fork or small wire whisk until just combined.

3 Heat a large, nonstick skillet with just enough oil to coat the bottom. Once the oil is hot, turn the heat down to medium-low and add a few tablespoons of the batter to form a pancake about 3¼ inches in diameter. Repeat so that you have 3 or 4 pancakes cooking in the skillet. Cook the pancakes until the edges change color and the underside is golden, then flip over and cook on the other side until golden. Transfer to a plate and cook the remaining batter as before.

4 Serve hot with maple syrup, yogurt, fruit, and chopped nuts.

TIPS & SWAPS

As you cook, put the pancakes on a baking sheet in a warm oven.

To make pancakes in bulk, triple the wet ingredients and mix into all the dry mix. Cook and store pancakes in the refrigerator in a sandwich bag for up to 3 days or in the freezer for up to 1 month. Thaw and warm up in the toaster.

For blueberry pancakes, pour the batter into the pan, then drop in a few blueberries.

MULTIGRAIN PANCAKES

FRENCH TOAST WITH MISO–DATE BUTTER

FRENCH TOAST WITH MISO–DATE BUTTER

Serves 2 to 3

MISO–DATE BUTTER
5 soft Medjool dates*
 or 6 Deglet Noor dates, pitted
5 tablespoons unsalted butter, softened
2 teaspoons miso, any kind

FRENCH TOAST
3 tablespoons all-purpose flour
 or chick pea (garbanzo bean) flour
pinch of salt
½ teaspoon ground cinnamon
3 green cardamom pods,
 seeds removed and ground
 in a mortar and pestle (optional)
¾ cup plus 1½ tablespoons milk or
 nondairy milk
2 teaspoons granulated sugar
 or maple syrup
1 teaspoon vanilla extract
olive oil or canola oil, for frying
4 to 6 slices of whole-wheat bread,
 stale is best

TO SERVE (OPTIONAL)
maple syrup
fruit

I have this pet peeve about that little tail of egg white that attaches the yolk to the albumen—it never mixes into French toast batter properly. But then I discovered how to make this dish without using eggs! Serve the French toast with a little salty, sweet miso–date butter for a great way to jazz it up.

1 Make the butter first. Place the dates in a medium bowl and mash into a coarse paste with the back of a fork. Add the butter and miso to the bowl and mix together until the dates are marbled through the butter. Spoon onto a piece of nonstick parchment paper in a line, then roll up into a log and twist the ends of the paper. Chill in the refrigerator for at least 30 minutes or the freezer for at least 10 minutes, until set.

2 For the French toast, in a shallow bowl, combine the flour, salt, cinnamon, and ground cardamom (if using). While whisking, gradually pour in the milk until fully combined, then stir in the sugar or maple syrup and vanilla extract.

3 Heat a large, nonstick skillet with just enough oil to lightly coat the bottom. Take 1 or 2 pieces of bread (depending on how large your bowl is) and submerge into the milk mixture, flipping to coat. Let soak for 2 minutes or so, then lift up the bread, letting the excess batter drip off. Place the battered bread in the skillet and let cook. Meanwhile, dunk another piece of bread into the batter and let soak for 2 minutes or so. Check on the piece of bread in the pan—when it's golden on the underside, flip it over and cook on the other side. Once it's golden, remove to a plate. Repeat the dunking and cooking with the rest of the bread as before until all the batter has been used up.

4 Serve the French toast hot with slices of the miso–date butter and maple syrup and fruit, if desired.

Vegan Use vegan spread or even cashew, almond, or peanut butter in the miso–date butter, and nondairy milk in the batter.

TIPS & SWAPS

To reheat cold French toast, slot into the toaster for a minute.

*To soften dates, soak them in boiling water for 15 minutes, then drain and let cool before mixing into the butter.

Store any extra French toast in the refrigerator or freezer in a sandwich bag for a weekday breakfast. Thaw the slices in the toaster.

LEFTOVERS: see pp. 228–233

● Dates
● Miso
● Bread

SALTY OR SWEET CRACKERS

Makes 8 large crackers (to be broken into smaller crackers)

2¼ teaspoons instant dry yeast
½ cup plus 2 tablespoons water
2 cups/9oz/250g whole-wheat pastry
   or whole-wheat flour, plus extra
   for dusting
½ teaspoon salt
¼ cup olive oil

SWEET FLAVOR MIX

2 tablespoons sesame seeds
1 tablespoon granulated sugar
1 teaspoon ground cinnamon

SAVORY FLAVOR MIX

3 teaspoons mixed dried herbs
1 teaspoon sea salt flakes
1 teaspoon smoked paprika

I always forget how moreish crackers are until I make them. They are a great snack eaten on their own, but they are also good served with dips and are a much healthier alternative to tortilla chips or potato chips. They store well in a sealed container, and if they start getting a little bendy, just place them on a baking sheet and put in an oven preheated to 350°F fan for a few minutes to crisp them up again.

1 In a medium bowl, mix together the yeast and water. Add the flour, salt, and oil, then mix with a spoon to form a coarse dough. Use your hands to knead the dough in the bowl until just smooth, then cover with a clean kitchen towel or plastic wrap and let rest at room temperature for 30 minutes.

2 Preheat the oven to 350°F

3 Divide the dough into 8 equal pieces. Roll each piece into a ball, then roll each ball out into long ovals as thinly as possible on individual strips of nonstick parchment paper, dusting the dough with a little flour as needed to stop it sticking to the rolling pin. Sprinkle on your choice of flavor mix, then lift the parchment paper and place on a baking sheet so that the cracker is still on top (I can usually fit 2 large crackers on a sheet).

4 Bake in the oven for 8 to 12 minutes, until golden. Remove from the oven and let cool on a wire rack. Bake the rest of the crackers.

SMOOTHIE BOX TRIO

Premade smoothie mixes are great to have on hand for rushed mornings—they'll keep in the freezer for a couple of months or in the refrigerator for a few days. Put a few ingredients in a freezer bag or plastic box and store until needed. Transfer the contents to a blender with a bit of liquid to get it going and you'll have a meal or snack in no time. Once blended, I pour my smoothie into a Thermos to take with me on particularly busy days.

I like to make sure there's a source of fiber (aside from the fruit), fat, and protein in my smoothies, so I have added veggies, yogurt, and nut butter to the recipes. They'll make you feel fuller for longer and prevent that dreaded mid-morning sugar crash.

FOR ANY OF THE BELOW RECIPES:

Assemble the smoothie mix ingredients and put in a freezer bag or small, lidded plastic box. Store in the freezer for up to 2 months.

For a thin smoothie (with a countertop or handheld blender): The night before, take the smoothie bag out of the freezer and place in the refrigerator. In the morning, transfer the contents of the bag to the blender, or a beaker if using a handheld blender. Add the "to blend" ingredients and blend until smooth.

For a thick smoothie (with a countertop blender only): No need to thaw the smoothie bag. When you are ready to make your smoothie, transfer the frozen contents of the bag to the blender. Add the "to blend" ingredients and blend until smooth, adding some extra liquid to get the blending going.

TOP LEFT: MANGO, BANANA & SPINACH
BOTTOM LEFT: CHOCOLATE
BELOW: CARROT & BERRY

(V) (VG) (GF)

CHOCOLATE

Serves 1

1 small sweet potato or ½ large one* (about 7oz/200g)
1 tablespoon unsweetened cocoa
1 teaspoon sugar, any kind, or 1 pitted dried date, chopped
1 tablespoon almond, cashew, or peanut butter,
    tahini, or creamed coconut
pinch of salt
pinch of ground cinnamon (optional)

TO BLEND
a glug (¼–⅓ cup) of milk or nondairy milk

1 Preheat the oven to 350°F. Prick the sweet potato all over with a fork, wrap in aluminum foil, and bake in the oven for 1 hour.

2 Unwrap the baked sweet potato and let cool for a few minutes, then cut in half lengthwise. Scoop out the flesh and discard the skin, then chop the sweet potato flesh into chunks. Mix with the rest of the ingredients (except the milk) in a zipper sandwich bag or plastic container. Stash in the freezer.

3 Follow the blending instructions opposite.

Vegan Use nondairy milk to blend.

TIPS & SWAPS

*If you only have large sweet potatoes, roast the whole potato but only use half and store the other half.

Roast 2 sweet potatoes to double up this recipe and keep the extra potato in a sealed container in the refrigerator until ready to use.

MANGO, BANANA & SPINACH

Serves 1

1 small, overripe banana, peeled and sliced into coins
½ cup/2¾oz/75g cubed fresh or frozen mango
⅔ cup/¾oz/20g cup baby spinach, washed
2 tablespoons old-fashioned rolled oats
2 teaspoons almond or cashew butter,
   tahini, or creamed coconut

TO BLEND
a glug (¼–⅓ cup) of milk or nondairy milk
2 tablespoons plain yogurt or unsweetened soy yogurt
squeeze of lemon, lime, or orange juice

1 Put the banana, mango, spinach, oats, and nut butter, tahini, or creamed coconut in a zipper sandwich bag or plastic container and stash in the freezer.

2 Follow the blending instructions on page 36.

Vegan Use nondairy milk and soy yogurt.

Gluten free If you can tolerate oats, make sure they are certified gluten free.

LEFTOVERS: see pp. 228–233

● Sweet potato (roasted or raw)
● Nut butter, creamed coconut, or tahini
● Dates

● Banana
● Mango (fresh or frozen)
● Spinach
● Yogurt

● Carrots
● Mixed berries (fresh or frozen)

CARROT & BERRY

Serves 1

1 medium carrot, washed
½ cup/1¾oz/50g mixed berries (I prefer strawberries and raspberries)
1 small, overripe banana, sliced into coins

TO BLEND
¼ cup whole Greek-style yogurt or unsweetened soy yogurt
milk or nondairy milk

1 Cut the carrot into coins about ⅟₁₆ inch thick or shred them on the coarse side of a box grater (if using a handheld blender to make the smoothie, you will need to shred the carrot). Put the carrot, berries, and banana in a zipper sandwich bag or plastic container and stash in the freezer.

2 Follow the blending instructions on page 36.

Vegan Use nondairy milk and soy yogurt.

TIPS & SWAPS

If you have a countertop (NOT a handheld blender), add a few handfuls of ice as you blend. It will make the smoothie thicker and colder—more like a milkshake!

Use fresh or frozen cubed pineapple instead of mango.

V

VG option

APPLE CINNAMON SCUFFINS

Makes 12

⅓ cup/2¼oz/60g red lentils, rinsed
2 eggs
6 tablespoons milk or nondairy milk
⅓ cup olive oil or canola oil
¼ cup plus 1 tablespoon/2¼oz/60g granulated or Demerara sugar, plus extra for sprinkling
¼ teaspoon salt
1 teaspoon ground cinnamon
1⅓ cups/5¾oz/160g whole-wheat pastry flour
⅔ cup/2¼oz/60g old-fashioned rolled oats
1 teaspoon baking powder
½ teaspoon baking soda
2½ cups/10½oz/300g (about 2 to 3) apples, peeled, cored, and chopped into cubes
12 walnuts

Scuffins are the shape and size of a scone, but with the texture of a muffin. They are ideal when you don't have a muffin pan to hand yet still want a cake breakfast bake. Don't stop at the flavor combo I've used here; try other flavors, such as blueberry and pecan, ground ginger and pear, or raspberry and almond extract.

1 Preheat the oven to 350°F. Line a baking sheet with nonstick parchment paper.

2 Put the lentils in a medium saucepan and cover well with water. Bring to a boil, then reduce the heat and simmer for 10 minutes.

3 Drain the lentils and return them to the pan off the heat. Stir in the eggs, milk, oil, sugar, salt, and cinnamon until well combined. Add the flour, oats, baking powder, baking soda, and apple cubes and stir until just combined.

4 Scoop mounds of the batter onto the prepared baking sheet. Each mound should be about 3 heaping tablespoons of batter spaced about 1¼ inches apart. I can usually fit all 12 onto a single baking sheet, but you may need to bake these in 2 batches of 6 if your baking sheet is small.

5 Top each one with a light sprinkle of sugar and a walnut, then bake in the oven for 17 to 20 minutes, until they spring back when poked in the middle. Let cool on a wire rack.

Vegan Replace the eggs with 2 tablespoons ground flax seed mixed with 6 tablespoons water. Use nondairy milk.

TIPS & SWAPS

Replace the apple with 2½ cups/10½oz/300g frozen blueberries, raspberries, or chopped pear.

Change the cinnamon for ground ginger, vanilla extract, or ½ teaspoon almond extract.

Swap the walnuts for pecans, pumpkin seeds, or chopped hazelnuts.

LEFTOVERS: see pp. 228–233

- Apples
- Red lentils
- Walnuts
- Eggs

BANOFFEE PEANUT BITES

When bananas are sliced and frozen, they transform into creamy, slightly chewy nuggets of sweetness, which are perfect on a hot summery day. I have jazzed them up with peanut butter, date "caramel," and a drizzle of dark chocolate—delicious and, oh, also adorable.

Makes 20 to 30

2 ripe bananas, peeled
3 tablespoons peanut, cashew,
   or almond butter
½ cup/2¾oz/75g dried dates, pitted*
1 teaspoon vanilla extract
pinch of salt
¼ cup milk or nondairy milk
handful of peanuts, almonds,
   or cashews, coarsely chopped
½ to 1 cup/1¾ to 3½oz/50 to 100g
   bar dark chocolate (at least 70%
   cocoa solids)

1 Line a plate or baking sheet with nonstick parchment paper. Cut the bananas into ½-inch-thick coins, then place on the prepared plate or baking sheet.

2 Spread a layer of nut butter on top of each piece of banana and freeze for 30 minutes.

3 Using a handheld blender or a countertop blender, blend the dates, vanilla, salt, and milk until smooth. Alternatively, cover the dates with ¼ cup water in a saucepan and cook over low heat until the water has mostly evaporated, 4 to 5 minutes. Mash with a fork until as smooth as possible, then stir in the vanilla, salt, and milk.

4 Spread the caramel over the frozen sections of banana, then sprinkle with the nuts and freeze again for 30 minutes.

5 Break the chocolate into small chunks and put in a heatproof bowl set over a saucepan of simmering water over a low heat (make sure the bottom of the bowl doesn't touch the water). Stir continously until just melted, then remove from the heat. Alternatively, melt the chocolate on low in a microwave-safe bowl in the microwave.

6 Transfer the melted chocolate to a sandwich bag; cut the tip off one corner and use it like a pastry bag to drizzle the chocolate over the frozen banana pieces. Freeze again for at least 1 hour before eating. Store them in an airtight container in the freezer for up to 2 weeks.

Vegan Use nondairy milk. Ensure your chocolate is suitable for vegans.

LEFTOVERS: see pp. 228–233

● Bananas
● Dates
● Nut butter

TIPS & SWAPS

Use ½ cup/4oz/120g Date Paste (see page 221) instead of the dates.

*If the dates aren't soft and sticky, let soak in boiling water for 15 minutes before removing the pits.

COCONUT & COCOA BITES

Makes 14 to 16

⅔ cup/3½oz/100g dried dates (with pits) or 5 tablespoons Date Paste (see page 221)
3 tablespoons unsweetened cocoa
1½ cups/5oz/140g dry unsweetened shredded coconut

These are a breeze to make and, considering they only have three ingredients, are pretty damn tasty! The raw mixture is as nice on its own, but I like to bake it briefly to create a kind of shell on the outside so that they aren't so sticky.

1 If using the Date Paste, skip this step. Put the dates in a saucepan and pour in enough water to cover. Bring to a boil, then cover with a lid, reduce the heat, and simmer for 10 minutes. Drain the dates and let cool for 5 minutes, then remove the pits and mash the dates with a fork in a bowl.

2 Add the cocoa and coconut and stir to combine into a dough.

3 Scoop tablespoons of the date mixture and roll into balls. Either enjoy as they are for a sticky treat OR arrange the balls on a nonstick parchment paper-lined baking sheet and bake in an oven preheated to 350°F for 4 minutes. Store in an airtight container for up to 5 days.

LEFTOVERS: see pp. 228–233

● Dates

TORTILLA OR PITA CHIPS 4 WAYS

Serves 2 to 4

2 whole-wheat pita breads
  OR 2 large whole-wheat tortillas
  (see page 214) or store-bought
  OR 3 small corn or whole-wheat
  tortillas
2 teaspoons olive oil or canola oil

SWEET & SMOKY FLAVOR MIX
½ teaspoon sweet smoked paprika
½ teaspoon ground coriander seeds
pinch of granulated sugar
pinch of salt
½ teaspoon ground sumac (optional)

HERBS & SALT FLAVOR MIX
2 teaspoons mixed dried herbs
pinch of salt (sea salt flakes are
  especially good here)

**GARLIC & PARMESAN FLAVOR MIX
(NOT VEGAN)**
1 large garlic clove, halved
2 tablespoons grated Parmesan
½ teaspoon mixed dried herbs

CINNAMON–SUGAR FLAVOR MIX
1 teaspoon granulated sugar
1 teaspoon ground cinnamon
pinch of salt

I am so obsessed with making my own chips for serving with dips. It's incredibly easy to do because they are baked (no messing around with a couple of quarts of hot oil, thanks) and it's up to you to choose the flavors. I have included a few savory flavor mixes for serving with guacamole or the Fattoush Dip on page 51, but there is also a cinnamon–sugar mix, which is definitely A+ snacking material on its own.

1 Preheat the oven to 425°F.

2 For pita breads, cut around the edge of each pita bread with a pair of kitchen scissors and separate them each into 2 thin halves. Cut each half into about 10 even pieces. On a baking sheet, toss with the oil, then lay them out in a single layer on the sheet.

3 For tortillas, use a pair of kitchen scissors to cut the tortillas in half. Stack the halves together and cut into quarters. Stack the quarters together and cut into eighths. On a baking sheet, toss the triangles with the oil, then spread them out in a single layer on the sheet.

4 Sprinkle on your choice of flavor mix and bake in the oven for 5 to 10 minutes, keeping a close watch, until they are just starting to turn golden. Remove from the oven and let cool and crisp up.

5 Store in an airtight container for up to 5 days. If they soften, just place them on a baking sheet and warm in an oven preheated to 350°F for 2 to 3 minutes.

Note For the Garlic & Parmesan flavor mix, rub the outside of the pita or surface of the tortilla with the cut side of the garlic clove before cutting into smaller pieces and sprinkling with the Parmesan and herbs.

TIPS & SWAPS
*Parmesan is not technically vegetarian—choose an alternative vegetarian hard cheese.

SWEET & SMOKY

GARLIC & PARMESAN

HERBS & SALT

CINNAMON–SUGAR

ROASTED CHICK PEAS

Serves 2

oil, for greasing
1½ cups/8½oz/240g cooked chick peas
(garbanzo beans)

CINNAMON–SUGAR FLAVOR MIX
2 teaspoons olive oil or rapeseed oil
pinch of salt
1 tablespoon ground cinnamon
2 tablespoons brown sugar

CURRY FLAVOR MIX
2 teaspoons garam masala
1 teaspoon ground cumin
1 teaspoon ground turmeric
¼ teaspoon salt
2 teaspoons olive oil

"BACON" FLAVOR MIX
1 tablespoon packed brown sugar
4 teaspoons smoked paprika
2 teaspoons olive oil
1 teaspoon soy sauce or tamari

If you're looking for a relatively healthy snack that will fill you up, then go for these roasted chick peas. You can flavor them in myriad ways and munch on them knowing that they are giving you lots of protein and fiber. Toss them into salad or sprinkle on soup for a healthier alternative to croutons.

1 Preheat the oven to 350°F. Lightly grease a baking sheet.

2 Drain the chick peas, but don't rinse. Toss with the flavor mix of choice (see note below). Transfer to the baking sheet and roast in the oven for 25 to 35 minutes, tossing every 10 minutes or so, until crisp. Let cool, then eat!

Gluten Free Ensure that your tamari or soy sauce is certified gluten free.

Note If using the cinnamon–sugar flavor mix, toss the drained chick peas with the oil and salt. Roast for 15 minutes. Mix the cinnamon–sugar in a bowl, then sprinkle over the chick peas. Toss, then return to the oven for 10 minutes.

TOP LEFT: CINNAMON–SUGAR
BOTTOM LEFT: "BACON"
BELOW: CURRY

LEFTOVERS: see pp. 228–233

● Canned chick peas

COCONUT–BANANA GRANOLA BARS

Makes 16

¼ cup olive oil or canola oil
2 tablespoons creamed coconut
1 tablespoon water
1 tablespoon honey or maple syrup
⅓ cup plus 1 tablespoon/3oz/85g
  packed brown sugar
1 small, ripe banana, mashed
1⅔ cups/5¾oz/160g old-fashioned
  rolled oats
¼ cup/1oz/30g whole-wheat pastry
  flour
½ teaspoon baking powder
pinch of salt
2 heaping tablespoons sunflower seed or
  1 heaping tablespoon pumpkin seeds
¼ cup/¾oz/20g dry unsweetened
  shredded coconut

With a slight banana flavor and a tropical aroma, these bars are a great, oaty snack for when you're on the go. You can make endless variations by mixing in your choice of nuts, dried fruit, chocolate, and nut butters. Try adding seeds and dry shredded coconut for something cheap and cheerful.

1 Preheat the oven to 350°F. Line an 8-inch square pan with nonstick parchment paper—no need to grease or flour it.

2 In a medium saucepan, heat the oil, creamed coconut, water, honey or maple syrup, and sugar over medium heat for 2 minutes, stirring continuously. Remove from the heat and stir in the mashed banana. Add the oats, flour, baking powder, salt, seeds, and coconut and stir together until combined.

3 Press the mixture into the prepared pan and bake for 15 minutes.

4 Remove from the oven and cut into 16 bars or squares, then let cool in the pan. Store in an airtight container at room temperature for up to 5 days.

Vegan Use maple syrup instead of honey.

TIPS & SWAPS

Replace the creamed coconut with a different nut butter and use finely chopped peanuts instead of the coconut.

Try using roasted pureed butternut squash instead of the banana.

Stir 3 tablespoons unsweetened cocoa into the mix.

Mix in dried fruits, such as chopped dates or raisins or chopped dark chocolate.

LEFTOVERS: see pp. 228–233

● Bananas
● Creamed coconut

A TRIO OF PUREES

These three purees are all extremely different in flavor and use, but are all creamy diplike items that I use to jazz up other recipes. They can also be used simply as a dip for fruits, vegetables, or crackers.

PEA HUMMUS

Serves 4 to 6

1 cup/5½ oz/150g frozen petite peas or peas
1 tablespoon tahini
good pinch of salt
juice of ½ lemon
1 garlic clove, crushed or minced

1　Put the peas in a heatproof bowl, cover with just-boiled water, and let stand for 2 minutes. Drain, return to the bowl, cover with cold water, and let cool for 5 minutes. Drain again and return to the bowl if using a handheld blender, or transfer to a food processor or countertop blender. Blitz with the other ingredients until smooth.

2　Store the dip in a lidded container in the refrigerator for up to 3 days.

WAYS TO USE
- With floured and pan-fried fish and roasted potatoes.
- On crostini (toasted baguette slices) with fried halloumi, thyme, and pea shoots.
- Use lime juice instead of lemon juice or add finely chopped red onion, cilantro, cherry tomatoes, and some hot sauce to make a fake guacamole (you can also add mashed avocado to make bulk it up).
- Use in tacos as you would salsa or guacamole.
- As a dip for quesadillas (see Spanakopita Quesadillas on page 78).

SQUASH & CINNAMON DIP

PEA HUMMUS

"CHORIZO" DIP

LEFTOVERS: see pp. 228–233

- Tahini
- Lemon
- Butternut squash
- Dates

- Sundried tomatoes
- Miso
- Cooked red kidney beans

GF LS

   NS

CHORIZO DIP

Serves 4 to 5

1 teaspoon fennel seeds
⅔ cup/2¾oz/75g sundried tomatoes in oil
3 tablespoons sundried tomato oil from the jar
1⅓ cups/8½oz/240g cooked red kidney beans, drained
  and rinsed
2 teaspoons sweet smoked paprika
¼ to ½ teaspoon crushed red pepper, or ¼ teaspoon cayenne
  pepper or grinding of black pepper
2 tablespoons miso paste, soy sauce, or tamari
2 teaspoons apple cider vinegar
2 garlic cloves, crushed
½ teaspoon granulated sugar or 1 dried date, pitted
¼ cup water

1 In a dry skillet, toast the fennel seeds over high heat,
   stirring frequently, until they begin to color and smell
   fragrant. Transfer them to a mortar and crush them
   with a pestle. Alternatively, pour them onto a cutting
   board and crush with the back of a spoon.

2 Using a handheld blender, food processor, or
   countertop blender, blitz the fennel seeds with
   the remaining ingredients until smooth.

3 Store in a lidded container in the refrigerator for up to
   3 days or, using a tablespoon, scoop blobs of the dip
   onto a baking sheet lined with nonstick parchment
   paper and freeze. Keep the blobs in a labeled and dated
   sandwich bag for up to 2 months, thawing as needed.

Gluten Free Make sure your soy sauce or tamari are
certified gluten free.

WAYS TO USE
- On toast, with an egg.
- With crunchy raw vegetables, crackers (see page 35),
  or pita chips (see page 42) for dipping.
- In a sandwich or on a flatbread with leftover roasted veg.
- Spoon into a frittata or onto pizza, or spread into tacos.
- In a savory galette (use instead of the pesto in the recipe
  on page 101).

SQUASH & CINNAMON DIP

Serves 4 to 6

½ small squash or ¼ large squash (about 9oz/250g), seeded
  and cut into 3 or 4 large chunks
2 dried dates, pitted, or 1 tablespoon Date Paste
  (see page 221)
½ teaspoon ground cinnamon
1 teaspoon vanilla extract

1 Preheat the oven to 350°F.

2 Put the squash on a baking sheet and roast in the oven
   for 45 minutes, until soft. Remove from the oven and
   let cool for 15 minutes, then scoop the flesh from the
   skin, discarding the skin.

3 Cover the dates with boiling water if they aren't already
   soft and let soak for 15 minutes, then drain.

4 Using a handheld blender, countertop blender, or food
   processor, blend the roasted squash, dates, cinnamon,
   and vanilla together until smooth.

5 Store in a lidded container in the refrigerator for up to
   3 days or, using a tablespoon, scoop blobs of the dip
   onto a baking sheet lined with nonstick parchment
   paper and freeze. Keep the blobs in a labeled and dated
   sandwich bag for up to 2 months, thawing as needed.

WAYS TO USE
- Serve with yogurt and granola.
- Use a large spoonful in your oatmeal with raisins, chopped
  apple, and pecans.
- Spoon onto Overnight Oats (see page 18).
- Spread on toast, after your butter or spread.
- Serve with sliced apple or pear, for dipping.
- Smear onto warm scones (see page 187), Scuffins
  (see page 39), or sliced banana bread (see page 194).
- Stir in 2 tablespoons unsweetened cocoa.
- If you have already roasted butternut squash to hand,
  use about 4½oz/125g instead. Just skip the first and
  second steps.

Light Bites

I always find it difficult to define the difference between lunch and dinner meals. I mean most of the time I eat the same stuff, but for lunch I'd just have a smaller portion or eat it cold. These light bites fall somewhere in between lunch and dinner—they're light mains or hearty sides. Usually if you pair them with some bread, dressed greens, or a poached egg, they'll do well as a meal. You can also combine two or three of them to make a mezze meal for dinner—whatever works for you!

GF option

FATTOUSH DIP

I prefer this purple dip made with red kidney beans to its more common chick pea-based cousin hummus, as it's easier to make it smooth, light, and creamy. (Seriously, I'm never going to hand-peel a bowl of cooked chick peas just to get smooth hummus.) I swirl the resulting pastel puree onto a platter and top it with a mixture of herbs, tomatoes, greens, and pomegranate seeds, with a cinnamon–lemon dressing inspired by the Middle Eastern salad called "fattoush." Serve with homemade pita chips (see page 42) and you have one impressive and beautiful sharing plate of food.

Serves 3 to 4

DIP
1 ⅓ cups/8½oz/240g cooked red kidney
   beans, drained (except for 3 tablespoons
   liquid from the can) and rinsed
2 tablespoons extra virgin olive oil
2 garlic cloves, coarsely chopped or
   crushed
salt
juice of ½ lemon

SALAD
handful of cherry tomatoes,
   halved or quartered
2 radishes, thinly sliced
handful of arugula or pea shoots
handful of cilantro, coarsely chopped
   (leaves and stems)
handful of mint leaves, coarsely chopped
1 scallion, finely sliced
handful of pomegranate seeds (optional)

DRESSING
2 tablespoons olive oil
½ teaspoon ground cinnamon
juice of ½ lemon
pinch of salt

TO SERVE
1 batch of pita chips (see page 42),
   a few pita breads (see page 215)
   or crackers (see page 35)

1 Using a handheld blender or a countertop blender, blend all the dip ingredients together until smooth. Transfer the dip to a serving plate, spread it out slightly, then top with the salad ingredients.

2 In a jar with a screw-on lid, combine all the dressing ingredients, put on the lid, and shake to mix.

3 Pour the dressing over the salad and dip, then serve with pita chips, pita bread, or crackers for dipping.

Gluten Free Serve with certified gluten-free crackers or corn tortilla chips.

TIPS & SWAPS
Use mixed salad greens or chopped Little Gem lettuce instead of pea shoots or arugula.

LEFTOVERS: see pp. 228–233

- Arugula or pea shoots
- Cherry tomatoes
- Cilantro
- Mint
- Pomegranate
- Scallions
- Cooked red kidney beans

SPICED SWEET POTATO FRIES WITH SMOKY DIP

Serves 1 to 2

1 large or 2 small sweet potatoes
1 tablespoon cornstarch (optional)*
½ teaspoon ground cinnamon
¼ teaspoon ground cayenne pepper
  or ½ teaspoon crushed red pepper
2 teaspoons olive oil
generous pinch of salt

SMOKY DIP

3 tablespoons plain yogurt
  or crème fraîche
1 tablespoon tahini
juice of ½ lemon
1 garlic clove, crushed or minced
½ teaspoon sweet smoked paprika
½ teaspoon honey or maple syrup, or
  1 teaspoon Date Paste
  (see page 221)

I've gotta say that when it comes down to a toss-up between regular and sweet potato fries, the latter always wins for me. There's no parboiling needed for these sunny wedges to caramelize and crisp up in the oven. It seems a shame to make some special homemade fries, then drown them in overly sweet ketchup, but this smoky dip is a nicer alternative, with a kick from the paprika and a creamy tang from the yogurt.

1 Preheat the oven to 350°F.

2 Peel the sweet potato and cut into slim wedges shaped like fries. Place on a baking sheet, add the cornstarch, if using, cinnamon, and cayenne pepper or crushed red pepper and toss until the sweet potato is coated. Drizzle with the oil, sprinkle with salt, and toss again to coat.

3 Bake the wedges in the oven for 30 minutes, flipping them halfway through cooking with a metal spatula.

4 In a bowl, stir the smoky dip ingredients together and serve with the warm sweet potato wedges.

Vegan Use Chick Pea Mayonnaise (see page 222), pureed silken tofu, or unsweetened soy yogurt instead of the yogurt. Use Date Paste or maple syrup instead of the honey.

TIPS & SWAPS

*Adding the cornstarch will make the sweet potato fries extra crispy.

Make some extra sweet potato wedges, tossed in oil and salt (but no spices or cornstarch); roast on a separate baking sheet.

LEFTOVERS: see pp. 228–233

- Sweet potato
- Tahini
- Yogurt or crème fraîche
- Lemon

SPICED SWEET POTATOES WITH RAW BEET & MISO DRESSING

Serves 2

2 small sweet potatoes (about 14oz/400g in total), peeled and cut into about 1¼-inch cubes
1 tablespoon olive oil
½ teaspoon ground coriander
½ teaspoon garam masala
¼ teaspoon ground cumin
pinch of salt
2 small or 1 large beet, rinsed
handful of mixed salad greens
handful of walnuts, coarsely chopped

MISO DRESSING
2 tablespoons miso, any kind
¼ cup olive oil
1 garlic clove, crushed or minced
1 shallot or ¼ red onion, finely diced
2 teaspoons granulated sugar or honey
1 tablespoon lemon juice, or apple cider vinegar or rice vinegar

Here, squidgy, stubby pieces of sweet potato are tossed together with wispy shreds of beet in a salty, addictive miso dressing. It's a satisfying warm salad, which is best eaten from a bowl while you snuggle under a blanket, cross-legged on the couch.

1 Preheat the oven to 350°F.

2 On a baking sheet, spread out the sweet potato cubes, drizzle with the oil, and sprinkle on the spices and a pinch of salt. Toss until the sweet potato is coated, then roast in the oven for 30 minutes, flipping halfway through cooking with a metal spatula.

3 Slice the beets as thinly as possible. Stack up a few slices at a time and cut into small matchsticks. Toss with the salad greens and chopped nuts.

4 In a jar with a screw-on lid, combine all the dressing ingredients, put on the lid, and shake to mix.

5 Drizzle some of the dressing over the salad greens and toss to coat, then divide between 2 bowls or plates and top with the warm roasted sweet potato and extra dressing, if desired.

Vegan Use sugar in the dressing.

TIPS & SWAPS
Use pumpkin or sunflower seeds instead of walnuts.

Use arugula, baby spinach, pea shoots, chopped Belgian endive, or chopped Little Gem lettuce instead of mixed salad greens.

LEFTOVERS: see pp. 228–233

● Sweet potatoes
● Miso
● Red onion

A TRIO OF SLAWS

Slaw is a bit of a weird concept. It's like an overdressed mayo salad without any actual salad greens. For a while this put me off, but when I discovered it can be made without the mayo and with loads of different vegetables, I was sold! These are lovely as a side dish, spooned on a (veggie) burger, topped on a bowl of grains with dressing and a poached egg, or tossed with some baby spinach for a ready-dressed salad—BOOM.

Serves 4 to 6

3 tablespoons sesame seeds
2 tablespoons tahini
juice of 1 lemon
1 garlic clove, crushed
½ teaspoon ground cumin
pinch of salt
3 tablespoons raisins or chopped dried
    apricots
2 large carrots, shredded
handful of cilantro (leaves and stems),
    finely chopped

TAHINI CARROT SLAW

1 In a small, dry skillet, toast the sesame seeds over high heat, stirring frequently, until browned.

2 Transfer them to a medium bowl with the tahini, lemon juice, garlic, cumin, and salt and add enough water to thin the mixture to a pourable consistency.

3 Add the raisins or apricots, carrots, and cilantro and stir to combine, then serve. Cover and store in the refrigerator for up to 3 days.

LEFTOVERS: see pp. 228–233

● Cilantro
● Tahini
● Carrots
● Lemon

VG option

MISO MANGO SLAW

Serves 4 to 6

1 tablespoon miso, any kind
juice of ½ lime
2 tablespoons olive oil or extra virgin olive oil
½ large mango, flesh scooped from the skin and thinly sliced
¼ head of red or white cabbage, shredded
handful of cilantro (leaves and stems), coarsely chopped
1 scallion, finely sliced

1 In a medium bowl, mix together the miso, lime juice, and oil.

2 Add the mango, cabbage, cilantro, and scallion and stir to combine, then serve. Cover and store in the refrigerator for up to 3 days.

BROCCOLI APPLE YOGURT SLAW

Serves 4 to 6

¼ cup plain yogurt
½ teaspoon granulated sugar or honey,
   or 1 teaspoon Date Paste (see page 221)
pinch of salt
2 teaspoons apple cider vinegar or lemon juice
½ head (about 3oz) of broccoli
1 apple, shredded
1 small red onion, finely diced
¼ cup coarsely chopped walnuts

1 In a medium bowl, mix together the yogurt, sugar, honey, or Date Paste, salt, and vinegar or lemon juice.

2 Thinly slice the broccoli, then cut the slices into thin matchsticks. It doesn't matter if the flowery part of the broccoli is crumbling everywhere. Sweep all of the broccoli into the bowl and add the shredded apple, red onion, and walnuts. Stir until everything is coated with the dressing, then serve. Cover and store in the refrigerator for up to 3 days.

Vegan Use Chick Pea Mayonnaise (see page 222) or unsweetened soy yogurt instead of the yogurt. Use sugar or Date Paste.

LEFTOVERS: see pp. 228–233

- Mango
- Scallions
- Cilantro
- Miso
- Lime
- Red or white cabbage

LEFTOVERS: see pp. 228–233

- Yogurt
- Apples

VG option

FALAFEL SMASH

Serves 3 to 4

1½ cups/8½oz/240g cooked chick peas
   (garbanzo beans), drained and rinsed
¼ teaspoon salt
1 teaspoon ground cumin
1 teaspoon ground coriander
¼ teaspoon crushed red pepper
juice of ½ lemon
1 tablespoon olive oil
¼ cup plain yogurt or unsweetened
   soy yogurt
a few handfuls of pea shoots or arugula
a few slices of Quick Pickled Red Onion
   (see page 223) or thinly sliced
   raw red onion
½ recipe for pita breads or flatbreads
   (see page 215) or 4 to 6 store-
   bought pita breads

CILANTRO SAUCE
1 garlic clove, crushed or minced
2 large handfuls of cilantro,
   finely chopped (including stems)
¼ cup olive oil (I like to use
   extra virgin, here)
2 tablespoons sesame seeds, toasted*
generous pinch of salt

This falafel smash comes together quickly using mainly pantry-friendly ingredients and makes a super-satisfying lunch or, when served with a fried egg and salad, a perfect dinner. I like to make my own bread, so if you fancy doing the same, make your own pita breads or flatbreads using the recipes toward the back of this book.

1 In a bowl, lightly mash the chick peas with the back of a fork, or pulse them briefly in a food processor or countertop blender if you have one. Stir in the salt, ground cumin, ground coriander, crushed red pepper, lemon juice, and olive oil.

2 In a small bowl, stir together all the ingredients for the cilantro sauce.

3 Layer up the yogurt, the pea shoots or arugula, chick pea mixture, cilantro sauce, and pickled or raw red onion on the breads and serve.

Vegan Use nondairy yogurt or Avocado Cream (see page 219) instead of the yogurt.

TIPS & SWAPS

*To toast sesame seeds, add them to a dry skillet and stir over high heat until they smell toasty and turn golden.

If you're cooking for only 1 or 2 people, keep leftovers in the refrigerator. It will make an easy lunch in the next couple of days, served with bread or a tortilla.

LEFTOVERS: see pp. 228–233

● Cooked chick peas
● Cilantro leaves
● Red Onion
● Yogurt
● Lemon
● Pea shoots or arugula

VG option

BEET FLATBREAD

This pretty little dish has a great combo of flavors—there is sweetness from the beets, salt from the feta, and the sugary balsamic vinegar mix gives the dish a lovely tart taste. I usually make this recipe when I've got some pizza or flatbread dough sitting in the refrigerator from a previous day so that I have less prep to do.

Serves 4 to 6

1 tablespoon olive oil, plus extra
  for greasing
4 small or 2 large beets
½ recipe for pizza dough (see page 220)
  or 1 recipe for unbaked pita bread
  dough (see page 215)
¼ cup balsamic vinegar
1 tablespoon granulated sugar
⅓ cup/1¾oz/50g crumbled feta cheese
5 sprigs of thyme
salt

1 Preheat the oven to 350°F.

2 Wrap the beets in aluminum foil and bake in the oven for 45 to 60 minutes, depending on size, until fork-tender. Unwrap and let them cool slightly.

3 Rub the beet skins under cool running water to remove them, then slice the beets into ⅟₁₆-inch-thick coins.

4 Meanwhile, prepare the dough according to the recipe on page 220 or page 215.

5 Preheat the oven to 350°F. Grease a baking sheet with a little oil.

6 Press the dough out on the prepared baking sheet into an oval shape about 9½ x 8 inches. Arrange slices of the beet on top, sprinkle with salt, and drizzle with the olive oil. Bake in the oven for 20 to 25 minutes, until the edges are golden.

7 In a small saucepan, heat the balsamic vinegar and sugar over medium heat until reduced and thick, 1 minute. Drizzle over the flatbread, then sprinkle on the feta and thyme to serve.

Vegan Use Sun Feta (see page 219) instead of the feta or chop a handful of pitted black ripe olives and sprinkle those over instead.

TIPS & SWAPS

Use 2 tablespoons "balsamic glaze" instead of the combo of the balsamic vinegar and sugar.

Roll out 9oz/250g vegetarian store-bought puff pastry on a lightly floured work surface to about ¼ inch thick. Prick all over with a fork, then top with the cooked beet slices and bake as in the recipe.

Roast extra beets and store in the the refrigerator for up to 3 days.

LEFTOVERS: see pp. 228–233

● Beet (raw or excess roasted)
● Feta cheese
● Thyme

CHILE-ROASTED POTATOES WITH GRANOLA & LIME–SOY DRESSING

Serves 3 to 4

2 medium regular potatoes
(e.g. Russet, Yukon Gold),
cut into about 1¼-inch cubes
2 medium sweet potatoes, peeled and
cut into about 1¼-inch cubes
1 tablespoon olive oil or canola oil
½ teaspoon crushed red pepper
a few handfuls of arugula
2 scallions, finely sliced
½ red chile, seeded and thinly sliced
salt

GRANOLA
4 tablespoons old-fashioned rolled oats
3 tablespoons pumpkin seeds
small handful of cashews or peanuts,
coarsely chopped
1 tablespoon olive oil or canola oil
1 teaspoon soy sauce or tamari
1 teaspoon honey, or maple syrup
or golden syrup

LIME–SOY DRESSING
1 tablespoon soy sauce or tamari
2 teaspoons honey, or maple syrup
or golden syrup
juice of 1 lime
1 tablespoon toasted sesame oil

If stovetop granola is a new concept to you, get ready for a revelation. It's super-quick to toast up oats with crunchy nuts and seeds, and coat them in a delicious mix of honey and soy sauce. It's then sprinkled on a combo of roasted sweet and regular potatoes with a dressing kissed with toasted sesame oil and lime. It's gorgeous warm or cold.

1 Preheat the oven to 350°F.

2 Add the regular potatoes to a large saucepan of boiling water. Salt well, then bring to a boil over high heat. Reduce the heat to a simmer and cook for 5 minutes. Drain the potatoes, return them to the pan, and cover with a lid. Let stand for 5 minutes so that the potatoes absorb excess moisture.

3 On a baking sheet, toss the cooked potatoes and raw sweet potato with the oil, a generous pinch of salt, and the crushed red pepper. Roast in the oven for 50 to 60 minutes, until golden, flipping them halfway through.

4 To make the granola, in a dry skillet, toast the oats, pumpkin seeds, and cashews or peanuts over medium-high heat, stirring frequently, until it all smells nutty and is beginning to brown. Reduce the heat to low, then pour in the oil and stir to coat the oats. Make a hollow in the center of the mixture, add the soy sauce or tamari and honey or syrup, and stir into the oats until coated. Transfer to a plate and let cool and crisp up.

5 In a small bowl, mix all the dressing ingredients together. Pour the mixture over the roasted potatoes and stir to coat with the dressing. Divide the arugula among serving plates, top with the dressed potatoes, then sprinkle with the granola, scallions, and sliced chile to serve.

Vegan Use maple syrup or golden syrup in the granola and dressing.

Gluten Free Make sure your oats and tamari or soy sauce are certified gluten free.

LEFTOVERS: see pp. 228–233

- Regular potatoes
  (raw or roasted)
- Sweet potatoes
  (raw or roasted)
- Scallions
- Red chile

TIPS & SWAPS

If you have roasted sweet potatoes and regular potatoes to hand, use them instead of the raw potatoes. Skip steps 2 and 3 and spread the potatoes on a baking sheet, then place in an oven preheated to 350°F for 10 minutes, until warmed through. Continue with the recipe.

SWEET MISO EGGPLANT & WALNUT SALAD

Serves 3 to 4

2 large eggplants, sliced into
   ¼-inch-thick coins
2 to 3 tablespoons toasted sesame oil
1 tablespoon sesame seeds, toasted*
handful of pea shoots
2 large handfuls of salad greens
   or baby spinach
small handful of walnuts,
   coarsely chopped

GLAZE
2 tablespoons miso, any kind
juice of ½ lime or lemon
1 garlic clove
1 tablespoon granulated sugar or
   honey, or 2 tablespoons Date Paste
   (see page 221)
¼ cup water

DRESSING
2 teaspoons minced or grated
   ginger root
juice of ½ lemon or lime
1 teaspoon honey or maple syrup
2 tablespoons soy sauce or tamari
1 scallion, finely sliced
2 tablespoons olive oil or rapeseed oil

You may have noticed that I love miso. I use it in so many dishes instead of salt to punch up the umami flavors. This salad is based on one of my favorite miso dishes, a Japanese recipe called "Nasu Dengaku." Instead of halving the eggplants and brushing them with glaze, I slice them into coins to create more area for that salty-sweet miso mixture to cling to.

1   Preheat the oven to 350°F.

2   Lay the eggplant slices on a baking sheet (you may need to do this in batches). Using the tip of a knife, score a shallow crosshatch pattern into the slices. Drizzle with sesame oil and bake in the oven for 10 minutes to soften.

3   Meanwhile, in a small saucepan, mix all the glaze ingredients together over medium heat, stirring frequently, for 1 minute. Remove from the heat and brush or spoon the glaze over the eggplant slices. Return to the oven for another 20 minutes, then sprinkle with toasted sesame seeds and let cool.

4   In a jar with a screw-on lid, combine all the dressing ingredients, put on the lid, and shake to mix.

5   Arrange the pea shoots and salad greens on a plate and pour over the dressing. Toss the salad, then adorn with the cooled eggplant and walnuts.

Vegan   Use sugar or Date Paste in the glaze. Use maple syrup in the dressing.

Gluten Free   Ensure your tamari or soy sauce is certified gluten-free.

LEFTOVERS: see pp. 228–233

● Eggplants
● Miso
● Baby spinach
● Pea shoots

TIPS & SWAPS

*Toast the sesame seeds in a dry skillet over high heat.

Can't find pea shoots? Use extra salad greens instead.

VG & GF options

LIME–CHILE CORN & CRISPY ONIONS

Serves 2

3 tablespoons canola oil or olive oil
½ red onion, thinly sliced
1 tablespoon all-purpose flour
2 ears of corn, kernels
   cut off with a knife
1½ teaspoons honey
juice of ½ lime
½ to 1 jalapeño, finely chopped
¼ cup/1oz/30g crumbled feta cheese
salt

Sautéed fresh corn is the ultimate way to eat corn in my opinion. It has that crisp bite that I want to describe as al dente, but in a nonpasta way. Coupled with a bit of balance from the lime juice and some addictively crispy slices of fried onion, this takes fresh corn to the next level. Sprinkle over crumbled feta for that salty, creamy something, but grated Parmesan or cheddar are also banging substitutions.

1 Line a plate with paper towels. In a small skillet, heat the oil over high heat. Reduce the heat to medium-low, then toss the onion with the flour and cook in the oil until golden. Remove the onion from the pan with a spoon or tongs, leaving behind some of the oil, and transfer them to the prepared plate. Sprinkle with salt and set aside.

2 Return the pan to the heat. Add the corn kernels and turn the heat up to high. Cook, stirring occasionally, until the corn is nice and hot. Add the honey, lime juice, and jalapeño and stir to combine. Season with salt to taste.

3 Remove the pan from the heat and transfer to a serving platter. Adorn with the crumbled feta and the crispy onions, and serve.

Vegan Use Sun Feta (see page 219) or ½ cubed avocado instead of the feta. Use maple syrup instead of honey.

Gluten Free Use cornstarch, rice flour, or chick pea (garbanzo bean) flour to coat the red onion before frying.

TIPS & SWAPS

No fresh corn? Use 1¼ cups/
7oz/200g drained, canned corn
kernels or thawed frozen corn instead.

Use an equal weight of grated
Parmesan or Gruyère instead of
the feta.

LEFTOVERS: see pp. 228–233

● Chile
● Feta cheese
● Red onion
● Lime

VG option

ROASTED BEET, CUMIN & CRISPY CHICK PEAS

Serves 2 to 3

2 small or 1 large beet
3 tablespoons olive oil
¾ cup/4¼oz/120g cooked chick peas (garbanzo beans), drained and rinsed
juice of ½ lemon
5 tablespoons Greek-style yogurt
1 teaspoon cumin seeds
½ teaspoon ground coriander
¼ teaspoon smoked paprika
small handful of mint leaves, coarsely chopped
salt

The fuchsia-pink vibrancy that you get from pureed beet always gives me heart-eye-emoji feelings when I see it. The addition of yogurt adds a slight piquancy and creaminess. The scattering of chick peas on top is needed to mop up that sexy sauce, while the tempered spices and a sprinkle of mint bring the whole dish together. Serve with flatbread (see page 215) or tortillas (see page 214) for a lunch to make you smile.

1 Preheat the oven to 350°F. Wrap the beets in aluminum foil and roast in the oven for 1 hour or until tender.

2 In a skillet, heat 1 tablespoon of the oil over high heat. Add the chick peas and season with a pinch of salt. Cook, stirring frequently, until the chick peas are just starting to brown.

3 Remove the beets from the oven. Let cool for at least 15 minutes, then rub the beets under cool running water to remove the skins. Chop half the beet into small cubes and toss with the lemon juice.

4 Blend the other half of the cooked beet with a handheld blender or countertop blender or mash with a potato masher until smooth. Mix the yogurt and a generous pinch of salt into the beet, pour onto a serving plate, and top with the cubed beet and chick peas.

5 In a dry skillet, toast the cumin seeds over high heat for 1 minute. Add the remaining oil, ground coriander, and smoked paprika, stir to mix, then remove from the heat. Pour over the beet and chick peas, then top with the mint and serve.

Vegan Use unsweetened soy yogurt or pureed silken tofu and 1 tablespoon lemon juice instead of the yogurt.

TIPS & SWAPS

If you have some whole, roasted beets to hand, use them. Skip step 1 and continue with the recipe.

This makes a great lunchbox dish, as it's delicious served cold with a tortilla.

Use cooked green or Puy lentils instead of chick peas.

LEFTOVERS: see pp. 228–233

● Beet (raw or roasted)
● Cooked chick peas
● Yogurt
● Lemon
● Mint

GINGER-PICKLED MUSHROOMS WITH DATE RICE

Serves 2

3½oz/100g mushrooms, cleaned
⅓ cup rice vinegar
   or apple cider vinegar
½ cup water
½ teaspoon salt
¾oz/20g piece of ginger root,
   peeled and cut into matchsticks
   (about 3 tablespoons matchsticks)
⅓ cup plus 1½ tablespoons/2¾oz/75g
   dry brown rice, rinsed, or ¾ cup/
   50oz/140g cooked
½ tablespoon olive oil
⅓ cup/1¾oz/50g frozen, shelled
   edamame
3 dried dates, pitted
   and coarsely chopped
1 garlic clove, very finely chopped
1 teaspoon dark soy sauce
   or tamari
handful of baby spinach
1 scallion, finely sliced

Pickling mushrooms seems a bit weird, I know. However, with the clean flavor from the rice vinegar and the spicy spears of ginger, you may just fall in love with them. A few pickled mushrooms will go a long way to bring a lift to whatever dish you add them to. Use them in noodle salads or miso-based soups, or here with some date-speckled brown rice.

1   If you have some larger mushrooms (cremini, button, shiitake), cut them into slices. Smaller mushrooms like enoki or shimeji mushrooms are fine to keep whole. Put the mushrooms in a small bowl or clean jar.

2   In a small saucepan, heat the vinegar, water, salt, and ginger until simmering. Pour the mixture over the mushrooms and let stand for at least 30 minutes.

3   If starting with uncooked brown rice, put the rice in a medium saucepan and pour in enough water until well covered. Season with salt and bring to a boil. Reduce the heat and simmer for 20 minutes for long-grain brown rice or 30 minutes for short-grain brown rice, adding more water if needed. Once cooked, drain the rice and return it to the pan. Cover with a lid and let stand for 5 minutes to absorb the excess moisture.

4   In a skillet, heat the oil over medium heat. Add the frozen edamame and sauté until hot, 2 minutes. Add the dates, cooked rice, and garlic and sauté for another minute, then add the soy sauce and stir until coated.

5   Put the spinach in a serving bowl and pour the rice over the top. Garnish with 3 tablespoons of the mushrooms, and some of the ginger from the pickle too, if desired. Finally, add the scallion. Eat warm.

Gluten Free   Ensure that you are using a certified gluten-free tamari or soy sauce.

LEFTOVERS: see pp. 228–233

● Mushrooms
● Brown rice (uncooked or cooked)
● Dates
● Scallions
● Baby spinach

TIPS & SWAPS

Top with a halved soft-boiled egg. Simmer the egg in its shell in boiling water for 5 to 6 minutes, then place it in a bowl of cold water before peeling.

Keep any excess mushrooms in a sterilized, sealed jar for up to 1 week in the refrigerator.

ROASTED CARROTS WITH COUSCOUS & PICKLED ONION

Serves 2 to 3

7oz/200g carrots
2 tablespoons olive oil
¾ cup plus 2 tablespoons/5½oz/150g
   couscous
¾ cup plus 1½ tablespoons just-boiled
   water
5 tablespoons pesto, homemade
   (see pages 224–225) or
   store-bought
juice of ¼ lemon
handful of Quick Pickled Red Onion
   (see page 223)
¼ cup/1¾oz/50g coarsely chopped
   pitted black ripe olives
salt

Sweet and soft coins of roasted carrot meet herby pesto and toasty couscous, while the salty, tangy nuggets of olives and Quick Pickled Red Onion bring some extra life to this dish. It's a great side salad at dinner or casual lunch (especially with a fried egg on top).

1 Preheat the oven to 425°F.

2 If you have baby carrots (the small ones with the greens still attached), cut off the carrot greens. For regular carrots, cut into coins about ⅛ inch thick. On a baking sheet, toss the baby carrots or carrot coins with 1 tablespoon of the oil and a pinch of salt, then roast in the oven for 20 to 25 minutes, flipping halfway through cooking. They should be soft and sweet.

3 Meanwhile, put the couscous in a large bowl and pour over the just-boiled water. Cover with a plate and let stand until all the water has been absorbed, about 5–10 minutes. Fluff the couscous with a fork and stir in the remaining oil, the pesto, and lemon juice. Season with salt to taste, then transfer to a plate. Top with the roasted carrots, pickled onion, and olives. Serve warm or cold.

Vegan If using store-bought pesto, make sure it is certified vegan.

Gluten Free Instead of couscous, cook the same quantity of quinoa or brown rice according to the table on page 11.

TIPS & SWAPS

Try cooked green or Puy lentils, orzo, or Israeli couscous (sometimes called pearl couscous or fregola) instead of regular couscous.

Use 5½oz ready-roasted carrots, butternut squash, or sweet potato instead of the raw carrots. Skip steps 1 and 2 and continue with the recipe.

Sprinkle some crumbled feta or dry-fried pieces of halloumi cheese over the top.

LEFTOVERS: see pp. 228–233

● Lemon
● Carrots (raw or roasted)
● Pesto

EGGPLANT, POMEGRANATE & CHICK PEA SALAD

Serves 2 to 3

2 medium eggplants, cut into about
   ⅛-inch coins
2 tablespoons olive oil or canola oil
2 tablespoons lemon juice
2 teaspoons granulated sugar or honey
pinch of salt
handful of mint, finely chopped
½ to 1 red chile, finely chopped
   (depending on taste)
2 large handfuls of baby spinach,
   rinsed if needed
¾ cup/4¼oz/120g cooked chick peas
   (garbanzo beans), drained and rinsed
seeds from ½ pomegranate
2 tablespoons tahini

TO SERVE
pita bread or crusty bread (optional)

Eggplants are definitely best a bit burned. Thinly slicing them means you increase the surface area of their spongy inner flesh so that they are the perfect receptacle for soaking up a tangy, sweet dressing.

1 Lay the sliced eggplants on a baking sheet or cutting board in a single layer. Use a spoon to drizzle half the oil over the top of the eggplant layers, then use your hands to spread it around to coat the top of the slices. Flip the slices over and repeat on the other side with the remaining oil.

2 In a medium bowl, mix together the lemon juice, sugar or honey, salt, mint, and chile to make a dressing.

3 Heat a stovetop grill pan or large, nonstick skillet over high heat. Once the pan is hot, add a few eggplant coins and cook until dark on the underside (we are talking verging on burned here), 3 to 4 minutes, then flip them over and cook until the other side is golden. Transfer the cooked eggplant to the bowl with the dressing and toss until the eggplant is coated all over. Continue until all the eggplant slices are cooked. Let cool for at least 30 minutes or up to 12 hours in the refrigerator.

4 Arrange the spinach on a serving platter and top with the marinated eggplant, drained chick peas, and pomegranate seeds. Drizzle with the tahini and serve. I like it with pita bread or crusty bread for lunch or as a side with dinner.

Vegan Use granulated sugar.

LEFTOVERS: see pp. 228–233

- Red chile
- Mint
- Cooked chick peas
- Pomegranate
- Baby spinach
- Tahini
- Eggplant
- Lemon juice

TIPS & SWAPS

Replace the pomegranate seeds with a handful of fresh raspberries.

Use zucchini instead of the eggplants. Trim 2 medium zucchini, then cut them into long slices about ⅛ inch thick.

To make the tahini easy to drizzle, give the jar a good stir or combine 2 tablespoons tahini with 1 tablespoon extra virgin olive oil.

Use cooked green or Puy lentils instead of chick peas.

GF & VG options

CHICK PEA "TUNA" SALAD

Serves 2 to 3

¾ cup/4¼oz/120g cooked chick peas
   (garbanzo beans), drained* and rinsed
1 apple, cored and coarsely chopped
1 celery stalk, finely chopped
½ small red onion, finely chopped
1 medium carrot, shredded
about ¼ cup plain yogurt, mayonnaise,
   or Chick Pea Mayonnaise
   (see page 222)
pinch of granulated sugar
juice of ½ lemon
2 tablespoons olive oil
handful of cilantro, coarsely chopped
salt and freshly ground black pepper

TO SERVE
crusty whole-wheat bread or tortillas

The idea of using canned chick peas instead of tuna is an idea I picked up from a few vegan blogs. It's just as convenient to mash up this mixture as it is to make a usual tuna salad, which I know many people rely on for quick lunches. The combo of flavors may sound weird, but my mom has been making this for years with canned albacore tuna instead of the chick peas.

1 In a bowl, lightly mash the chick peas with a fork until they are still slightly chunky. Add the apple, celery, onion, and carrot and stir together. Mix in the yogurt or mayonnaise, the sugar, lemon juice, and oil and stir to combine, then season with salt and pepper to taste.

2 Top the salad with the chopped cilantro and serve with crusty bread or tortillas.

Vegan Use Chick Pea Mayonnaise (see page 222).

Gluten Free Serve with warmed gluten-free corn tortillas instead of bread.

TIPS & SWAPS

*If making the vegan Chick Pea Mayonnaise, reserve the liquid from the canned chick peas (or the cooking liquid, if you have cooked them yourself) to use in the recipe.

Replace the chick peas with cannellini (white kidney) or navy beans.

LEFTOVERS: see pp. 228–233

● Cooked chick peas
● Apples
● Celery
● Carrots
● Lemon
● Yogurt
● Cilantro
● Red onion

CANNELLINI BEANS WITH BALSAMIC ONIONS

Serves 2 as a side

½ cup/2¾oz/75g string or green beans
   trimmed and cut into
   about 1¼-inch lengths
1 tablespoon olive oil or canola oil
1 red onion, cut into
   ¹⁄₁₆-inch-thick slices
pinch of salt
2 tablespoons balsamic vinegar
1 cup/7oz/200g quartered cherry
   tomatoes
⅔ cup/4¼oz/120g cooked cannellini
   (white kidney) beans, drained and
   rinsed
pinch of granulated sugar
handful of basil leaves, torn

This light summer stew of sorts makes the most of seasonal produce. The cherry tomatoes break down slightly into a barely cooked sauce to keep the dish fresh and quick. In the winter, use green or red cabbage in place of the beans and half a can of diced tomatoes in place of the cherry tomatoes.

1 In a small saucepan, cover the green beans with just-boiled water. Bring to a boil, then reduce the heat and simmer for 3 minutes. Drain and set aside.

2 In a skillet, heat the oil over medium heat. Add the onion and salt and cook, stirring frequently, until the onion begins to darken in color. Splash in a few tablespoons of water and continue to cook, stirring, until the water has mostly evaporated. Add the balsamic vinegar and stir again.

3 Add the cherry tomatoes and a few more tablespoons of water and cook until the water has evaporated and the tomatoes have softened, about 7 to 10 minutes. Stir in the cooked green beans and the cannellini beans and cook just until heated through, about 1 minute. Stir in the sugar and serve warm with the torn basil.

TIPS & SWAPS

For a main-size salad for 2, double the recipe and serve with steamed spinach or kale and whole-wheat bread.

For a simple lunch, double everything except the green beans and cannellini beans. Cook 3½oz/100g dried whole-wheat pasta until al dente, reserving some of the pasta water. Follow the recipe as above, then stir in the cooked pasta and loosen it with some of the reserved pasta water.

Use cooked green or Puy lentils instead of cannellini beans.

LEFTOVERS: see pp. 228–233

● Green beans
● Cherry tomatoes
● Cannellini beans
● Basil

BEET, HAZELNUT & CRISPY SAGE SALAD

Serves 2 to 3

2 medium or 3 small beets,
  thinly sliced
3 tablespoons olive oil or canola oil
6 to 10 sage leaves, depending on size
⅔ cup/4¼oz/120g cooked cannellini
  (white kidney) or navy beans, drained
  and rinsed
¼ cup/1oz/30 g hazelnuts
generous pinch of granulated sugar
3 tablespoons balsamic vinegar
2 tablespoons extra virgin olive oil
juice of ½ lemon
salt

This is a salad for embracing the fall. The ingredients seem to be made for each other with their earthy flavors. I love to combine both raw and cooked thinly sliced beets because the textures are so different but complement each other so well. If you manage to find some pretty Chioggia beets (those "candy stripe" ones), this is a great way to display their stunning interiors.

1 Preheat the oven to 350°F.

2 Toss half the sliced beets in 1 teaspoon of the olive or canola oil and a pinch of salt. Spread in a single layer over a baking sheet and bake in the oven for 10 minutes, until softened.

3 In a small skillet, heat the remaining olive or canola oil over medium heat. Add the sage leaves and cook until crispy, then remove with a slotted spoon and drain on paper towels.

4 Keeping the skillet on the heat, add the beans and a pinch of salt and cook until the beans are slightly crisp and beginning to color. Transfer the beans to a bowl.

5 Return the skillet to medium heat and add the hazelnuts. Toast for 1 minute, then add the sugar, balsamic vinegar, and a pinch of salt and then stir until thickened and sticky, 2 minutes. Turn off the heat and let cool.

6 Add the baked beet and raw beet to the bowl with the beans. Pour in the extra virgin olive oil, lemon juice, and candied hazelnuts and toss together. Transfer to a serving plate and top with the crispy sage.

LEFTOVERS: see pp. 230–233

- Beets
- Sage leaves
- Lemon
- Cannellini beans

TIPS & SWAPS

Replace the hazelnuts with walnuts or pumpkin seeds.

Use an equal quantity of lentils instead of the cannellini beans. Refer to the cooking table on page 11 if you need guidance.

If you can't find sage, use (unfried) basil or thyme instead.

CHARRED LETTUCE WITH BAKED TOFU & PEANUT DRESSING

Serves 2

7oz/200g firm tofu
1 tablespoon olive oil or canola oil, plus
4 teaspoons
1 tablespoon soy sauce or tamari
2 teaspoons sesame seeds
2 heads of Little Gem lettuce
1 radish, thinly sliced
1 scallion, finely chopped
1 red chile, finely chopped (optional)

PEANUT GINGER DRESSING
2 tablespoons peanut, almond, or
    cashew butter, or tahini
1 teaspoon granulated sugar
    or honey, or 1 tablespoon
    Date Paste (see page 221)
juice of ½ lime
1 tablespoon soy sauce or tamari
1 teaspoon grated ginger root

If you're not convinced by tofu, try it baked. It's less fuss and healthier than fried tofu and produces the cutest crisp, golden cubes. I like to double the recipe and keep the extra tofu in the refrigerator for a few days—it provides a great protein boost for salads, stir-fries, or tacos. Grilling the lettuce may seem weird but I love it—you get half the lettuce charred, warm, and wilted and the rest still crisp and cooling.

1 To press the tofu, wrap it in a clean kitchen towel and place on a flat surface. Cover with a cutting board, then weigh the cutting board down with something heavy, such as a stack of cookbooks or a saucepan full of water. Let stand for 30 minutes to drain.

2 Preheat the oven to 350°F. Line a baking sheet with nonstick parchment paper.

3 Unwrap the tofu, cut it into ½-inch cubes, and put in a bowl. Add the 1 tablespoon oil and soy sauce or tamari and toss until the tofu is coated all over. Sprinkle over the sesame seeds and toss again. Spread out on the prepared baking sheet and bake in the oven for 30 minutes, until golden.

4 Cut the lettuce heads in half and drizzle the cut sides with the remaining oil. Place them cut side down in a skillet, or stovetop grill pan if you have one, over the highest heat. I can fit 2 halves at a time into my pan. Cook until the underside is blackened, about 4 minutes. Transfer to a plate.

5 In a bowl, mix all the dressing ingredients together until smooth. Add a bit of water to thin the dressing into a drizzle-able sauce.

6 Drizzle the sauce over the charred lettuce and top with the baked tofu, thinly sliced radish, chopped scallion, and chile to serve.

Vegan Use sugar or Date Paste.

Gluten Free Make sure that you are using a certified gluten-free tamari or soy sauce.

TIPS & SWAPS
If you drain and bake double the tofu, double up on the olive oil, soy, and sesame seeds. Use the extra tofu as snacks or with steamed veg for a quick dinner.

Asian markets will usually have tofu in their chiller cabinets. Drain before using.

Serve with brown rice for a more filling dish.

LEFTOVERS: see pp. 228–233

- Red chile
- Nut butter or tahini
- Scallions
- Lime
- Firm tofu

GF option

SQUASH, POTATO & CHILE CAKES

Makes 6 to 8

about ⅙ large or ⅓ small butternut
squash (7oz/200g), peeled and
seeded
7oz/200g potatoes (about 2 medium),
peeled
3 tablespoons all-purpose flour
2 scallions, minced
½ red chile, minced, or ¼ teaspoon
crushed red pepper
generous pinch of salt
olive oil or canola oil, for cooking

Both butternut squash and potatoes can be stored at room temperature for quite a while. I always feel happy knowing I have a stock of squash, which I buy in the fall, sitting on my windowsill to use for a few months. These fritters are very basic, but I love the bite of the chile and the fresh flavor of the scallions. They are great with a fried egg and some greens for lunch or with rice, Tahini Dressing (see page 226), chopped cilantro, and steamed greens for dinner.

1 Line a plate with paper towels.

2 Shred the butternut squash and potato and place on a square of cheesecloth or a clean kitchen towel. Gather up the edges at the top to make a little bundle, then squeeze over the sink to remove as much liquid as possible. Transfer the squeezed squash and potato to a medium bowl, add the flour, scallions, chile, and salt and use your hands to combine it all together.

3 In a nonstick skillet, heat just enough oil to coat the bottom over medium heat. Once the oil is hot, add heaping tablespoons of the mixture— I can fit 3 to 5 in my skillet depending on how strategically I place them. Flatten each mound down with the back of the spoon so that you have small fritters, then cook them until dark golden and crispy on the underside. Flip them over and cook until the other side is golden too. Transfer to the prepared plate and cook the remaining mixture as before, adding more oil to the pan as needed.

Gluten Free Use chick pea (garbanzo bean) flour instead of the all-purpose flour.

LEFTOVERS: see pp. 228–233

● Butternut squash (raw)
● Potatoes
● Scallions
● Red chile

TIPS & SWAPS

Use shredded raw
sweet potato instead of
the butternut squash.

SPANAKOPITA QUESADILLAS

Makes 3

7oz/200g baby spinach
7oz/200g Tuscan kale (cavolo nero)
 (weighed with the stems)
½ cup/1¾oz/50g shredded cheddar
 cheese
⅓ cup/1¾oz/50g crumbled feta cheese
1 teaspoon mixed dried herbs or 3 sprigs
 of fresh thyme, stems removed
1 egg
generous pinch of salt
3 teaspoons olive oil or canola oil
3 large whole-wheat tortillas
 or 6 small whole-wheat tortillas

TO SERVE
Pea Hummus (see page 46)

This stroke of genius happened when my friend Sam couldn't find phyllo pastry to make me a birthday spanakopita. He used tortillas instead and I'm glad he did—they were so good!

1 Put the spinach and Tuscan kale in a large saucepan with a bit of water over medium heat. Cover with a lid, reduce the heat to low, and cook until wilted, a few minutes.

2 Once wilted, rinse the greens under cold running water, then squeeze as much water out as possible. Coarsely chop the greens and add to a medium bowl with the cheeses, herbs, egg, and salt and stir until evenly mixed.

3 In a large skillet, heat 1 teaspoon of the oil over medium heat. Tilt the pan so that the oil spreads to cover the bottom of the skillet. Add 1 tortilla and cover half of it with a third of the spinach mixture. Fold the tortilla in half up and over the filling and press down to seal. Cook over medium-low heat until the underside is golden, then flip over and cook the other side until golden. Transfer to a plate and repeat with the rest of the filling and tortillas.

4 Cut the tortillas into wedges and eat hot with Pea Hummus!

ZUCCHINI & GARLIC QUESADILLA

Serves 2

1 tablespoon olive oil
1 medium zucchini, shredded
1 garlic clove, crushed or minced
2 large whole-wheat tortillas
handful of shredded cheddar cheese
a few basil leaves, torn
salt

TO SERVE
plain yogurt (optional)

Simple, quick and tasty, this is my go-to lunch when I need something hot and carby to fill me up. By shredding the zucchini you'll go from zero to food in about 10 minutes.

1 In a medium skillet, heat the oil over medium heat. Add the zucchini and garlic and sauté until softened, 1 to 2 minutes. Season with salt to taste and transfer to a plate. Wipe out the pan and return it to the heat.

2 Place a tortilla in the skillet, then sprinkle half the cheese over the surface of the tortilla. Sprinkle the basil over the cheese, then spread half the cooked zucchini over half the tortilla. Fold the tortilla in half to cover the filling and cook until golden on the underside. Flip over and cook until the other side is golden. Remove from the pan and cut into 2 wedges. Repeat with the last tortilla and remaining filling. Eat warm with yogurt for dipping!

TIPS & SWAPS

Spanakopita Quesadillas can be kept in the refrigerator in plastic wrap for up to 3 days. Reheat in a dry skillet over medium heat to serve.

Use shredded or chopped mozzarella cheese instead of the cheddar in the Spanakopita Quesadillas for a more gooey quesadilla.

LEFTOVERS: see pp. 228–233

- Feta cheese
- Baby spinach
- Tuscan kale
- Thyme

- Zucchini
- Basil
- Yogurt

VG option

ROASTED TOMATOES & CARROTS WITH BLACK BEANS & TAHINI

Serves 2 to 3

7oz/200g carrots
7oz/200g cherry tomatoes, halved
1 tablespoon olive oil or canola oil
⅔ cup/4¼oz/120g cooked black beans, drained and rinsed
handful of cilantro, coarsely chopped
handful of mint, coarsely chopped
5 to 6 dried dates, pitted and coarsely chopped
1 tablespoon pomegranate molasses

SAUCE
2 tablespoons tahini
½ teaspoon ground turmeric
3 tablespoons plain yogurt
juice of ½ lemon
pinch of salt

Roasting carrots is something I never used to do, but then I realized they are the quicker, cheaper cousin to sweet potatoes or butternut squash. When I find them, I like to use baby carrots that come tied in a bunch with a head of luscious carrot greens—I wash the greens and use them instead of arugula in my Basil & Arugula Pesto (see page 224).

1   Preheat the oven to 425°F. Line a baking sheet with nonstick parchment paper.

2   If you have baby carrots, just wash them and remove the greens. If you have regular carrots, cut them into about ¼-inch-thick coins.

3   Toss the tomatoes and carrots in the oil and spread out on the prepared baking sheet. Roast in the oven for 30 minutes, tossing them with a spatula halfway through.

4   In a small bowl, mix together all the ingredients for the sauce. Spread the mixture onto a serving plate. Top with the black beans, the roasted tomatoes and carrots, the herbs, and dates, and drizzle with the pomegranate molasses.

Vegan Use Chick Pea Mayonnaise (see page 222) or unsweetened soy yogurt in the sauce.

LEFTOVERS: see pp. 228–233

- Tahini
- Lemon
- Yogurt
- Carrots (raw or roasted)
- Cherry tomatoes (raw or roasted)
- Cilantro
- Mint
- Dates
- Cooked black beans

TIPS & SWAPS
Omit the pomegranate molasses and cook ¼ cup balsamic vinegar with 2 teaspoons granulated sugar in a small saucepan over low heat until reduced and syrupy, 1 to 2 minutes.

Instead of fresh, use 1 cup/4¼oz/120g drained sundried tomatoes in oil and toss in at the end.

Use any beans here. I like chick peas (garbanzo beans) or red kidney beans.

A sprinkle of pomegranate seeds is a colorful, crunchy addition.

GF option

CORN, PEACH & PEARL BARLEY SALAD

Serves 2 to 3

⅓ cup/2¼oz/60g dry pearl barley or scant 1¼ cups/6½oz/180g cooked pearl barley
2 ears of corn*, corn kernels cut off with a knife
1 peach, pitted and cut into eighths
½ red onion, thinly sliced
handful of sorrel leaves or baby spinach
3 tablespoons pumpkin seeds
juice of ½ lime
¼ teaspoon smoked paprika
salt

BASIL AVOCADO DRESSING
½ avocado, pitted and peeled
a large handful of basil leaves
pinch of salt
3 tablespoons water
juice of ½ lime

If you have half an avocado slowly turning brown in the refrigerator and you know you're not going to smash it onto some toast, why not turn it into dressing? It's a great way to use it up. Having that creamy, light dressing on chewy pearl barley with fresh peaches and corn is a summer salad delight.

1 Put the pearl barley in a small saucepan and cover with cold water. Bring to a boil, reduce the heat, and simmer until cooked, 30 to 40 minutes. Drain, rinse, drain again well, and spread out on a serving plate to cool.

2 Meanwhile, for the dressing, in a bowl, mash the avocado with a fork until smooth, then finely chop the basil and stir it into the avocado with the salt, water, and lime juice. It will be quite a thick consistency. Alternatively, use a handheld blender in a beaker or a countertop blender to blend.

3 Sprinkle the corn kernels over the pearl barley along with the peach and onion, then toss with the sorrel or spinach and a pinch of salt until combined.

4 In a small, dry skillet, toast the pumpkin seeds over high heat, stirring frequently, until they start to pop. Remove from the heat and transfer to a bowl. Squeeze over the lime juice, then add the paprika and a pinch of salt and stir until the seeds are coated in the mixture. Sprinkle over the salad and drizzle with the avocado dressing to serve.

Gluten Free Swap the pearl barley for cooked quinoa, brown rice, or millet.

TIPS & SWAPS

*No fresh corn? Use 1¼ cups/ 7oz/200g drained, canned corn kernels or thawed frozen corn.

A firmer peach works best in this salad.

Instead of raw red onion, use Quick Pickled Red Onion (see page 223).

LEFTOVERS: see pp. 228–233

● Avocado
● Basil
● Red onion
● Sorrel or baby spinach
● Peaches
● Lime

CARROT RIBBON, CINNAMON & HALLOUMI SALAD

Serves 2

3 large carrots
¼ red onion, thinly sliced
handful of cilantro, finely chopped
2 tablespoons sesame seeds
4oz/115g halloumi cheese,
  cut into ¼-inch-thick slices
2 handfuls of baby spinach

DRESSING

juice of ½ lime or lemon
½ teaspoon honey or granulated sugar
¼ teaspoon ground cinnamon
½ teaspoon ground cumin
1 teaspoon olive oil
pinch of salt

The lip-smacking salinity of the halloumi is tempered here by the sweet carrot ribbons and lime-pepped dressing. This salad is quick to assemble and looks super-impressive thanks to the undulating ribbons of carrot. Don't forget to add the sesame seeds, which bring toasty pops of flavor to each bite!

1 In a medium bowl, mix all the dressing ingredients together until smooth. Set aside.

2 Using a vegetable peeler, peel the carrots into lots of lovely ribbons and add them to the bowl with the sliced onion and chopped cilantro. Toss the mixture together with your hands until everything is well coated in the dressing and set aside.

3 In a dry skillet, toast the sesame seeds over medium-high heat, stirring frequently, until golden. Transfer to a bowl and set aside.

4 Set the skillet back on the heat and add the sliced halloumi. Cook until light golden on the underside, 2 to 4 minutes, then flip over and cook on the other side. Remove and let cool slightly, then tear into coarse chunks.

5 Place a handful of spinach in the bottom of each serving bowl and top with the carrot mixture, a sprinkle of sesame seeds, and the torn halloumi chunks.

TIPS & SWAPS

Replace the baby spinach with arugula, mixed salad greens, or sliced Little Gem lettuce.

Use ⅓ cup/1¾oz/50g crumbled feta instead of halloumi. Don't fry it—just sprinkle over the salad.

LEFTOVERS: see pp. 228–233

- Lime
- Halloumi cheese
- Red onion
- Cilantro
- Carrots
- Baby spinach

WARM ROASTED CAULIFLOWER & CHICK PEA SALAD

Serves 2 to 3

1 large head of cauliflower, outer leaves removed, head cut into medium florets
1 tablespoon olive oil
1½ cups/8½oz/240g cooked chick peas (garbanzo beans), drained and rinsed
2 heads of Belgian endive, separated into leaves
salt

DRESSING

2 tablespoons miso, any kind
¼ cup olive oil
1 garlic clove, crushed or minced
1 shallot or ¼ red onion, finely diced
2 teaspoons granulated sugar or honey
1 tablespoon lemon juice, or apple cider vinegar or rice vinegar

I can (and have) happily eaten this dish for dinner on a dark, wintery evening. It's a homely combination of slightly chewy chick peas, crisp-yet-soft cauliflower, and hardy spears of crisp endive. I have found that I prefer endive when it's subjected briefly to heat, as it loses its bitter edge but stays crisp and juicy. If you are a fan of the bitterness that endive brings, by all means skip the grilling and toss them in raw.

1 Preheat the oven to 350°F.

2 Place the cauliflower on a baking sheet or in a roasting pan, drizzle with the oil, and sprinkle with salt. Toss until the cauliflower is coated in the oil, then roast in the oven for 45 minutes.

3 Twenty minutes into roasting the cauliflower, add the chick peas to the baking sheet and toss using a metal spatula to coat them in the oil. Return to the oven for the remaining 25 minutes of cooking time.

4 In a jar with a screw-on lid, combine all the dressing ingredients, put on the lid, and shake to mix.

5 Heat a skillet or stovetop grill pan over very high heat. Working in batches, add the endive leaves to the pan and let the heat slightly wilt the leaves, which will remove their bitterness, then transfer them to a large bowl.

6 Add the warm cauliflower and chick peas to the bowl with the endive and the dressing. Toss to coat, then serve warm.

Vegan Use granulated sugar in the dressing.

LEFTOVERS: see pp. 228–233

- Cauliflower
- Miso
- Cooked chick peas
- Lemon (if you used lemon juice in the dressing)
- Red onion

TIPS & SWAPS

If you have roasted cauliflower florets to hand, use about 10½oz/300g instead of the raw cauliflower. Skip step 1 and just roast the chick peas for 20 minutes, tossing the cauliflower onto the baking sheet in the final 5 minutes.

CANNELLINI BEAN & APPLE SALAD WITH APPLE YOGURT DRESSING

Serves 3 to 4

2 carrots
1 apple, thinly sliced
juice of 1 lemon
1 head of Little Gem lettuce, rinsed
⅔ cup/4¼oz/120g cooked cannellini
  (white kidney) beans, drained and
  rinsed
handful of sunflower seeds
2 scallions, finely sliced

APPLE YOGURT DRESSING

1 apple, shredded
1 tablespoon honey
generous pinch of salt
⅓ cup extra virgin olive
  oil or olive oil
6 tablespoons plain yogurt
  or crème fraîche
2 tablespoons apple cider vinegar

This salad is nothing fancy in itself—just a crunchy, bright thing to eat in the fall. The real star is the dressing made with cooked, blended apple and creamy yogurt.

1 First, make the dressing. In a small skillet, cook the apple and honey over low heat until softened. Remove from the heat and let cool. Transfer the apple and honey mixture to a beaker with the salt, olive oil, and yogurt. Using a handheld blender, blend until smooth. Alternatively, add it all to a countertop blender and blend until smooth. Stir in the vinegar and add enough water as needed to make a pourable dressing.

2 Using a vegetable peeler, peel the carrots into ribbons and put them in a bowl. Add the thinly sliced apple and lemon juice and toss until coated.

3 Shred the lettuce into bite-size chunks and toss with the apple, carrots, and beans in a salad bowl. Add half the dressing and toss until everything is coated, then top with the sunflower seeds and scallions. Serve with more dressing as needed.

TIPS & SWAPS

Store extra dressing in the refrigerator in a sealed jar for up to 1 week—handy for quick lunches or salads.

Use pears instead of the apples in both the salad and dressing.

Replace the Little Gem lettuce with 3⅓ cups/3½oz/100g baby spinach, mixed salad greens, or arugula.

LEFTOVERS: see pp. 228–233

● Cooked cannellini beans
● Yogurt or crème fraîche
● Apples
● Carrots
● Scallions

PEAR, RICOTTA & ENDIVE SALAD WITH THYME DRESSING

Serves 2 to 3

1 pear, thinly sliced
2 large handfuls of mixed salad greens
2 heads of Belgian endive,
   separated into leaves
¼ cup/1oz/30g sunflower seeds
¼ cup/2¼oz/60g ricotta cheese
Parmesan*, shaved with
   a vegetable peeler

HONEY–THYME DRESSING
2 teaspoons honey
3 tablespoons olive oil
juice of 1 lemon
pinch of salt
¼ red onion, finely chopped
4 sprigs of thyme, leaves picked

Creamy ricotta spooned into the gentle curves of Belgian endive leaves and that always satisfying sweet and salty combo coming from pears, honey, and wisps of Parmesan is just delicious. If you're unconvinced by salad, try this one out —it may just make you reconsider.

1 In a jar with a screw-on lid, combine all the dressing ingredients, put on the lid, and shake to emulsify.

2 Place the sliced pear and mixed salad greens on a large serving plate. Drizzle over some of the dressing and toss gently until coated (the lemon juice in the dressing will help prevent the pear browning).

3 Heat a skillet or stovetop grill pan over very high heat. Working in batches, add the endive leaves to the pan and let the heat slightly wilt the leaves, which will remove their bitterness, then transfer them to the serving plate. Return the empty pan to the heat and add the sunflower seeds. Toast over high heat, stirring frequently, until lightly golden and smelling toasty. Scatter them over the endive.

4 Dot the salad with spoonfuls of ricotta and a few big flakes of shaved Parmesan. Drizzle over some more dressing, if desired, and serve.

TIPS & SWAPS

*Parmesan is not technically vegetarian—choose an alternative vegetarian hard cheese.

Replace the pear with apple, peach, or grapes.

Chopped walnuts or almonds are fab instead of the sunflower seeds.

Omit the endive and replace it with a few more handfuls of mixed salad greens.

LEFTOVERS: see pp. 228–233

● Red onion
● Ricotta cheese
● Thyme

Bigger Meals

These heartier dishes are definitely what you would want at the end of a long day. There are rib-sticking stews, thick soups, all sorts of pasta dishes, and some lighter, more saladlike meals. I think the key to not getting exhausted from cooking every night is to batch-cook certain ingredients on the weekends, such as chick peas or roasted vegetables and salad dressings. It makes stepping into the kitchen in the evening seem like less of a monotonous task, as you get most of the hard work out of the way on a single evening. I've left gentle reminders in the "Tips" sections at the end of each recipe to get you to start cooking extra food while you are making a recipe so that you can make your future life a bit easier. Once you get into the habit, it'll become second nature, and, trust me, you'll be happier for it.

VG option

ROASTED SQUASH WITH BROWN RICE & HALLOUMI

Serves 2

about ½ small butternut squash or
   ¼ large one (14oz/400g), peeled,
   seeded, and cut into about 1¼-inch
   chunks
½ tablespoon olive oil or canola oil
¾ cup plus 1 tablespoon/5½oz/150g
   dry brown rice, rinsed, or 1½ cups/
   10½oz/300g cooked
4½oz/125g halloumi, cut into ⅛-inch-
thick slices
a few handfuls of pomegranate
   seeds or raisins
2 handfuls of baby spinach
½ red onion, finely sliced
large handful of cilantro or cilantro
   microgreens, finely chopped
salt

TAHINI DRESSING
2 tablespoons tahini
1 garlic clove, crushed or minced
pinch of salt
juice of ½ lemon

I hoard butternut squash in fall and winter. It will keep on a windowsill or in a cupboard for a month or two without spoiling (until you cut it, then you need to refrigerate it), so it's perfect to buy in season and store for later in the year. I'm not a fan of steamed butternut squash, but roasted squash? UH, 1,000 times YES. It's a pretty sweet vegetable, so I love love love it with salty, squeaky halloumi and earthy tahini dressing. The pomegranates add a pop of color, but you can just use raisins or even cubed apple for the same effect.

1   Preheat the oven to 350°F.

2   On a baking sheet, toss the squash with the oil and a pinch of salt. Roast in the oven for 45 minutes, turning it halfway though cooking, until it starts to brown.

3   If starting with dry brown rice, put in a medium saucepan and pour in enough water until well covered. Season with salt and bring to a boil. Reduce the heat and simmer for 20 minutes for long-grain brown rice or 30 minutes for short-grain brown rice, adding more water if needed. Once cooked, drain the rice and return it to the pan. Cover with a lid and let stand for 5 minutes to absorb the excess moisture.

4   In a small bowl, mix together all the tahini dressing ingredients. Add enough water to make a drizzle-able sauce and set aside.

5   Heat a dry, nonstick skillet over medium heat. Add the sliced halloumi and cook until it is light golden on the underside, 2 to 4 minutes, then flip over and cook on the other side. Remove from the pan.

6   Mix the pomegranate seeds or raisins and roasted squash into the cooked rice. Arrange a bed of spinach in each bowl, add the rice mixture, drizzle with the tahini sauce, and top with the halloumi, red onion, and cilantro.

Vegan   Leave out the halloumi or replace with Sun Feta (see page 219).

LEFTOVERS: see pp. 228–233

● Butternut squash (raw or roasted)
● Brown rice (dry or cooked)
● Tahini
● Red onion
● Baby spinach
● Cilantro
● Halloumi cheese
● Pomegranate
● Lemon

TIPS & SWAPS

Use Little Gem lettuce, mixed salad greens, arugula, or pea shoots instead of baby spinach.

Swap the pomegranate seeds for some apple! Leave the skin on; just core and coarsely chop before using.

Use cooked pearl barley or quinoa instead of the rice.

Replace the squash with an equal weight of cubed sweet potato or carrots cut into $1/8$-inch-thick coins.

CHICK PEA, DATE & GINGER TAGINE WITH HUMMUS

Serves 2 to 3

¼ cup olive oil
1 medium eggplant, cut into
    about 1¼-inch cubes
1 red onion, cut into about
    ⅛-inch-thick slices
1 red, yellow, or orange bell pepper,
    seeded and cut into eighths
1 tablespoon grated or minced
    ginger root
2 teaspoons garam masala
1 teaspoon Chinese five spice
½ teaspoon ground cinnamon
¼ teaspoon cayenne pepper
3 tablespoons water
1 tablespoon miso, any kind,
    soy sauce, or tamari
4 to 6 dried dates, pitted and coarsely
    chopped (depending on your taste)
14oz/400g canned diced tomatoes
2¼ cups/12½oz/360g cooked chick
    peas (garbanzo beans)—don't drain
    yet
1 garlic clove, crushed or minced
1 tablespoon lemon juice
¾ cup plus 1 tablespoon/5½oz/150g
    dry brown rice, rinsed, or 1½ cups/
    10½oz/300g cooked, warmed
salt
sprigs of cilantro, to serve

Loosely based on a tagine, this chick pea dish is packed with flavor thanks to a hit of ginger and spices. The hummus seems to round out the flavors and textures, plus it cuts through the sticky sweetness of the dates.

1 In a large skillet, heat 1 tablespoon of the oil over medium heat. Add the eggplant and sauté until slightly browned, 10 minutes. Add another tablespoon of oil, then the onion, bell pepper, and ginger and cook until the onion starts to brown, about an additional 10 minutes. Add the spices and cook, stirring, for 1 minute, then add the water and cook until the water has evaporated and the onion has softened, 1 to 2 minutes. Add the miso, dates, and tomatoes and stir until combined.

2 Reserve ¼ cup of liquid from the canned chick peas and set aside. Now completely drain the chick peas and mix half of them into the pan. Simmer the stew until the eggplant has softened, 15 to 20 minutes.

3 Meanwhile, place the other half of the chick peas in a countertop blender or food processor (or a beaker if using a handheld blender) with the remaining oil, garlic, lemon juice, and a generous pinch of salt, and blitz until smooth, thinning with the reserved chick pea liquid.

4 If using dry rice, put in a medium saucepan and cover with water. Season with salt and bring to a boil. Reduce the heat and simmer for 20 minutes for long-grain brown rice or 30 minutes for short-grain brown rice, adding more water as needed. Once cooked, drain the rice and return it to the pan. Cover with a lid and let stand for 5 minutes to absorb the excess moisture.

5 Serve the stew over the rice with the hummus and a handful of cilantro.

Gluten Free Make sure that you are using a certified gluten-free tamari or soy sauce.

LEFTOVERS: see pp. 228–233

● Cooked chick peas
● Dates
● Miso
● Tomatoes, canned
● Lemon
● Brown rice (dry or cooked)
● Cilantro

TIPS & SWAPS

Double up on the hummus and keep the extra in the refrigerator for another day.

Serve with pita or flatbreads (see page 215) instead of rice.

Cool and store any extra rice as quickly as possible by rinsing it under cold running water or spreading it out on a plate. Once cooled, keep in the refrigerator for 1 day or in a sandwich bag in the freezer for 2 months. When reheating, make sure it is piping hot before serving.

EGGPLANT, RED LENTIL & COCONUT CURRY

Serves 2 to 3

1 medium eggplant
3 tablespoons olive oil
½ red onion or 1 shallot, chopped
½ teaspoon crushed red pepper
2 teaspoons garam masala
1½ teaspoons ground cinnamon
½ teaspoon ground cumin
1 teaspoon ground turmeric
1 star anise (optional)
¼ cup/3½oz/100g dry red lentils, rinsed
½ block (3½oz/100g) creamed coconut
　or ½ can (7oz/200g) coconut milk
2½ cups vegetable stock or 1⅓ cups if
　using coconut milk
1 teaspoon granulated sugar
　or honey, or 2 teaspoons Date
　Paste (see page 221)
juice of ½ lemon or lime
salt
cooked brown rice or No-yeast
　Flatbreads (see page 214)

TO GARNISH
large handful of cilantro, chopped
3 scallions, sliced
¼ cup toasted coconut flakes

I know it looks like a lot of ingredients, but trust me I'm not trying to trick you into making something super-complicated. Most of the ingredients are individual spices—I like making my own spice mixes for curries rather than using premixed "curry powder," which can become too same-y. The red lentils make this dish easy for a weeknight meal, as they cook quickly and are chockablock with protein and fiber.

1 Cut the top off the eggplant, slice it in half lengthwise, and then cut into ¾-inch cubes.

2 In a deep skillet, heat 2 tablespoons of the oil over high heat. Add the eggplant and cook, stirring occasionally, until it has started to turn golden, 15 minutes. Transfer to a plate and set aside.

3 Reduce the heat to medium-low, add the remaining oil, onion, and all the spices to the pan. Cook, stirring, until the onion has softened, 2 minutes.

4 Add the lentils, creamed coconut or coconut milk, stock, and sugar, honey, or Date Paste to the pan and stir until the creamed coconut has fully melted and mixed into the other ingredients. Bring to a boil, then reduce the heat and simmer, stirring occasionally, until thickened, 20 to 25 minutes.

5 Remove and discard the star anise, if using, then season the curry with the lemon or lime juice and salt to taste. Stir in the eggplant. Serve the curry piping hot with some cooked brown rice or No-yeast Flatbreads, garnished with the cilantro, sliced scallions, and toasted coconut flakes.

Vegan Use granulated sugar or Date Paste.

TIPS & SWAPS

Split yellow peas work well instead of red lentils, but cook the curry for another 20 minutes and add a bit of water to stop it becoming too dry.

Add extra veggies—stir in 3⅓ cups/3½oz/100g baby spinach at the end.

LEFTOVERS: see pp. 228–233

- Creamed coconut
　or coconut milk
- Red onion
- Lemon or lime
- Cilantro
- Scallions
- Brown rice, cooked

ROASTED (SWEET OR REGULAR) POTATO 3 WAYS

If you know you're going to be too exhausted to cook during the week, a good habit to get into is to roast floury or sweet potatoes on the weekend to store in the refrigerator. When it comes to crunch time, just reheat your potato in the microwave or oven and make one of the easy fillings overleaf OR use the leftovers table on pages 228–233.

1 Preheat the oven to 350°F.

2 Sweet potato (7 to 10½oz/200 to 300g): Prick all over with a fork, then wrap in a piece of aluminum foil and roast in the oven for 1 to 1¼ hours (depending on size and shape), until completely tender.

3 Regular potato (7 to 10½oz/200 to 300g): Prick all over with a fork, rinse with water but don't dry, then rub with sea salt. Put on a baking sheet and bake in the oven for 1 to 1¼ hours (depending on size and shape), until knife tender.

4 Speed it up: Preheat the oven to 350°F. Prick either potato all over with a fork, place on a plate, and microwave on high for 5 minutes. Rub with salt, put on a baking sheet, and finish cooking by baking in the oven for 20 to 30 minutes.

CANNELLINI BEANS, TOASTED BREAD CRUMBS & SPINACH

LEFTOVERS: see pp. 228-233

- Whole sweet potato (baked)
- Whole regular potato (baked)

MISO, MUSHROOMS
& CRISPY TUSCAN KALE

SALSA & COUSCOUS

TIPS & SWAPS

Bake some extra potatoes and keep
them in the refrigerator for up
to 3 days. Reheat in the microwave or
oven. See the leftovers table, on
pages 228–233, for other
recipes to use them in.

MISO, MUSHROOMS & CRISPY TUSCAN KALE

Serves 1

2 large Tuscan kale (cavolo nero) leaves, tough stems removed
and leaves cut into bite-size pieces
1 tablespoon olive oil or canola oil
1 tablespoon sesame seeds
1 cup/2¾oz/75g sliced button or cremini mushrooms
1 teaspoon miso, any kind
salt

1 Preheat the oven to 275°F.

2 Put the Tuscan kale on a baking sheet. Drizzle with half
the oil and sprinkle with salt, then toss and massage
together until all the leaves are coated. Bake in the oven
for 12 to 15 minutes, until crisp.

3 In a dry skillet, toast the sesame seeds over high heat,
stirring, until golden, then transfer to a bowl and set aside.

4 Return the skillet to the stove over medium heat and
add the remaining oil. Add the mushrooms and sauté
until darkened and soft, 5 to 7 minutes. Add the miso
and a good splash of water—smush the miso into the
water with the back of a spoon to make a miso sauce,
then stir to coat the mushrooms. Remove the pan from
the heat.

5 Cut the sweet potato in half and coarsely mash the
flesh with a fork. Top with the mushrooms, crispy
Tuscan kale, and sesame seeds, then serve.

LEFTOVERS: see pp. 228–233

- Tuscan kale
- Miso
- Mushrooms

CANNELLINI BEANS, TOASTED BREAD CRUMBS & SPINACH

Serves 1

3 teaspoons olive oil
2 tablespoons dry bread crumbs (see page 218)
½ cup/3½oz/100g cooked cannellini (white kidney) beans, drained and rinsed
1 garlic clove, crushed or minced
2 handfuls of baby spinach
few basil leaves, coarsely chopped
salt

1 Drizzle 1 teaspoon of the oil over the halved baked (sweet) potato, sprinkle with some salt, and lightly mash it into the flesh with a fork.

2 In a skillet, toast the bread crumbs with another teaspoon of the oil over medium heat, stirring continuously, until golden, 1 to 2 minutes. Pour into a bowl and set aside. Wipe out the skillet and return to the heat.

3 Add the remaining oil to the skillet over medium heat. Add the beans and garlic and sauté for 1 minute. Add the spinach, reduce the heat to low, and stir until wilted. Season with salt to taste.

4 Pour the beans over the halved (sweet) potato and garnish with the bread crumbs and basil.

SALSA & COUSCOUS

Serves 1

2 tablespoons dry couscous
3 tablespoons just-boiled water
4 to 5 cherry tomatoes, finely chopped
juice of ½ lime
handful of cilantro, finely chopped
1 scallion, finely sliced,
    or ¼ red onion, finely chopped
pinch of crushed red pepper
1 tablespoon pumpkin or sunflower seeds,
    coarsely chopped
pinch of salt

1 Put the couscous in a small bowl with the just-boiled water, cover with a plate, and set aside for 5 minutes. Fluff with a fork.

2 Meanwhile, in a bowl, mix together the tomatoes, lime juice, cilantro, scallion or red onion, crushed red pepper, and salt.

3 Spoon the couscous and tomato salsa over the halved (sweet) potato and sprinkle on the chopped seeds.

LEFTOVERS: see pp. 228–233
- Cannellini beans
- Basil leaves
- Baby spinach

LEFTOVERS: see pp. 228–233
- Lime
- Cherry tomatoes
- Scallions or red onion
- Cilantro

TIPS & SWAPS

Serve with a side of vegetables or a simple salad for a hearty main meal.

If you have cubed, roasted sweet potato to hand, you can use that. Skip steps 2 and 3 and scatter the potato over the spinach in step 6, before baking.

Double up on the pie dough and store half of it in the refrigerator or freezer for another day.

VG option

PESTO, SPINACH & SWEET POTATO GALETTE

Makes 1 galette
(serves 3 to 4 as a main)

1 recipe for Half-Oat Pie Dough
(see page 217) or Olive Oil Pie Dough
(see page 217), or 9oz/250g store-
bought pie dough

1 large or 2 small sweet potatoes
(about 10½oz/300g total)

all-purpose flour, for dusting

3 tablespoons homemade Pesto
(see pages 224–225)
or store-bought

3⅓ cups/3½oz/100g baby spinach,
rinsed

1 teaspoon olive oil

2 tablespoons crumbled feta cheese

salt and freshly ground black pepper

Galettes are a godsend when you don't have a tart pan or pie dish (of which I had neither for a few months at university). They also look fancy and, as far as handling pie dough goes, they are simple to master, as you don't have to worry about it shrinking or cracking inside a pan. This recipe is quick to make if you have a microwave (or a bit slower if you don't!) and, thanks to the fancy fanned pattern of the sweet potatoes, makes you look like a boss at tart making.

1 Prepare the pie dough according to the recipe on page 217.

2 Prick the sweet potato all over with a fork. Microwave it on high for 4 minutes or wrap in aluminum foil and cook in an oven preheated to 350°F for 30 minutes. It should be slightly softened, but it will cook more when you bake the tart. Keep the oven on.

3 Slice the sweet potato in half lengthwise and remove the skin. Cut each half into ⅛-inch-thick slices so that they look like little half-moons. If your oven isn't already on, preheat it to 350°F.

4 Cut a piece of parchment paper slightly larger than the size of your baking sheet. Lightly dust the parchment paper with flour and roll the dough out to about a 10 to 12-inch circle. Spread the pesto in the center of the dough, with a 1¼-inch bare border around the edge.

5 Put the spinach in a microwave-safe or heatproof bowl and either microwave it for 1 minute or cover with just-boiled water to wilt. Drain and rinse under cold running water, then squeeze to remove any excess moisture. Tear into clumps and spread out over the pesto.

6 Arrange the sweet potato in semicircles over the spinach. It's fine if bits are overlapping. Fold the bare edge of the dough up around the tart, folding in pleats as needed. Drizzle over the oil, then season with salt and pepper.

7 Bake for 25 to 30 minutes, then remove from the oven and serve with the crumbled feta.

Vegan Use the Olive Oil Pie Dough (see page 217). Make sure your pesto is vegan or use one of the recipes on pages 224–225. Use Sun Feta (see page 219) instead of the feta.

LEFTOVERS: see pp. 228–233

● Half-Oat Pie Dough
● Sweet potatoes (raw or roasted)
● Pesto
● Baby spinach
● Feta cheese

CAULIFLOWER MISO MAC & CHEESE

Serves 2

1 medium head of cauliflower
   (about 12oz/350g when leaves are
   removed), outer leaves removed
   and head cut into medium florets
5½oz/150g dry whole-wheat pasta (I
   like penne here) or 10½oz/300g
   cooked
1 tablespoon olive oil
3 tablespoons all-purpose flour
1½ cups milk or nondairy milk
¼ teaspoon smoked paprika
1 garlic clove, crushed or minced
1 cup/4¼oz/120g shredded sharp
   cheddar
1 tablespoon miso, any kind
salt

You might be wondering whether putting miso into cheese sauce is going to work, but trust me, it's great! I know I do use miso a lot, but here it makes the sauce special, as that salty, umami twang brightens the flavor. I add cauliflower in two ways here—whole chunks and pureed. The whole chunks help to bulk up the dish and, for me, bring back memories of the incredibly indulgent cauliflower cheese that my dad used to make. The puree is mixed into the cheese sauce because, hey, it's always good to have more vegetables.

1 Bring a large saucepan of salted water to a boil. Add the cauliflower and simmer for 5 minutes. Scoop the cauliflower out and set aside.

2 If using dry pasta, add the pasta to the same pan and bring to a boil, then reduce the heat and simmer for 4 minutes less than the time specified in the package directions. Drain and return to the pan.

3 Mix half the cooked cauliflower into the cooked pasta, then pour this into a medium casserole dish and set aside.

4 Preheat the oven to 350°F.

5 Return the pan to the stove with the oil over medium heat. Add the flour and cook, stirring, for about 1 minute. Add the milk, drizzling it in a bit at a time and stirring well between additions. Add the smoked paprika, garlic, and most of the cheese, reserving a heaping tablespoon for sprinkling.

6 If using a handheld blender, put the reserved, cooked cauliflower and miso into a beaker with a few tablespoons of the hot milk mixture and blend until smooth. Return to the pan, stir until smooth, then pour over the pasta and cauliflower in the casserole dish.

7 If using a countertop blender or food processor, pour the hot milk mixture into the blender with the reserved, cooked cauliflower and miso and blend carefully until smooth. Pour over the pasta and cauliflower in the dish.

8 Sprinkle with the reserved cheese and bake in the oven for 30 to 40 minutes, until the cheese on top has melted and browned.

LEFTOVERS: see pp. 228–233

● Cauliflower
● Pasta (dry or cooked)
● Miso

TIPS & SWAPS

For extra crunch, toast bread crumbs with a bit of oil or butter in a skillet until golden. Sprinkle over the pasta just before baking.

Don't have any miso? Leave it out, but just be sure to add extra salt to the sauce.

For a lighter version, reduce the cheese down to ⅔ cup/2½oz/70g in total.

Replace the cauliflower with an equal quantity of butternut squash, peeled, seeded, and chopped into chunks.

VG option

POTATO, HALLOUMI & ZUCCHINI BAKE

Serves 2

about 3 medium (14oz/400g) potatoes (e.g. Russet, Yukon Gold), unpeeled
1 tablespoon olive oil
2 medium zucchini, cut into chunks
2 red bell peppers, seeded, halved, and cut into 4 to 5 strips
4½oz/125g halloumi cheese, cut into ⅛-inch-thick slices
salt

BASIL OIL

large handful of basil (leaves and stems), reserving a few leaves to scatter over the veg
⅓ cup extra virgin olive oil

I remember being at my friend's house for dinner when her mom brought this out of the oven, much to my delight, covered in bronzed halloumi. It's a simple traybake meal that is jazzed up by a vibrant basil oil.

1 Cut the potatoes into about 1¼-inch chunks and put in a medium saucepan. Cover with just-boiled water and add a generous pinch of salt, then bring to a boil. Reduce the heat and simmer for 5 minutes. Drain the potatoes, then return them to the pan and cover with a plate or a lid. Let stand for 5 minutes to remove any excess moisture.

2 Preheat the oven to 350°F.

3 Transfer the cooked potatoes to a large baking sheet or roasting pan and toss in the olive oil. Bake in the oven for 40 minutes. Add the zucchini and bell pepper and toss until coated in the oil. Return to the oven for another 20 to 25 minutes. Finally, lay the halloumi slices over the veg, turn the oven broiler on, and broil for a few minutes until the halloumi is golden.

4 Using a handheld blender and beaker or countertop blender, blitz the basil and olive oil together*. Drizzle 2 tablespoons of the basil oil over the roasted vegetables and halloumi. Sprinkle the reserved basil leaves on top and serve.

Vegan Omit the halloumi and roast the veg for 40 minutes, then top with Sun Feta (see page 219) or coarsely chopped pitted olives and drizzle with the basil oil, before returning the baking sheet or roasting pan to the oven.

TIPS & SWAPS

Serve with "Chorizo" Dip (see page 47) or some crusty bread for dipping.

*If you don't have a blender, chop the basil as finely as possible and mix with the olive oil.

Double up on the roasted vegetables and use them in another recipe (see the leftovers table, pages 228–233) or wrap in tortillas for a quick lunch the next day.

Use sweet potatoes instead of regular potatoes. Peel them and skip step 1. Reduce the initial roasting time to 15 minutes.

Store leftover basil oil in the refrigerator and use for pesto, pasta, or salad dressings.

LEFTOVERS: see pp. 228–233

- Halloumi cheese
- Bell peppers
- Zucchini
- Potatoes
- Basil

LENTIL & YOGURT PITA DIP

Serves 2

½ cup/3¼oz/90g Puy or green lentils, rinsed or ⅔ cup/4oz/110g cooked
2 bell peppers, seeded and cut into wide strips
1 teaspoon olive oil
2 whole-wheat pita breads, homemade (see page 215) or store-bought
⅔ cup/5½oz/150g plain yogurt
1 garlic clove, crushed
1 tablespoon tahini (optional but really good)
handful of mint leaves, finely chopped
1 tablespoon sesame seeds
½ teaspoon sweet smoked paprika
salt

I made this based on a Middle Eastern dish called "fatteh," of which there are many versions. Some include cooked chicken or ground lamb, chick peas, eggplant, and pine nuts, but this is my own version with roasted bell pepper, lentils, and sesame seeds. It sounds more like a side dish, but believe me it is quite filling. If you serve this as a main with a side of cooked vegetables or a simple dressed salad, you should be content. Conversely, you could make a big batch to serve at a dinner party as a fun, shared appetizer.

1 Preheat the oven to 350°F.

2 If starting with dry lentils, put them in a small saucepan and pour in enough water to cover. Bring to a boil and cook until soft, 20 to 25 minutes. Drain and set aside.

3 Meanwhile, on a baking sheet, toss the bell peppers in the oil. Roast in the oven for 20 minutes.

4 Cut the pita bread in half as if you were going to fill it, then split each half into 2 thin pieces. Cut each thin piece into around 6 strips.

5 Once the bell peppers have been roasting for 20 minutes, add the pita bread pieces to the baking sheet and toss to coat the bread in some of the oil. Return to the oven and bake for another 5 to 8 minutes, until the pita pieces are crisp.

6 In a small bowl, combine the yogurt, garlic, tahini, and a pinch of salt.

7 Transfer the pita pieces and bell peppers to a serving bowl. Spoon the yogurt mixture and lentils over the top (I like to leave some pita chips exposed around the edges for some crunch). Sprinkle over the chopped mint, sesame seeds, and smoked paprika and serve right away.

Vegan Use unsweetened soy yogurt instead of the yogurt.

LEFTOVERS: see pp. 228–233

- Bell peppers
- Yogurt
- Tahini
- Mint

TIPS & SWAPS

Extra lentils can be stored for
5 days in the refrigerator and are
great cold in salads or stirred into
a pasta sauce or soup.

Roast extra vegetables, such as sweet
potato or some cauliflower florets, or
make some pita chips (see page 42)
for another meal.

VG option

SQUASH, CAULIFLOWER & ROASTED GARLIC GRATIN

Serves 2 to 3

1 small or ½ large butternut squash (1lb/450g), peeled, seeded, and cut into 1¼-inch chunks
½ large head of cauliflower (about 9oz/250g, once outer leaves are removed), outer leaves removed and cut into florets
1 head of garlic, pointy tip sliced off
2 tablespoons olive oil or canola oil
salt

SAUCE
1½ tablespoons olive oil
3 tablespoons all-purpose flour
1¼ cups vegetable stock
1 bay leaf
4 sprigs of thyme, leaves picked

TOPPING
1 tablespoon olive oil
⅓ cup/1oz/30g dry bread crumbs
2 tablespoons grated Parmesan*

Classic comfort food right here—caramelized, roasted veg snuggled into a bubbling sauce with a crispy bread crumb topping. There's a whole head of garlic in there too, which is roasted so that it mellows into a soft, sticky, sweet pulp. This is great as an entree with crusty bread and some steamed vegetables. I sometimes tip in cooked cannellini beans to make it heartier, or replace the butternut squash with an equal quantity of sweet potato.

1 Preheat the oven to 350°F.

2 In a large, deep baking dish, toss the squash, cauliflower, garlic head, oil, and a pinch of salt together. Roast in the oven for 30 minutes, turning the vegetables over halfway through. Once cooked, let cool slightly, then squeeze the cooked garlic cloves out of their papery casing and into the roasted veg. Discard the papery casing and keep the oven on.

3 To make the sauce, in a medium saucepan, heat the oil and flour over medium heat, stir to make a paste, and cook for 1 minute. Reduce the heat and gradually drizzle in the stock, stirring until smooth between additions, until it's all added. Add the bay leaf and reduce the heat to low. Cook, stirring occasionally, for 15 minutes. Pour the sauce over the cooked vegetables and squeezed garlic in the baking dish and sprinkle over the thyme leaves.

4 To make the topping, in a small skillet, heat the oil over medium heat. Add the bread crumbs and cook, stirring, for 1 minute. Mix in the Parmesan and remove the pan from the heat. Sprinkle over the saucy veg in the baking dish and bake for 20 minutes.

Vegan Leave the Parmesan out of the bread crumb topping and season with salt instead.

TIPS & SWAPS

Add ⅔ cup/4¼oz/120g cooked cannellini (white kidney) beans, drained and rinsed, after the veg is roasted or serve with whole-wheat bread for a more substantial meal.

Replace the butternut squash with an equal quantity of peeled and cubed sweet potato. The roasting time will remain the same.

*Parmesan isn't technically vegetarian—choose a vegetarian alternative hard cheese.

LEFTOVERS: see pp. 228–233

● Butternut squash
● Cauliflower
● Thyme

PESTO CRUMB ZUCCHINI WITH WEEKNIGHT FOCACCIA

Serves 2 to 3

FOCACCIA

¾ cup plus 2 teaspoons lukewarm water*

1 teaspoon instant dry yeast

2 tablespoons olive oil, plus extra for greasing

1 cup/4½oz/125g whole-wheat pastry or whole-wheat flour

¾ cup plus 1 tablespoon/3½oz/100g all-purpose flour or ¾ cup/ 3½oz/100g bread flour

pinch of granulated sugar

½ teaspoon salt

1 teaspoon mixed dried herbs or dried thyme or dried oregano

FOR THE ZUCCHINI

2½ tablespoons pumpkin seeds

2 large handfuls of basil (leaves and stems)

grated zest and juice of ½ lemon

3 medium zucchini

1 teaspoon olive oil

1 garlic clove, crushed

grated Parmesan, for sprinkling (optional)**

salt

My friend Rhiannon and I often eat this as a comforting, easy weeknight dinner when we have a friend date. It gets so cold in Leeds, north east England, where our university is located, so this is the perfect solution. The focaccia dough is extremely wet, which means it requires little kneading. The pesto-crumb zucchini is my solution to them becoming too watery when shredded and sautéed—the crumb has no liquid in it, so it absorbs all the moisture and becomes a chunky pesto.

1 In a medium bowl, mix together the lukewarm water and yeast. Add 1 tablespoon of the oil, the flours, sugar, and salt and mix well. Shape your hand like a claw and use it to beat the mixture in the bowl for 1 minute.

2 Grease an 8-inch square baking pan well with some oil. Using oiled hands, press and stretch the dough into the pan. Cover with plastic wrap or a clean kitchen towel and let rise in a warm place until almost doubled in size, about 30 to 45 minutes.

3 Preheat the oven to 350°F.

4 Uncover the dough and use your fingers to gently poke a few dimples into the surface. Drizzle with the remaining 1 tablespoon oil and sprinkle on the dried herbs. Bake in the oven for 30 to 35 minutes, then unmold onto a board and cut into 6 pieces.

5 Meanwhile, chop the pumpkin seeds finely—around the size of a grain of couscous is best—then sweep them to the side of the cutting board. Finely chop the basil with a generous pinch of salt and the lemon zest. Mix the chopped seeds and basil on the board and run through chopping once more with your knife.

6 Lay a box grater on its side with the large holes facing toward the ceiling. Drag each zucchini along the large holes of the grater in long strokes to create ribbons of zucchini.

7 In a skillet, heat the oil over medium heat. Add the zucchini and garlic and sauté for a few minutes until they have just softened and released a little liquid. Add the pesto crumb and stir to combine. Remove from the heat and season with salt and the lemon juice, to taste. Top with the Parmesan, if using, and serve with the focaccia.

Vegan Don't serve with Parmesan.

LEFTOVERS: see pp. 228–233

● Zucchini
● Basil
● Lemon

TIPS & SWAPS

*Ensure the water is just slightly warm to the touch.

**Parmesan isn't technically vegetarian—choose a vegetarian alternative hard cheese.

Pulse together the pesto crumb ingredients in a food processor until finely chopped but not pasty.

Use cashews, almonds, or sunflower seeds instead of pumpkin seeds. Rinse salted cashews before using.

For garlic bread, in a small skillet, heat 2 tablespoons butter or olive oil with 2 crushed garlic cloves for 1 minute, then brush over the baked focaccia.

GF option

CRISPY BROCCOLI & BARLEY BOWL WITH TAHINI DRESSING

Serves 2

¾ cup/5½oz/150g dry pearl barley
  or 2⅓ cups/13oz/375g cooked,
  warmed
1 large head of broccoli,
  cut into medium florets
1 tablespoon olive oil
3 tablespoons pumpkin seeds
  or sunflower seeds
1 teaspoon soy sauce or tamari
¼ teaspoon granulated sugar
  or maple syrup
handful of cilantro, chopped
salt

TAHINI DRESSING
2 tablespoons tahini
juice of ½ lemon
1 garlic clove, crushed
pinch of salt

Chewy pearl barley meets crunchy fronds of roasted broccoli in a simple, quick bowl meal. The tahini dressing is creamy and tangy and the sweet crunch of the pumpkin seeds adds a pop of texture.

1   Preheat the oven to 350°F.

2   If starting with uncooked pearl barley, put the barley in a medium saucepan and pour in enough water to cover. Bring to a boil, then reduce the heat and simmer until chewy but soft, 35 to 40 minutes. Drain, rinse, and return to the pan, and cover with a kitchen towel and a lid. Let stand for 10 minutes.

3   Meanwhile, toss the broccoli in the oil and a sprinkle of salt on a baking tray. Roast in the oven for 20–30 minutes until golden and crispy.

4   In a nonstick skillet, toast the pumpkin seeds over medium heat, stirring frequently, until they start to pop. Add the soy sauce or tamari and sugar or syrup, then stir until the seeds clump together. Transfer to a plate or cutting board and let cool.

5   In a small bowl, stir the tahini, lemon juice, garlic, and salt together. Add enough water to make a drizzle-able dressing.

6   Divide the cooked pearl barley, crispy broccoli, pumpkin seeds, and tahini dressing among 2 bowls, sprinkle over the cilantro, and serve warm.

Gluten Free Cook a heaping ¾ cup quinoa or rice instead of the pearl barley. Make sure that you are using a certified gluten-free tamari or soy sauce.

TIPS & SWAPS
Use cauliflower instead of broccoli and roast for 30 to 40 minutes.

Any extra broccoli and cooked pearl barley can be stored in the refrigerator in a container for up to 3 days.

LEFTOVERS: see pp. 228–233

● Pearl barley (dry or cooked)
● Cilantro
● Tahini
● Lemon

LAZY POTATO HASH
WITH KALE, PESTO & EGGS

Serves 2

2 medium potatoes* (about 14oz/400g),
   cut into ½-inch-thick coins
2 tablespoons light olive oil
   or canola oil
4 large leaves of Tuscan kale (cavolo
   nero), tough stems removed and
   leaves shredded into thumb-size
   strips
⅔ cup/4oz/120g cooked cannellini
   (white kidney) beans, drained and
   rinsed
¼ cup homemade Pesto (see pages
   224–225) or store-bought
2 eggs
salt and freshly ground black pepper

I'm one of those people who likes to use the same pan as much as possible when cooking so that I have less washing up to do. Here, I slice the potatoes before parboiling, making it possible to parboil them in the skillet, which is then used for sautéing them—and one less pot to wash, TICK! Back in the skillet, I whack in Tuscan kale until it wilts and becomes a slightly crispy, and add in pesto for flavor, beans for texture, and eggs for those saucy yolks!

1 Arrange the potatoes in a deep, nonstick skillet and pour in enough water to cover. Salt well and bring to a boil. Once boiling, reduce the heat and simmer for 5 minutes, then drain and set aside.

2 Rinse and wipe out the skillet, then return to medium heat. Heat half the oil, add the potato slices, and season well with salt and pepper, then break them up into bite-size chunks with a wooden spatula. Let cook until golden on the underside (resist any temptation to nudge them around), then flip over and cook until the other side is golden, about 10 minutes in total.

3 Add the Tuscan kale strips to the skillet with the remaining oil and sauté until it starts to wilt slightly, then add the beans and pesto and stir to coat. Make 2 fist-size hollows in the hash and crack an egg into each. Cover with a lid or large plate, reduce the heat, and cook until the whites are set and the yolk is still runny, about 2 to 3 minutes. Season with more salt and pepper, then divide between plates and serve.

Gluten Free If using store-bought pesto, make sure it is certified gluten free.

Dairy Free If using store-bought pesto, make sure it is dairy free.

LEFTOVERS: see pp. 228–233

● Potatoes
● Tuscan kale
● Cooked cannellini beans
● Pesto

TIPS & SWAPS
*I like Russet potatoes for
this recipe.

TIPS & SWAPS

Quinoa, pearl barley, or cooked soba,
udon, or rice noodles will also work well.

Use creamed coconut instead of coconut milk.
Stir 2 tablespoons into ¼ cup hot water.

Cool and store any extra rice as quickly as possible
by rinsing it under cold running water or spreading
it out on a plate. Once cooled, keep in the
refrigerator for 1 day or in a sandwich bag
in the freezer for 2 months. When
reheating, make sure it is piping hot
before serving.

RICE BOWL WITH GREENS & CILANTRO–COCONUT DRESSING

Serves 2

½ cup plus 1 tablespoon/3½oz/100g dry brown rice, rinsed, or 1 scant cup/6oz/180g cooked, warmed

2 eggs

3½oz/100g broccolini or ½ head of regular broccoli, cut into medium florets

⅓ cup/1¾oz/50g frozen petite peas or peas

3 large Tuscan kale (cavolo nero) leaves

handful of sesame seeds

1 scallion, finely sliced

CILANTRO–COCONUT DRESSING

2 handfuls of cilantro leaves

¼oz/10g piece of ginger root, peeled and minced or grated

juice of 1 lemon or lime

2 tablespoons soy sauce or tamari

1 tablespoon granulated sugar or honey, or 2 tablespoons Date Paste (see page 221)

⅓ cup coconut milk

This is the type of simple meal I like to make on a stressful weekday. It has greens to keep me feeling my best, a wicked dressing, and, of course, an oozy soft-boiled egg. I have used broccoli, Tuscan kale, and frozen petite peas here, but any greens will work. Try sautéing your greens briefly in a drizzle of toasted sesame oil and a crushed garlic clove after cooking for a flavor punch.

1 If starting wtih dry rice, place it in a medium saucepan and cover with water. Season with salt and bring to a boil. Reduce the heat and simmer for 20 minutes for long-grain brown rice or 30 minutes for short-grain brown rice, adding more water as needed. Drain the rice and return it to the pan. Cover with a lid and let stand for 5 minutes to absorb the excess moisture.

2 Using a handheld blender or a countertop blender, blend together all the dressing ingredients. If you don't have a blender, chop the cilantro leaves as finely as possible and stir into the rest of the dressing ingredients.

3 Bring a medium saucepan of water to a boil. Gently lower in the eggs and simmer over medium-low heat for 5 to 6 minutes. Use a spoon to scoop the eggs out of the pan (keep the pan on the heat) and transfer to a bowl of cold water. Set aside. Add the broccolini or broccoli to the pan and cook for 2 minutes, then stir in the frozen peas and Tuscan kale and cook until the kale is softened, 3 to 5 minutes. Drain the vegetables and return to the empty pan; cover with a lid or plate to keep warm.

4 Gently fracture the egg shells and carefully peel them.

5 In a dry skillet, toast the sesame seeds over medium heat, stirring continuously, until golden. Transfer to a plate or bowl.

6 Divide the rice between 2 bowls. Top with the vegetables, a drizzle of the dressing, the sliced scallion, and the sesame seeds. Halve the eggs and add to the bowl.

Gluten Free Make sure that you are using a certified gluten-free tamari or soy sauce.

LEFTOVERS: see pp. 228–233

● Brown rice (dry or cooked)
● Tuscan kale
● Petite peas or peas
● Cilantro
● Coconut milk
● Scallions
● Lemon or lime juice

MISO–GARLIC–CHILE BROCCOLI 3 WAYS

I love to display the versatility of miso. It has an umami salinity that works well in many types of dishes. Using it with chile and garlic makes a simple, sauced-up broccoli side dish, which can then be turned into a main dish by adding a few more ingredients (see overleaf).

Serves 2 as a side

1 medium head of broccoli, cut into medium florets, or about 9oz/250g broccolini
1 tablespoon olive oil or canola oil
2 garlic cloves, crushed
½ to 1 red chile (depending on strength) or a few pinches of crushed red pepper
1 tablespoon miso, any kind, mixed with ¼ cup water to make a paste

1 In a deep skillet, steam the broccoli or broccolini in a small amount of water, covered with a lid, for 5 minutes. Drain and set aside.

2 Return the skillet to medium heat, add the oil, garlic, and chile and sauté for 30 seconds, then add the drained broccoli or broccolini. Sauté for another 30 seconds, then add the miso–water mixture to the pan. Stir until the broccoli or broccolini is coated and cook until the liquid has reduced by half, an additional 1 to 2 minutes.

3 Serve on its own as a side or turn into a main meal by keeping it in the pan and using one of the recipes overleaf.

LEFTOVERS: see pp. 228–233
- Miso
- Red chile

SOY SAUCE & GINGER & RICE

PASTA & TOMATOES & SPINACH

ONION & CUMIN & BEANS

WITH SOY SAUCE & GINGER & RICE

Serves 2

¾ cup plus 1 tablespoon/5½oz/150g
   dry brown rice, rinsed, or 1⅓ cups/
   9¼oz/270g cooked
1 teaspoon toasted sesame oil
2 teaspoons grated or minced ginger
   root
1 tablespoon soy sauce or tamari
good pinch of granulated sugar
   or a small squeeze of honey
1 recipe for Miso–Garlic–Chile Broccoli
   (see page 118); keep it in the pan

1 If starting with dry brown rice, put the rice in a medium saucepan and pour in enough water until well covered. Season with salt and bring to a boil. Reduce the heat and simmer for 20 minutes for long-grain brown rice or 30 minutes for short-grain brown rice, adding more water if needed. Once cooked, drain the rice and return it to the pan. Cover with a lid and let stand for 5 minutes to absorb the excess moisture.

2 Add the oil, ginger, soy sauce or tamari, and sugar to the skillet with the Miso–Chile–Garlic Broccoli. Cook over medium heat for 1 minute to take the raw edge off the ginger, then serve over the cooked rice.

Gluten Free   Make sure that you are using a certified gluten-free tamari or soy sauce.

Vegan   Use granulated sugar.

TIPS & SWAPS

Not enough of a meal? Add a sweet potato, steamed or mashed with lime juice and a pinch of salt, on the side.

Cool and store any extra rice as quickly as possible by rinsing it under cold running water or spreading it out on a plate. Once cooled, keep in the refrigerator for 1 day or in a sandwich bag in the freezer for 2 months. When reheating, make sure it is piping hot before serving.

LEFTOVERS: see pp. 228–233

- Brown rice (dry or cooked)

- Cannellini, black, or red kidney beans
- Cilantro
- Yogurt or crème fraîche
- Lime

- Pasta (dry or cooked)
- Lemon
- Baby spinach
- Cherry tomatoes
- Basil

WITH ONION & CUMIN & BEANS

Serves 2

1 red onion, thinly sliced
1 recipe for Miso–Garlic–Chile Broccoli
   (see page 118); keep it in the pan
1½ teaspoons ground cumin
1 teaspoon sweet smoked paprika
juice of ½ lime
1⅓ cups/8½oz/240g cooked black,
   cannellini (white kidney), or red kidney
   beans, drained and rinsed
salt

TO SERVE
2 tablespoons plain yogurt
   or crème fraîche
large handful of cilantro,
   coarsely chopped

1 Add the thinly sliced onion to the skillet with the Miso–Chile–Garlic Broccoli. Stir and cook for 2 minutes to soften the onions. Add the cumin, paprika, lime juice, beans, and a good splash of water to the skillet and cook over medium-low heat, stirring gently to mix everything together, for 5 minutes. Season with salt to taste and divide between 2 plates. Serve with the yogurt and cilantro.

Vegan Use unsweetened soy yogurt or Avocado Cream (see page 219) instead of the yogurt.

TIPS & SWAPS
Poached, soft-boiled, or fried eggs are amazing with this dish.

WITH PASTA & TOMATOES & SPINACH

Serves 2

5½oz/150g dry whole-wheat or spelt
   spaghetti, or 10½oz/300g cooked
1 recipe for Miso–Garlic–Chile Broccoli
   (see page 118)
grated zest and juice of ½ lemon
2 large handfuls of baby spinach
handful of basil leaves, coarsely chopped
5 to 6 cherry tomatoes, quartered
grated Parmesan, to serve (optional)*

1 If starting with dry pasta, put in a medium saucepan and cover with just-boiled water from the kettle. Bring to a boil and cook until al dente (this will generally be the shorter cooking time specified in the package directions). Drain, reserving a small mugful of the pasta water.

2 Add the pasta to the skillet with the Miso–Garlic–Chile Broccoli along with a good splash of the reserved pasta water, the lemon juice and zest, and the spinach. Cook over medium heat, stirring, until the spinach has wilted and there is still some liquid left in the pan (you can add more pasta water if needed).

3 Remove from the heat and stir in the basil and tomatoes. Divide between 2 bowls and serve with Parmesan, if desired.

TIPS & SWAPS
*Parmesan isn't technically vegetarian—choose a vegetarian hard cheese instead. Omit if vegan.

Cook some extra pasta and store in the refrigerator in a container for up to 3 days—handy for a quick lunch.

SPINACH & FETA BALLS
WITH SPAGHETTI

Serves 2 to 4

14oz/400g baby spinach or 9oz/240g frozen, cooked spinach, thawed

⅔ cup/3½oz/100g crumbled feta cheese

1 tablespoon mixed dried herbs (I like herbes de Provence)

1 egg

½ cup Oat Flour/2oz/55g (see page 216) or dry bread crumbs

¼ cup olive oil, for cooking (optional)

10½oz/300g dry spaghetti or 1¼lb/600g cooked

a pat of unsalted butter or 2 tablespoons extra virgin olive oil

2 tablespoons soy sauce or tamari

1 medium zucchini, shredded

freshly ground black pepper

You may look at me with squinted, questioning eyes when I tell you to use soy sauce, butter, and shredded zucchini to coat your pasta, but it does taste good. This recipe makes around 20 spinach and feta balls, enough for 4 people, so if you are only cooking for 1 or 2 people, the leftovers can be repurposed as a falafel substitute the next day in a sandwich!

1 If using fresh baby spinach, add to a large saucepan with a small splash of water. Place over medium-low heat and cover with a lid. Cook until wilted, 3 to 5 minutes, then rinse under cold running water. Squeeze the spinach out over the sink to remove as much liquid as possible, then coarsely chop and set aside.

2 In a medium bowl, mix the feta, dried herbs, a generous amount of pepper, the egg, and flour or bread crumbs together. Stir in the chopped spinach, then scoop heaping tablespoons of the mixture and roll into balls. You should get about 20 balls. You can either place them on a baking sheet lined with nonstick parchment paper and bake in an oven preheated to 350°F for 20 to 25 minutes, or fry them over medium heat in 2 batches, in 2 tablespoons oil per batch, turning, until golden on both sides, 3 to 5 minutes.

3 If starting with dry pasta, put in a medium saucepan and cover with just-boiled water from the kettle. Bring to a boil and cook until al dente (this will generally be the shorter cooking time specified in the package directions). Drain, reserving a small mugful of the pasta water.

4 Return the pasta to the pan off the heat, then stir in the butter, soy sauce or tamari, and shredded zucchini. Serve the pasta with the spinach balls.

Gluten Free If you can tolerate oats, make sure you use certified gluten-free oats in your Oat Flour. Use gluten-free pasta (e.g. brown rice pasta) and tamari or soy sauce.

LEFTOVERS: see pp. 228–233

- Baby spinach
- Feta cheese
- Bread crumbs, if using
- Pasta (dry or cooked)
- Zucchini

TIPS & SWAPS

For 2 people, make the whole recipe but only serve half. Keep the extra pasta (without zucchini) in the refrigerator for up to 3 days. Warm up the spinach and feta balls for lunch the next day; serve stuffed into pita with Quick Pickled Red Onion (page 223), Tahini Dressing (page 226), and salad greens.

Instead of using shredded zucchini and soy, make the No-cook Pizza Sauce (see page 220) and heat in a saucepan over low heat until reduced by half.

GF option

CRISPY TORTILLA STRIPS WITH CORN & QUINOA

Serves 2 to 3

1 large or 2 small corn or whole-wheat tortillas, homemade (see page 214) or store-bought
2 tablespoons olive oil or canola oil
⅔ cup/4¼oz/120g dry quinoa, rinsed, or 1⅓ cups/9oz/250g cooked
2 ears of corn,* kernels cut off
juice of ½ lemon
pinch of granulated sugar
pinch of salt
½ teaspoon sweet smoked paprika
4 to 5 sundried tomatoes in oil**, coarsely chopped
½ avocado, pitted, peeled, and cubed
handful of cilantro, coarsely chopped
2 scallions, thinly sliced

Crispy tortilla strips are something that can be sprinkled on to anything and immediately make it better. I like to use corn tortillas when I can, as they have a better color and flavor than wheat ones, but either will do. The most important thing is that you make extra strips for snacking on while you cook because, trust me, you'll want them.

1 Preheat the oven to 350°F.

2 Cut the tortillas in half and then into strips about ¼ inch wide. On a baking sheet, toss with half the oil and cook in the oven for 3 to 4 minutes, until just turning golden. Remove and let cool and crisp up.

3 If starting with dry quinoa, put in a medium saucepan and pour in enough water to cover. Bring to a boil, then reduce the heat and simmer for 10 minutes. Drain, return to the pan, and cover with a lid or plate. Let stand for 5 minutes to absorb any excess moisture.

4 In a medium skillet, heat the remaining oil over medium heat. Add the corn kernels and sauté until hot, 2 minutes, then remove the pan from the heat.

5 Mix the lemon juice, sugar, salt, and paprika into the quinoa and transfer to a serving plate. Top with the cooked corn, sundried tomatoes, cubed avocado, chopped cilantro, sliced scallions, and crispy tortilla strips.

Gluten Free Use gluten-free corn tortillas.

TIPS & SWAPS

*Use about 1½ cups/9oz/250g drained, canned or thawed frozen corn kernels.

**If using dry-packed sundried tomatoes, cover with boiling water and let soak for 15 minutes to rehydrate, then drain.

In place of sundried tomatoes, halve and roast cherry tomatoes in a drizzle of olive oil in an oven preheated to 325°F for 40 to 60 minutes.

Instead of avocado, top with a heaping ¼ cup/1½oz/40g crumbled feta cheese.

LEFTOVERS: see pp. 228–233

● Sundried tomatoes
● Avocado
● ½ lemon
● Scallions

GF option

ORZO WITH SQUASH, CHILE, LEMON & PEAS

Serves 2 to 3

½ small or ¼ large butternut squash (10½oz to 14oz/300 to 400g), peeled, seeded, and cut into bite-size chunks
3 tablespoons olive oil or canola oil
1 teaspoon fennel seeds
½ red chile, seeded and finely chopped
¾ cup/3½oz/100g frozen petite peas or peas
1 red onion, sliced about ⅛-inch thick
1 tablespoon balsamic vinegar
¾ cup/5½oz/150g dry orzo pasta (or any small pasta shapes)
grated zest and juice of ½ lemon
handful of basil, coarsely chopped
salt

Orzo is probably the cutest pasta shape around. The little ricelike grains are perfect additions to brothy soups, hearty green salads, or just simply dressed with some vegetables like this. Eat warm for dinner today and save the rest to have cold for lunch tomorrow.

1 Preheat the oven to 350°F.

2 On a baking sheet, toss the squash with 1 tablespoon of the oil and a pinch of salt. Roast in the oven for 35 to 45 minutes, flipping halfway through, until golden and soft.

3 In a dry skillet, toast the fennel seeds over medium heat until they pop, about 2 minutes. Pour in 1 tablespoon of the oil, then add the chile and frozen peas. Cook until the peas are heated through, 2 minutes, then transfer to a small bowl and set aside. Return the skillet to the heat.

4 Add the onion with the remaining oil and a pinch of salt and cook over low heat for 10 minutes. Splash in a few tablespoons of water and cook until the water has evaporated and the onion is soft, about another 10 minutes. Stir in the balsamic vinegar and remove the skillet from the heat.

5 If using dry orzo, bring a medium saucepan of salted water to a boil. Add the orzo and cook until al dente (this is usually the shorter cooking time specified in the package directions). Drain, then add the pasta to the skillet with the onion and stir together. Stir in the roasted squash and the fennel–chile–pea mixture from the bowl. Finally, stir through the lemon zest and juice, the basil, and a pinch of salt, and serve warm.

Gluten Free Use quinoa instead of the orzo.

Omnivores Chuck 4½oz/125g cooked, shelled shrimp (fresh or frozen) into the pan with the onion right at the end of cooking and cook until warmed through. Stir into the pasta with the other ingredients.

LEFTOVERS: see pp. 228–233

● Butternut squash (raw or roasted)
● Basil
● Pasta (dry or cooked)
● Lemon

TIPS & SWAPS

Swap the butternut squash for roasted sweet potato.

Replace the orzo with cooked quinoa or Israeli (pearl) couscous.

Swap the squash for cubed sweet potato or carrots, cut into ⅛-inch coins. Roast the sweet potato in oil and salt for 30 minutes in an oven preheated to 350°F, or the carrots in oil and salt for 20 minutes in an oven preheated to 425°F.

QUICKIE CHILI

MINESTRONE

SHAKSHOUKA

CHICK PEA STEW 3 WAYS

Serves 2 to 3

BASE STEW

2 tablespoons olive oil
1 carrot, finely diced
1 celery stalk, finely diced
1 red onion, finely diced
3 garlic cloves, crushed or minced
1½ cups/8½oz/240g cooked, chick peas
   (garbanzo beans), drained and rinsed
14oz/400g canned diced tomatoes
¾ cup plus 1 tablespoon water or
   vegetable stock
½ tablespoon granulated sugar
   or honey, or 1 tablespoon
   Date Paste (see page 221)
salt

Having a simple stew recipe like this is super-useful for weekday batch cooking. You can double or triple this base stew, then keep it in the refrigerator or freezer to use throughout the week. It can easily become boring if you're always eating the same flavor combos again and again, so by simply adding a couple of extra ingredients (see overleaf), you can have a completely different meal!

1 In a large saucepan, heat the oil over medium-low heat. Add the carrot, celery, onion, garlic, and a generous pinch of salt and cook, stirring frequently, until the vegetables are softened, 15 to 20 minutes.

2 Add the chick peas, tomatoes, water, and sugar to the saucepan. Stir together, then bring to a boil. Reduce the heat to a simmer and continue according to one of the recipes overleaf.

Vegan Use granulated sugar or Date Paste.

TIPS & SWAPS

Use an equal quantity of fresh tomatoes instead of canned.

Make a double or triple batch of stew base and store in the freezer in a container for up to 2 months. Thaw to use in one of the recipes on pages 130–131.

LEFTOVERS: see pp. 228–233

- Cooked chick peas
- Tomatoes (canned)
- Celery
- Carrots

QUICKIE CHILI

Serves 2

1 tablespoon olive oil or canola oil
3 teaspoons ground cumin
2 teaspoons ground coriander
1 teaspoon ground cinnamon
¼ teaspoon smoked paprika
½ teaspoon cayenne pepper
1 recipe for Chick Pea Stew (see page 129)
1 teaspoon mixed dried herbs
2 tablespoons soy sauce or tamari
handful of cilantro, finely chopped

TO SERVE
tortillas or cooked rice
plain yogurt or Avocado Cream (see page 219)

1 In a small skillet, heat the oil over low heat. Mix in the spices and cook, stirring continuously, for 1 minute.

2 Transfer this mixture to the pot of Chick Pea Stew and stir through along with the mixed herbs and soy sauce or tamari. Simmer until thickened, 15 minutes. Sprinkle the chopped cilantro over and serve with tortillas or cooked rice and yogurt.

Vegan Serve with Avocado Cream.

Gluten Free Use certified gluten-free tamari or soy sauce. Serve with gluten-free corn tortillas or brown rice.

MINESTRONE

GF & VG options

Serves 4

2 teaspoons fennel seeds
2½ cups vegetable stock
1 bay leaf
1 tablespoon mixed dried herbs
1 recipe for Chick Pea Stew (see page 129)
about ¾ cup/2¾oz/75g dry short-cut pasta (e.g. macaroni) or
    1 scant cup/5½oz/150g cooked
2 handfuls of baby spinach or 2 Tuscan kale (cavolo nero) leaves,
    stems removed and leaves coarsely chopped
salt

TO SERVE
Parmesan shavings (optional)

1 In a dry skillet, toast the fennel seeds over medium heat until they pop, about 2 minutes, then remove the skillet from the heat.

2 Mix the fennel seeds, stock, bay leaf, and dried herbs into the pot of Chick Pea Stew. If using dry pasta, add that in now. Bring to a boil, then reduce the heat and simmer until the pasta is al dente. If you're using precooked pasta, simmer the stew for 10 minutes, then stir in the cooked pasta. Remove and discard the bay leaf, then stir in the spinach or Tuscan kale and season with salt to taste. Divide among 4 bowls and serve topped with shavings of Parmesan, if desired.

Vegan Serve without the Parmesan cheese.

Gluten Free Use certified gluten-free pasta.

SHAKSHOUKA

DF option

Serves 2 to 3

1 teaspoon olive oil
1 red, yellow, or orange bell pepper,
  seeded and cut into thick strips
2 teaspoons smoked paprika
½ teaspoon crushed red pepper
1 recipe for Chick Pea Stew (see page 129)
3 to 4 eggs
3 tablespoons crumbled feta cheese, or Sun Feta
  (see page 219)
handful of cilantro, coarsely chopped
salt

TO SERVE
crusty bread

1 In a large skillet, heat the oil over medium heat. Add the bell pepper and cook for 5 minutes. Stir in the paprika and crushed red pepper and cook for another minute.

2 Add the Chick Pea Stew and stir together. Bring to a boil, then reduce the heat and simmer for 10 minutes.

3 Once thickened, make 3 or 4 hollows in the mixture. Crack an egg into each hollow, then cover with a lid (I often just use a large plate or another skillet) and cook over low heat until the egg whites are set and the yolks are still runny.* Sprinkle over the feta and cilantro. Serve with crusty bread, for dipping.

Dairy Free Use Sun Feta or chopped olives instead of the feta, or just omit the feta.

TIPS & SWAPS

*If you don't have a lid or large plate to cover the pan, cook the mixture on the stove for 5 minutes, then place under a hot preheated broiler with the rack at the top. Cook until the whites are set and the yolks are still runny. Alternatively, carefully cover the pan with aluminum foil.

LEFTOVERS: see pp. 228–233

● Feta cheese
● Bell pepper
● Cilantro

● Pasta (dry or cooked)
● Baby spinach or Tuscan kale

TIPS & SWAPS

Just make the filling and serve as
a stew with thick whole-wheat bread.

If you have roasted cauliflower to hand
use about 10½oz/300g instead of raw
cauliflower and skip step 1.

Double up on the pie dough and store half in
the refrigerator or freezer for another day.

Use cooked red kidney beans or chick
peas (garbanzo beans) instead
of cannellini beans.

VG option

CAULIFLOWER, LEEK & SAGE PIE

Serves 4

1 recipe for Half-Oat Pie Dough
(see page 217) or Olive Oil Pie Dough
(see page 217)
1 large cauliflower, outer leaves
removed, cut into medium florets
(about 1lb/450g once leaves are
removed)
2 tablespoons olive oil
6 sage leaves, finely sliced
2 leeks
1 carrot, finely chopped
1 celery stalk, finely chopped
3 tablespoons all-purpose flour,
plus extra for dusting
2 cups vegetable stock
2 teaspoons miso, any kind
1⅓ cups/8½oz/240g cooked cannellini
(white kidney) beans, drained and
rinsed
salt

When you live somewhere that gets pretty cold from October through April, like I do, you're gonna need a hearty pie recipe to pull you through. This is my veggie-friendly version of a chicken and leek pie, with cauliflower and cannellini beans in place of the meat. My special trick here is to stir miso into the sauce, which seasons it and brings in an extra layer of flavor.

1 Prep the pie dough according to the recipe on page 217.

2 Preheat the oven to 350°F.

3 Put the cauliflower in a deep roasting pan or casserole dish (you'll be baking the pie in this later) and toss with 1 tablespoon of the oil, the sage leaves, and a pinch of salt. Roast in the oven for 30 minutes. Remove and keep the oven on.

4 Cut the leeks in half and rinse under cold running water to remove any dirt, then shake dry. Chop the leeks into short ¾-inch-wide strips.

5 In a medium saucepan, heat the remaining oil over medium heat. Add the leeks, carrot, and celery and cook, stirring frequently, until the leeks have softened, 10 minutes. Add the flour and cook, stirring, for 1 minute. Pour in the stock and stir together.

6 Mix the miso with about 3 tablespoons of the liquid from the saucepan to thin it out, then pour into the pan. Cook over medium-low heat, stirring occasionally, until thickened. Stir in the cannellini beans, then pour the mixture over the roasted cauliflower in the roasting pan or casserole dish.

7 Cut a piece of nonstick parchment paper a little larger than the size of your roasting pan or casserole dish. Dust the parchment paper lightly with flour and place your pie dough on it, dusting the dough with some flour too. Roll it out so that it's a little larger than the size of your pan or dish. Lift the parchment paper up and invert it over the pan or dish, then peel the paper off. Cut a few slits in the center of the pie crust so that the steam can escape and bake the pie for 40 to 50 minutes, until the crust is dry.

Vegan Use Olive Oil Pie Dough.

Omnivores Cut 1 to 2 boneless, skinless chicken breasts into 1¼-inch chunks and cook with the leeks, carrot, and celery. Use chicken stock instead of the vegetable stock. Another delicious tip is to roast the cauliflower with ½ cup diced smoked pancetta.

LEFTOVERS: see pp. 228–233

- Sage
- Leeks
- Celery
- Carrots
- Cannellini beans
- Pie dough (Half-Oat or Olive Oil)
- Miso

GF option

PAPRIKA BEAN STEW

Serves 2

1 tablespoon olive oil
1 red onion, finely diced
1 carrot, finely diced
1 celery stalk, finely diced
about ⅓ cup water
1 orange, yellow, or red bell pepper,
    deseeded and cut into thin strips
1 garlic clove, crushed or minced
½ to 1 red chile, finely chopped (keep
    the seeds in if you like it spicy)
2 tablespoons all-purpose flour
1 tablespoon smoked paprika
1 tablespoon miso, any kind, or
    2 tablespoons soy sauce or tamari
1⅔ cups vegetable stock
1⅓ cups/8½oz/240g cooked red
    kidney beans, rinsed and drained
½ teaspoon granulated sugar or honey,
    or 1 teaspoon Date Paste (see
    page 221)
juice of ½ lemon
salt

One night when my flatmate Anna and I were craving something substantial and comforting, we cooked up this stew by cobbling together what we had in the refrigerator. We served it with a huge Yorkshire pudding, of course. The next time we made it, we added some chorizo, which really amped up the rich, smoky flavor, so omnivores take note.

1 Heat the oil in a large saucepan over medium heat. Add the onion, carrot, and celery and sauté, stirring frequently, until the onion is translucent, 5 minutes. Add the water to the pan and stir until evaporated.

2 Add the bell pepper, garlic, and chile and cook for another 5 minutes, stirring frequently. Sprinkle over the flour and paprika, then cook for 2 minutes, stirring continuously.

3 Stir in the miso, soy, or tamari, the stock, beans, sugar, honey, or Date Paste, and lemon juice. Reduce the heat to low and simmer for 30 minutes, stirring occasionally to prevent it from burning. The stew should now be quite thick. Season with salt to taste and divide the stew between 2 bowls to serve.

Vegan Use granulated sugar or Date Paste.

Gluten Free Use chick pea (garbanzo bean) flour or cornstarch instead of the all-purpose flour. Make sure you are using a certified gluten-free tamari or soy sauce.

Omnivores Chop about 2oz chorizo into chick pea-size chunks and sauté them with the vegetables at the beginning of the recipe.

LEFTOVERS: see pp. 228–233

● Miso
● Bell pepper
● Cooked red kidney beans
● Lemon
● Celery
● Carrots
● Chile

TIPS & SWAPS
Serve with chunky brown
bread or mashed potatoes
and cauliflower.

RICOTTA GNOCCHI

Serves 2

⅔ cup/3oz/80g all-purpose flour,
    plus extra for dusting
1 cup/9oz/250g ricotta cheese
1 egg
2 tablespoons grated Parmesan*

I find making my own fresh pasta extremely gratifying. I love the flavor, but sometimes I find it a bit too much effort to make tagliatelle due to the time required for kneading, resting, and rolling it out. Ricotta gnocchi is an exception, and although making it can look like an arduous task, it's actually pretty speedy.

1 Dust a baking sheet lightly with flour and set aside.

2 Line a plate with 3 layers of paper towels. Place the ricotta on the paper towels and top with another 3 layers of paper towels. Press down and pat the ricotta out into a circle about ½ inch thick. Remove the top layers of paper towels, then transfer the ricotta to a bowl.

3 Add the egg and Parmesan to the ricotta and stir to combine. Add the flour and gently mix in until just combined.

4 Dust a work surface or a large cutting board with some flour. Scoop the dough onto the floured surface and sprinkle a bit more flour over it and on your hands. Flatten the dough slightly and cut into quarters. Roll one of the quarters out gently into a ¾-inch-wide rope, then cut it into ¾-inch pieces. Carefully place the gnocchi on the prepared baking sheet and repeat with the remaining dough.

5 If your sauce is ready to go, cook the gnocchi immediately by dropping them gently into a pot of boiling water and cooking until they puff up and start to float to the surface, 2 to 3 minutes. Alternatively, put the baking sheet in the freezer until the gnocchi are frozen, about 2 hours. Transfer them all to a zipper freezer bag, label and date it, and freeze for up to 3 months. You don't have to thaw them before cooking; just add them directly to a pot of boiling water and cook as above.

TIPS & SWAPS

*Parmesan isn't technically vegetarian—choose a vegetarian alternative hard cheese.

Replace half the all-purpose flour with Oat Flour (see page 216) to increase the fiber content.

LEFTOVERS: see pp. 228–233

● Ricotta cheese

RICOTTA GNOCCHI
WITH PESTO & ZUCCHINI

Serves 2

2 tablespoons olive oil
2 medium zucchini, cut
   into ½-inch-thick coins
1 recipe for Ricotta Gnocchi
   (see page 137)
3 tablespoons Basil & Arugula Pesto
   (see page 224) or store-bought
salt

TO GARNISH
handful of basil leaves
Parmesan, shaved*

**Simple and quick to make, this is the main way I serve gnocchi.
I like to let it brown in the pan a bit before stirring in the wet
ingredients because that crispy shell it gains is to die for.**

1 In a large skillet, heat half the oil over medium heat. Add the zucchini and
   season with salt. Cook until golden on the underside, then flip the coins over
   and cook until the other side is golden, about 10 to 15 minutes in total.

2 Meanwhile, bring a large pot of salted water to a boil. Once the zucchini are
   cooked, transfer them to a plate and take the skillet off the heat.

3 Add the gnocchi to the boiling water and cook until they puff up and start to
   float to the surface, 2 to 3 minutes. Reserve a mugful of the water from the
   gnocchi pot, then drain the gnocchi.

4 Add the gnocchi to the skillet with the remaining oil and return to the heat.
   Let the gnocchi sit undisturbed in the skillet until they start to color and
   crisp up, then add the zucchini, pesto, and a splash of the reserved pasta
   water. Gently stir to coat the gnocchi, then remove from the heat and divide
   between 2 plates. Top with basil and Parmesan shavings, and serve.

TIPS & SWAPS
*Parmesan isn't technically
vegetarian—choose a vegetarian
alternative hard cheese.

LEFTOVERS: see pp. 228–233

● Zucchini
● Pesto
● Basil

TIPS & SWAPS

*Parmesan isn't technically vegetarian—
choose a vegetarian alternative hard cheese.

Don't have sage? Don't worry! Omit or sprinkle
with thyme or chopped basil instead.

Most vegetables will work—try cubed zucchini
fried in a bit of olive oil, roasted butternut
squash, or steamed broccoli.

VG option

PASTA WITH MUSHROOMS, CRISPY SAGE & GARLIC BREAD CRUMBS

Serves 2

4½oz/125g dry pasta or 9oz/250g cooked
¼ cup olive oil or canola oil
1 tablespoon all-purpose flour
1¼ cups vegetable or chicken stock
¼ cup/¾oz/20g grated Parmesan*
1 bay leaf
4 large sage leaves
1½ cups/3½oz/100g sliced cremini or button mushrooms
3 tablespoons dry bread crumbs
1 garlic clove, crushed or minced
salt

As I have an Italian–American mom, I've grown up eating lots of pasta, and it is my go-to food for a weeknight when I don't feel like cooking. This is a pantry-friendly meal, as you can use whatever veg you have around (top tip: Use frozen peas if you don't have any fresh veggies), and you don't even need to have milk because you use vegetable stock for the sauce. The garlic bread crumbs are not to be missed—they amp up the dish and make it feel special.

1 If starting with dry pasta, put in a medium saucepan and cover with just-boiled water from the kettle. Bring to a boil and cook until al dente (this will generally be the shorter cooking time specified in the package directions). Drain, reserving a small mugful of the pasta water.

2 In a medium saucepan, heat 1 tablespoon of the oil over medium heat. Add the flour and cook, stirring, for 1 minute, then reduce the heat to low and gradually pour in the stock, stirring well between additions, until it has all been added. Stir in the Parmesan and add the bay leaf. Let simmer for 5 minutes, stirring occasionally, then season with salt to taste.

3 In a small skillet, heat the remaining oil over medium-high heat. Add the sage leaves and cook until crisp. Drain on paper towels and set aside.

4 Add the sliced mushrooms to the skillet and cook over medium heat until dark and soft, 5 to 7 minutes. Transfer the cooked mushrooms to the sauce and return the skillet to the heat.

5 Add the bread crumbs, garlic, and a pinch of salt to the skillet and toast, stirring continuously but gently, for 2 minutes so that the garlic cooks and the bread crumbs are crisped.

6 Remove the bay leaf from the sauce and pour it over the cooked pasta. Stir together and splash in a little of the reserved pasta water to loosen the mixture, if needed. Divide between 2 dishes and top with the mushrooms, bread crumbs, and crispy sage, then serve.

Vegan Use vegetable stock. Replace the cheese in the sauce with 2 tablespoons nutritional yeast flakes.

Omnivores This is a great recipe to add shrimp to! Omit the Parmesan from the sauce and don't use sage; just sprinkle chopped parsley over the finished dish. If using frozen, peeled, cooked shrimp, simply add them to the sauce in the last minute of simmering to thaw them. If using fresh, cooked, peeled shrimp, just stir them into the sauce right at the end.

LEFTOVERS: see pp. 228–233

● Mushrooms
● Pasta (dry or cooked)
● Sage leaves
● Bread crumbs

ROASTED CAULIFLOWER & GARLIC SOUP

Serves 3 to 4

1 large head of cauliflower, outer leaves removed (about 1lb/450g once leaves are removed)
2 tablespoons olive oil
1 red onion, thickly sliced
3 garlic cloves, crushed
1 cup vegetable stock
2 cups milk or nondairy milk
2 teaspoons miso, any kind, or 2 tablespoons soy sauce or tamari
¼ teaspoon ground cayenne
¼ teaspoon smoked paprika
½ teaspoon ground turmeric
⅔ cup/4¼oz/120g cooked cannellini (white kidney) beans, drained and rinsed
4 sprigs of thyme, leaves picked
1 tablespoon lemon juice
2 tablespoons plain or unsweetened soy yogurt or crème fraîche (optional)
handful of chive sprouts or finely chopped chives
salt and freshly ground black pepper

If you've never had roasted cauliflower before, you're about to meet a game changer. The bitterness fades away to leave a deep and cozy flavor, while the cannellini beans make the soup more filling and add to the creamy texture. It's even dairy free if you opt for nondairy milk, which I usually do.

1 Preheat the oven to 350°F.

2 Cut the cauliflower into large florets. In a roasting pan or on a baking sheet, toss the cauliflower florets in 1 tablespoon of the oil. Roast in the oven for 30 minutes, turning occasionally, until soft and starting to turn golden.

3 Meanwhile, in a large pot, heat the remaining oil over medium heat. Add the onion and sauté until translucent, 5 minutes. Add the garlic and cook for 1 minute. Stir in the stock, milk, miso, soy, or tamari, cayenne, smoked paprika, turmeric, and beans. Bring to a boil, then remove from the heat.

4 Add the roasted cauliflower, thyme, and lemon juice to the pot. Blend the soup. This can either be done directly in the pan using a handheld blender, or transfer the soup to a countertop blender to blend. Just be careful not to overfill your blender, so you may need to blend in batches. Season with salt and pepper to taste.

5 Divide among serving bowls, then top with the yogurt or crème fraîche, if using, and the chive sprouts or chopped chives.

Vegan Use nondairy milk and unsweetened soy yogurt (if using).

Gluten Free Make sure that you are using a certified gluten-free tamari or soy sauce.

LEFTOVERS: see pp. 228–233

● Cannellini beans
● Yogurt or crème fraîche
● Lemon
● Thyme
● Miso

TIPS & SWAPS

Make a quick, creamy pasta sauce from leftover soup—thin it out with a bit of vegetable stock and some butter or olive oil.

If you have roasted cauliflower to hand, use about 10½oz/300g. Skip step 1 and continue with the recipe.

THAI GREEN CURRY PEA SOUP

Serves 3 to 4

2 cups/10oz/280g frozen petite peas or peas

1 cup coconut milk (or 3½oz/100g creamed coconut stirred into 1 cup just-boiled water), a bit reserved for drizzling later

3⅓ cups/3½oz/100g baby spinach or scant ¼ cup/1oz/30g frozen spinach

juice of 1 lime

1 to 3 tablespoons Thai green curry paste, homemade (see page 221) or store-bought

handful of cilantro leaves, coarsely chopped

1 scallion, finely sliced

TIPS & SWAPS

Turn leftover soup into curry! Boil chopped regular or sweet potatoes, broccoli, and green beans and mix them into the soup when reheating it. You could also add roast veggies, frozen shrimp, or cold chicken from a roast. Serve with cooked brown rice and cilantro.

I like to make my own curry paste because I can control the heat and salt levels, but you can buy some pretty good store-bought green curry pastes now. If I'm buying it, I usually go to Asian grocery stores, as supermarket paste seems more expensive and less flavorsome. My top tip for this soup is to make excess and freeze it—I like to repurpose it into a riff on Thai green curry by serving it with rice, potatoes, string beans, snow peas, and broccoli.

1   In a medium saucepan, combine the frozen peas and coconut milk (or creamed coconut and hot water mixture). Cook over medium heat until the peas have thawed and the mixture is gently steaming.

2   Stir in the spinach until wilted and cooked (or thawed if using frozen spinach) and add the lime juice, then blend the soup. This can either be done directly in the pan using a handheld blender, or transfer the soup to a countertop blender to blend. Just be careful not to overfill your blender, so you may need to blend in batches.

3   Blend or stir in the curry paste. Start with 1 tablespoon and add more if needed. I recommend this because if you're using store-bought paste, it can vary wildly in strength of flavor, level of heat, and salinity. Serve the soup hot, drizzled with the reserved coconut milk, the cilantro, and scallion.

Vegan   The recipe for the Thai curry paste is vegan, but if using store-bought paste, then make sure you check the label.

LEFTOVERS: see pp. 228–233

- Baby spinach
- Thai green curry paste
- Coconut milk or creamed coconut
- Cilantro
- Scallions

VG option

CURRIED TOMATO–COCONUT SOUP

Serves 2 to 3

1 tablespoon olive oil
1 small red onion, diced
1 tablespoon grated or minced
    ginger root
2 garlic cloves, crushed or minced
1¾oz/50g creamed coconut or
    ½ (14oz) can coconut milk
¾ cup just-boiled water (if using the
    creamed coconut)
14oz/400g canned diced tomatoes
1 tablespoon miso, any kind,
    or soy sauce or tamari
½ teaspoon granulated sugar
    or honey, or 1 teaspoon Date
    Paste (see page 221)
about ½ cup/3½oz/100g dry red
    lentils, rinsed
¾ cup cold water
½ teaspoon garam masala
½ teaspoon ground turmeric
2½ teaspoons sweet smoked paprika
1 teaspoon coriander seeds, ground

TO SERVE
handful of cilantro, chopped

This is a humble tomato soup, jazzed up with coconut milk and spiced and thickened with red lentils. It's a thrifty, filling recipe for cold evenings, and is a lot more special than your usual tomato soup.

1   In a medium saucepan, heat the oil over medium heat, add the onion, and sauté until translucent, 7 to 10 minutes. Add the ginger and garlic, reduce the heat, and sauté for another minute.

2   If using creamed coconut, put it in a mug and pour over the just-boiled water. Stir until melted and combined.

3   Set aside 2 tablespoons of the creamed coconut–water mixture or coconut milk for drizzling at the end. Add the remaining coconut mixture or milk to the pan with the diced tomatoes, miso, soy, or tamari, sugar, honey, or Date Paste, red lentils, and the cold water. Stir, then bring to a boil. Reduce the heat and simmer for 20 minutes, stirring occasionally. Add the spices, stir, and cook for another 2 minutes.

4   Blend the soup until smooth. This can either be done directly in the pan using a handheld blender, or transfer the soup to a countertop blender to blend. Just be careful not to overfill your blender, so you may need to blend in batches. Alternatively, keep as is for something more like dahl. Serve the soup drizzled with the reserved coconut mixture or milk and sprinkled with the chopped cilantro.

Vegan Use sugar or Date Paste.

Gluten Free Make sure that you are using a certified gluten-free tamari or soy sauce.

LEFTOVERS: see pp. 228–233

- Coconut milk or creamed
  coconut
- Cilantro
- Miso

ONE-PAN CREAMY PASTA WITH ASPARAGUS, LEMON & BASIL

Serves 2

5½oz/150g dry pasta, such as
　　spaghetti*
1 tablespoon olive oil
2 garlic cloves, crushed or minced
2½ cups just-boiled water
3½oz/100g asparagus
¼ head of white cabbage, sliced into
　　¼ inch wide ribbons
handful of basil leaves,
　　finely chopped
1 egg, lightly beaten
grated zest of 1 lemon and
　　small squeeze of juice
⅓ cup/1oz/30g grated Parmesan,
　　Grana Padano, or cheddar
salt and freshly ground black pepper

This pasta dish is a dream come true—the method cooks the pasta by water absorption so that you don't have to drain it. What you're left with is perfectly cooked pasta and vegetables coated in a slick of starchy water. By vigorously stirring a beaten egg into the pasta just as it finishes cooking, you create a luscious yet light sauce in a matter of seconds.

1　In a deep skillet, put the pasta, oil, garlic, and just-boiled water. Bring to a boil over medium heat, then reduce the heat and simmer, pushing the pasta into the pan to submerge it as it softens, for 6 minutes, stirring occasionally to prevent clumping.

2　Snap the woody ends off the asparagus, then cut into small pieces. Put the asparagus and cabbage on top of the pasta in the skillet. Cover with a lid or a large plate and cook for 5 minutes.

3　Carefully uncover and take the skillet off the heat. Immediately add the basil and egg, and quickly toss and stir into the pasta with a couple of forks until the egg has thickened into a lovely, creamy sauce. If the egg doesn't look like it's thickening up, return the skillet to the heat briefly, while still mixing, to help it cook through. At this point, add a bit of water to thin the sauce out a little, if needed.

4　Stir most of the lemon zest and cheese into the pasta, reserving some for sprinkling, and season with salt and pepper. Divide between 2 plates, top with the reserved cheese and lemon zest, and add the lemon juice.

LEFTOVERS: see pp. 228–233

● White cabbage

TIPS & SWAPS

*Use whole-wheat spaghetti to help you feel fuller for longer.

If asparagus isn't in season, replace with an equal quantity of broccoli, string beans, or fava beans.

Grana Padano is often cheaper than Parmesan and works just as well!

TIPS & SWAPS

*Parmesan isn't technically vegetarian—choose a vegetarian alternative hard cheese.

This dish works with any pasta shape you like!

Use a spiralizer, vegetable peeler, or box grater to create long ribbons of raw zucchini, then toss in with the pasta at the end to bulk up the dish and add more vitamins.

GF option

CREAMY TUSCAN KALE, LEEK & PEA PASTA

Serves 2

1 large or 2 small leeks
5½oz/150g Tuscan kale (cavolo nero)
   (weighed with stems)
1 tablespoon olive oil
5½oz/150g dry whole-wheat
   tagliatelle or 10½oz/300g cooked
¾ cup/3½oz/100g frozen petite peas
   or peas
4 sprigs of thyme, leaves picked
¼ cup crème fraîche or ricotta cheese
salt
grated Parmesan, to serve (optional)^

Tuscan kale (cavolo nero) is my favorite green to cook. Its texture is better than curly kale in my opinion and it doesn't wither away into nothingness like spinach tends to do. Combined with the soft sweetness of leeks and peas plus the zing of crème fraîche, this is a light, fresh pasta dish packed with veggies. If you own a spiralizer, tossing in raw, spiralized zucchini will add even more vitamins and bulk to this dish.

1 Cut the leek in half lengthwise and wash under cold running water to remove any dirt between the layers. Shake off the excess water, place on a cutting board, and cut into ¾-inch-thick strips. Rinse again in a colander.

2 Strip the leaves off the stems of the Tuscan kale and coarsely chop the leaves, discarding the stems. Set aside.

3 In a large skillet, heat the oil over medium-low heat. Add the leek with a generous pinch of salt and cook for 15 minutes, stirring frequently so that it softens but doesn't color.

4 Meanwhile, if starting with dry pasta, put in a medium saucepan and cover with just-boiled water from the kettle. Bring to a boil and cook until al dente (this will generally be the shorter cooking time specified in the package directions). Drain, reserving a small mugful of the pasta water.

5 Add the Tuscan kale and frozen peas to the leek and cook, stirring, over medium heat until the kale has softened slightly. Add the thyme, a good splash of the reserved pasta water (or just some water from the faucet if you're using precooked pasta), and the crème fraîche or ricotta. Cook, stirring, until the kale is fully softened, then mix in the pasta. Season with salt to taste and add more pasta water if needed to make it saucier. Divide between 2 plates and top with Parmesan, if using.

Gluten Free Use gluten-free pasta (e.g. brown rice pasta) instead of the tagliatelle.

LEFTOVERS: see pp. 228–233

- Tuscan kale
- Leeks
- Pasta (dry or cooked)
- Crème fraîche or ricotta cheese
- Frozen petite peas or peas
- Thyme

EASY SUMMER PASTA

Serves 2

1¾ cups/10½oz/300g halved cherry tomatoes

2 medium zucchini

1 aubergine, cut into ¾-inch cubes

1 tablespoon olive oil or canola oil

2 teaspoons mixed dried herbs (I like herbes de Provence)

2¾oz/75g fresh mozzarella cheese, torn into medium strips

1½ cups/5½oz/150g dry whole-wheat penne pasta or 3 cups/11oz/ 300g cooked

3 tablespoons crème fraîche or ricotta cheese

salt

By roasting tomatoes, eggplant, and zucchini together, you end up with a ratatouillelike mixture. Just whack it all in the oven for an hour and come back when you are ready to cook the penne. Throw on some torn mozzarella near the end so that it melts over the vegetables and combine with the pasta and some crème fraîche or ricotta.

1 Preheat the oven to 350°F.

2 Reserve about ½ cup of the cherry tomatoes for later. Add the rest to a roasting pan. Cut the zucchini in half along their lengths, then cut the lengths into half-moons about ¾ inch thick and add them to the roasting pan with the zucchini, oil, herbs, and a pinch of salt. Toss together and roast in the oven for 1 hour, tossing halfway through cooking. After 45 minutes, scatter the torn mozzarella over the top of the vegetables and return to the oven for the final 15 minutes of cooking time so that the cheese melts.

3 Meanwhile, if starting with dry pasta, put in a medium saucepan and cover with just-boiled water from the kettle. Bring to a boil and cook until al dente (this will generally be the shorter cooking time specified on the package directions). Drain, reserving a small mugful of the pasta water, and return the pasta to the saucepan.

4 Once the vegetables and mozzarella have finished roasting, add them to the drained pasta along with the crème fraîche and a splash of the reserved pasta water (or just some water from the faucet if you're using precooked pasta). Season with salt to taste and divide between 2 plates. Scatter the reserved cherry tomatoes over the pasta and serve.

Vegan Omit the mozzarella and replace the crème fraîche with 2 tablespoons extra virgin olive oil and a squeeze of fresh lemon juice.

Gluten Free Use gluten-free pasta (e.g. brown rice pasta).

TIPS & SWAPS

Roast some extra tomatoes and cook extra pasta to use for lunch or dinner the next day. Keep in the refrigerator in a container for up to 3 days. See the leftovers table, pages 228–233, for how to use them.

LEFTOVERS: see pp. 228–233

- Eggplant
- Zucchini
- Cherry tomatoes
- Mozzarella cheese
- Pasta (dry or cooked)
- Crème fraîche or ricotta cheese

V

VG & GF options

LENTIL & FENNEL RAGU WITH BALSAMIC ONIONS

Serves 4

2 tablespoons olive oil
1 red onion, cut into ¹/₁₆-inch-thick slices
about ½ cup water, plus 1 tablespoon
2 tablespoons balsamic vinegar
1 fennel bulb
3 garlic cloves, coarsely chopped
    or crushed
2 teaspoons coriander seeds, ground
1 tablespoon fennel seeds
2 teaspoons mixed dried herbs
2 teaspoons granulated sugar
    or honey, or 1 tablespoon Date
    Paste (see page 221)
14oz/400g canned diced tomatoes
3⅓ cups vegetable stock
½ cup white or red wine or water
½ cup/3¼oz/90g dry Puy lentils, rinsed
½ cup/1¾oz/50g finely chopped
    walnuts (optional)
1 tablespoon miso, any kind, or
    2 tablespoons soy sauce or tamari
3 tablespoons Worcestershire sauce*
10½oz/300g dry pasta or 1¼lb/600g
    cooked
salt
grated Parmesan, to serve**

Even if you don't think you'd enjoy a vegetarian ragu, this one might surprise you... in a good way. I don't really like fennel bulb raw, as I find the anise flavor too intense and the texture a bit tough. But when, on impulse, I cooked it down into a stewy sauce, it softened in flavor and texture. I'm such a fan of the tomato and fennel combo with the lentils and walnuts.

1   In a large saucepan, heat half the oil over medium heat. Add the sliced onion and pinch of salt and cook for 5 minutes, stirring frequently. Pour in ¼ cup of the water and stir until the water has evaporated, then reduce the heat to low and cook for another 3 minutes. Add in another ¼ cup water and cook for another 3 minutes. Stir in half the balsamic vinegar, then transfer the onion to a plate and set aside.

2   Heat the rest of the oil in the same pan over medium-low heat. Trim the bottom of the fennel bulb, then cut in half from top to bottom. Slice each half into about ¹/₈-inch-thick slices. Add to the pan with the garlic. Cook, stirring constantly, for 1 minute. Add the coriander and fennel seeds and stir through for another minute. Add the herbs, sugar, honey or Date Syrup, tomatoes, stock, and wine or water. Stir in the lentils and walnuts, then bring the mixture to a boil. Reduce the heat to low, cover, and simmer until the lentils are tender but not mushy, about 40 to 50 minutes.

3   Uncover the saucepan. In a small bowl or mug, mix the miso, soy or tamari with the remaining tablespoon of water, then add to the saucepan and stir through with the remaining tablespoon of balsamic vinegar and the Worcestershire sauce. Taste the sauce and add salt, if needed. Cook, uncovered, until it is reduced to a thick sauce.

4   Meanwhile, if starting with dry pasta, put in a medium saucepan and cover with just-boiled water from the kettle. Bring to a boil and cook until al dente (this will generally be the shorter cooking time specified in the package directions). Drain, reserving a small mugful of the pasta water.

5   Stir most of the thickened sauce into the cooked pasta together with a good splash of the reserved pasta water. Divide among 4 bowls, top with more sauce and some of the onions, and serve with Parmesan, if desired.

Vegan   Use granulated sugar or Date Paste. Make sure your wine (if using) is vegan. Use vegan Worcestershire sauce or Marmite or Vegemite instead. Don't serve with Parmesan.

Gluten Free   Use gluten-free pasta (e.g. brown rice pasta). Make sure your tamari or soy sauce is certified gluten free.

LEFTOVERS: see pp. 228–233

● Pasta (dry or cooked)
● Miso

TIPS & SWAPS

*Conventional Worcestershire sauce contains fish—find vegetarian or vegan alternatives online or in health-food shops, or use Marmite or Vegemite instead.

**Parmesan isn't technically vegetarian—choose a vegetarian alternative hard cheese.

Replace the fennel with 2 celery stalks, chopped.

This sauce also makes a great pie filling.

Make a double batch and store in the freezer in a container for up to 3 months.

TIPS & SWAPS

Replace the mango with thinly sliced apple, cubed pineapple, or peach.

Use frozen (then thawed) mango cubes instead of fresh.

For the dressing, use creamed coconut instead of coconut milk. Stir 2 tablespoons into ¼ cup hot water. This is much more convenient than using a small amount of canned coconut milk, which goes off within a few days.

VG & GF options

HALLOUMI & MANGO NOODLE SALAD

Halloumi and mango may seem an unlikely pairing, but it's a good combo, trust me. Sweet and salty, chewy and juicy, this is a light meal for a summery day. If you don't eat dairy, then I have good news—the baked tofu from page 75 swaps in perfectly in place of the halloumi!

Serves 2

⅔ cup/5½oz/100g frozen, shelled edamame

5½oz/150g dry soba or udon noodles

4½oz/125g halloumi cheese, cut into ⅛-inch-thick slices

½ large ripe mango, peeled and cubed

2 scallions, thinly sliced

handful of basil, coarsely chopped

handful of cashews or peanuts, coarsely chopped

CILANTRO–COCONUT DRESSING

2 handfuls of cilantro leaves

¼oz/10g piece of ginger root, peeled and minced or grated

juice of 1 lemon

2 tablespoons soy sauce or tamari

1 tablespoon granulated sugar or honey, or 2 tablespoons Date Paste (see page 221)

1 to 2 pinches of crushed red pepper

⅓ cup coconut milk

1 Put the frozen edamame in a colander in the sink. Add the noodles to a saucepan of boiling water over medium heat. Cook for the length of time specified in the package directions, then pour the noodles and cooking water over the frozen edamame in the colander. Let sit for 30 seconds (to thaw the edamame), then rinse under cold running water to prevent the noodles from clumping.

2 Heat a dry, nonstick skillet over medium heat. Add the sliced halloumi and cook until light golden on the underside, 2 to 4 minutes, then flip over and cook on the other side. Remove from the pan.

3 Blend all the dressing ingredients together. This can be done in a beaker using a handheld blender or in a countertop blender. If you don't have a blender, just chop the cilantro leaves as finely as possible and stir into the remaining dressing ingredients.

4 Toss the noodles and edamame with the cubed mango, scallions, basil, and cashews or peanuts. Divide the salad between 2 plates and top with the dressing and halloumi slices.

Vegan Replace the halloumi with the baked tofu from the recipe on page 75. Use granulated sugar or maple syrup in the dressing.

Gluten Free If you can find gluten-free soba noodles, use those, otherwise use flat rice noodles (the ones usually used for pad Thai) instead. Make sure your soy sauce or tamari is certified gluten free.

LEFTOVERS: see pp. 228–233

- Halloumi cheese
- Basil
- Cilantro
- Coconut milk
- Scallions
- Mango

ORANGE, FENNEL, OLIVE & PEARL BARLEY STEW

Serves 2 to 3

1 fennel bulb
2 tablespoons olive oil
2 teaspoons fennel seeds
2 red onions, coarsely diced
1 red, yellow, or orange bell pepper,
    seeded and thinly sliced
5 garlic cloves, crushed or minced
½ teaspoon smoked paprika
½ teaspoon ground cinnamon
½ teaspoon ground turmeric
1 bay leaf
1 large orange (grated zest
    of ½, juice of whole)
14oz/400g canned diced tomatoes
⅓ cup/2½oz/70g coarsely chopped
    black ripe or green pitted olives
1 quart vegetable stock or chicken stock
⅓ cupplus 1 tablespoon/3oz/80g
    dry pearl barley
½ cup white or red wine, or more stock
1 tablespoon sherry vinegar, apple
    cider vinegar, or balsamic vinegar
2 teaspoons granulated sugar
    or 1 tablespoon Date Paste
    (see page 221)
salt
basil leaves, torn, to serve

My dad makes a chicken stew with olives, lots of orange juice, and a cinnamon stick thrown in. It's a surprising combination of flavors, but it works. This is my university version of it (basically just minus the meat) with some chewy pearl barley and fennel added in. It's a salty, sweet, and fragrant stew that is light enough to suit a slightly cold summer's evening.

1 Trim the bottom of the fennel, then cut in half from top to bottom. Slice each half into about ⅛-inch-thick slices.

2 In a large saucepan, heat the oil over medium heat. Add the fennel seeds and onions and cook, stirring frequently, until the onions are translucent, about 5 minutes. Add the fennel with the bell pepper and garlic and cook, stirring occasionally, until the fennel starts to soften, 7 to 10 minutes.

3 Stir in the paprika, cinnamon, turmeric, bay leaf, and orange zest and cook for 30 seconds, then pour in the orange juice, tomatoes, olives, stock, pearl barley, and wine. Stir together, then bring to a boil. Once boiling, cover with a lid, reduce the heat, and simmer for 20 minutes.

4 Uncover and stir in the vinegar and sugar or Date Paste, then season with salt to taste. If the mixture seems too watery, cook uncovered for 5 to 10 minutes until it is your preferred consistency. Serve with torn basil.

Vegan If using wine, make sure it's vegan, otherwise use more stock.

LEFTOVERS: see pp. 228–233

● Bell pepper
● Pearl barley
● Basil

TIPS & SWAPS
If fresh fennel is out of season,
use 2 celery stalks, coarsely
chopped, instead.

VG option

ZINGY CARROT & RICE NOODLE SALAD

Serves 2

2 large carrots, peeled into ribbons
3½oz/100g dry rice vermicelli (thin rice noodles)
1¼ cups/7oz/200g frozen corn kernels, thawed, or canned, drained corn kernels
large handful of cilantro, coarsely chopped
handful of cashews, coarsely chopped
2 scallions, finely sliced
handful of Quick Pickled Red Onion (see page 223)

DRESSING
½ teaspoon salt
juice of 2 limes
¼ cup apple cider vinegar or rice vinegar
2 tablespoons honey or granulated sugar
2 teaspoons grated or minced root ginger
1 garlic clove, crushed or minced
½ red chile, seeded and finely chopped
1 star anise (optional)

In this dish, a hot, spicy, and punchy dressing is heated up and poured over ribboned carrots, effectively quick-pickling them. They are tossed into rice vermicelli (which only require a quick soak to "cook" them) and some other flavorsome additions to make an incredibly fast meal. You don't have to spend much time at the stove, so this recipe is ideal for when it's too hot to bear being in the kitchen for too long.

1 To make the dressing, in a small saucepan, heat all the ingredients until the mixture begins to steam. Remove from the heat and pour the hot dressing over the carrots. Let cool.

2 Put the rice vermicelli in a medium heatproof bowl and pour in enough just-boiled water to cover them well. Let stand for 5 minutes, then drain.

3 Remove and discard the star anise, if using, from the bowl of carrots. Toss the noodles, dressing, carrots, and corn together. Transfer to a plate and sprinkle with the cilantro, cashews, scallions, and Quick Pickled Red Onion.

Vegan Use granulated sugar.

TIPS & SWAPS
Replace the rice vermicelli with cooked soba or udon noodles. You can also use wide, flat rice noodles (like the ones in pad Thai).

LEFTOVERS: see pp. 228–233

● Carrots
● Red chile
● Cilantro

Clear the Fridge

At the end of the week, my once bountiful refrigerator is usually looking bare. There will be scraps of raw or cooked vegetables, cut lemons, wilting herbs, and the likes, and so it can be very uninspiring to try and cook. This is where these template recipes come in. Use them as guides for how to use up all those random pieces of food that you have left. For each of the templates I have also included three structured recipes so that you can see how I use the templates as a guide. Hopefully they can spark some creativity and give you and your refrigerator an end-of-the-week boost to get you through to your weekend food shop.

PIZZA TEMPLATE

Makes 3 medium pizzas

1 recipe for Pizza Dough (see page 220)
all-purpose flour, for dusting
olive oil, for drizzling
salt

SAUCE
(2 TO 4 TABLESPOONS PER PIZZA)
1 recipe for No-cook Pizza Sauce
   (see page 220)
Pesto (see pages 224–225)
puréed, cooked corn kernels
puréed, roasted butternut squash
   or sweet potato

VEGETABLES
(A HANDFUL PER PIZZA)
pureed cooked corn kernels
pureed roasted butternut squash
   or sweet potato
raw zucchini or asparagus, peeled
   into ribbons
diced zucchini or eggplant, sautéed in
   olive oil with a pinch of salt until golden
roasted cubed sweet potato or
   butternut squash
roasted sliced carrots
roasted cherry tomatoes
wilted spinach or Tuscan kale
   (cavolo nero)
small florets of steamed or roasted
   broccoli or cauliflower
thinly sliced and parboiled white
   potatoes
frozen peas, thawed
bell pepper, seeded and thinly sliced
mushrooms, thinly sliced and sautéed
   in olive oil with a pinch of salt

This template makes enough for 3 medium pizzas. If you are cooking for one or two people, just divide the recipe quantities as needed.

1   Heat a medium skillet over the highest heat. Heat the oven broiler to the highest setting and place the rack in the top third of the oven.

2   Take a quarter of the pizza dough, flour it, and stretch into a circle about the size of your skillet. To do this, I lift the pizza dough up, hold it with both my hands, and stretch it all the way around the perimeter of the dough. Once the dough is the right size, carefully lay it in the hot skillet. Reduce the heat to medium and let the pizza dough cook until it starts to change color and looks dry in patches on top.

3   Spread over the pizza sauce and sprinkle on any vegetables you are using. Dot or sprinkle with any "special additions" (see page 161)—I personally add mozzarella followed by a grating of Parmesan to my pizzas.

4   Drizzle your pizza with some olive oil and sprinkle with some salt. Place under the broiler with the door ajar and the skillet handle sticking out. Cook until the crust is browned and, if using mozzarella, the cheese is browned, 4 to 6 minutes.

5   Remove from the broiler (make sure you use a kitchen towel or oven mitt to grab the handle, as it may be hot) and let cool on a heatproof surface for a second. Slide the pizza onto a cutting board, top with any "uncooked sprinkles," (see page 161) and slice into wedges. Repeat with the remaining pizza dough and toppings, as desired.

TOP LEFT: POTATO, CARAMELIZED ONION & THYME
TOP RIGHT: EGG, SPINACH & CHERRY TOMATO
BOTTOM: BLITZED CORN, CILANTRO & SCALLION

PIZZA: BLITZED CORN, CILANTRO & SCALLION

Makes 2

about 1 cup cooked corn kernels
  (if canned, drained; if frozen,
  thawed)
½ recipe for Pizza Dough (see page 220)
5½oz/150g fresh mozzarella cheese,
torn
grated Parmesan, for sprinkling
olive oil, for drizzling
½ recipe for "Chorizo" Dip (see page 47)
handful of cilantro, finely chopped
1 scallion, thinly sliced
2 radishes, thinly sliced
salt

A slightly unusual sauce here. It's so simple to do, though, and my boyfriend Andy loves it. The vibrant corn base is offset by shards of thinly shaved radish, pungent scallion, and cilantro. Don't forget about the smoky "Chorizo" Dip (see page 47)—you will be a fan of it if you usually opt for a meaty pizza.

1   Blitz the corn in a countertop blender or in a beaker with a handheld blender to form a coarse paste.

2   Follow the pizza template method (see page 158) to make and cook the pizzas. Dot the "Chorizo" Dip and blitzed corn along with the mozzarella cheese and Parmesan over the pizzas, but don't add the cilantro, scallions, and radishes yet. Once the pizzas have been cooked, sprinkle them on top.

PIZZA: POTATO, CARAMELIZED ONION & THYME

Makes 2

1 floury potato (about 3½oz/100g),
  thinly sliced
2 tablespoons olive oil,
  plus extra for drizzling
1 red onion, cut into about
  ¹⁄₁₆-inch-thick slices
about ¼ cup water
1 tablespoon balsamic vinegar
½ recipe for Pizza Dough
  (see page 220)
½ recipe for No-cook Pizza Sauce
  (see page 220) or ¾ cup
  your favorite tomato pizza sauce
4 sprigs of thyme
5½oz/150g fresh mozzarella cheese,
  torn
grated Parmesan*, for sprinkling
salt

Carbs on carbs! This is my idea of heaven. I love putting sliced potatoes on pizza because, in my eyes, you can never have too much carb on one plate. Some balsamic-tangy caramelized onion sets it off beautifully and the thyme adds freshness.

1   Put the potato slices in a small saucepan and cover with water. Bring to a boil, then reduce the heat to a simmer and cook for 5 minutes. Drain and set aside.

2   In a medium skillet, heat the oil over medium heat. Add the red onion and a pinch of salt and cook, stirring frequently, over medium-low heat until softened, about 5 to 10 minutes. Add the water and stir until it has evaporated, then cook for another 5 minutes until the onion is completely soft. Stir in the balsamic vinegar, then remove from the heat and set aside.

3   Follow the pizza template method (see page 158) to make and cook the pizzas, sprinkling on the thyme and mozzarella and adding the potato and onions. Serve with a sprinkling of Parmesan.

PIZZA: EGG, SPINACH & CHERRY TOMATO

Makes 2

1 tablespoon olive oil, plus a little
    extra for drizzling
2 garlic cloves, crushed or minced
5½oz/150g baby spinach
½ recipe for Pizza Dough
    (see page 220)
½ recipe for No-cook Pizza Sauce
    (see page 220) or ¾cup of your
    favorite tomato pizza sauce
5½oz/150g fresh mozzarella cheese,
    torn
grated Parmesan*, for sprinkling
2 eggs
⅓ cup/3½oz/100g halved or quartered
    cherry tomatoes
torn basil, for sprinkling

Whoever came up with baking an egg right on top of a pizza was a genius. That runny yolk just gives you more sauce to mop up with each slice. Technically, I think this also makes this a brunch-appropriate pizza—yes...?

1   Heat the oil in a large saucepan over medium heat. Add the garlic, reduce the heat to low, and cook, stirring, for 1 minute, then add the spinach. Continue to cook, stirring, until the spinach has wilted. Remove from the heat and set aside. Give the spinach a little squeeze to remove any excess water before using on the pizzas.

2   Follow the pizza template method (see page 158) to cook the pizzas, but don't add the eggs, cherry tomatoes, or basil yet. Once the pizza has been under the broiler for 2 minutes, crack an egg onto the pizza, then place back under the broiler for the remaining 3 minutes or until cooked.

3   Once the pizza is cooked, top it with the cherry tomatoes and a sprinkling of torn basil.

TIPS &
SWAPS

*Parmesan is not technically
vegetarian—choose an
alternative vegetarian hard
cheese.

SPECIAL ADDITIONS

Choose between 1 and 3 and use 2 to 3 tablespoons each per pizza: "Chorizo" Dip (see page 47), Pea Hummus (see page 46), sliced chiles, sundried tomatoes, pitted black ripe olives, feta cheese or Sun Feta (see page 219), balsamic onions (see Lentil & Fennel Ragu on page 150), ricotta, mozzarella, Parmesan, or cheddar cheese, sage leaves, thyme leaves

UNCOOKED SPRINKLES

Use 1 to 2 tablespoons per pizza: Basil or cilantro, scallions, Avocado Cream (see page 219), crème fraîche, cherry tomatoes, arugula or pea shoots, Parmesan, Quick Pickled Red Onion (see page 223)

LEFTOVERS: see pp. 228–233

- Mozzarella cheese
- Basil
- Tomatoes
- Baby spinach

- Mozzarella cheese
- Thyme

- Cilantro

FRITTATA TEMPLATE

Serves 2 to 3

BASE
6 to 8 eggs
¼ teaspoon salt
2 garlic cloves, crushed (optional)
½ to ¾ cup/3½oz to 7oz/100 to 200g
ricotta cheese (optional)
olive oil, for cooking
freshly ground black pepper

1 In a large bowl, whisk the eggs with the salt and some black pepper. If using garlic and/or ricotta, mix that in now. Set aside.

2 Heat a large, nonstick skillet with 2 tablespoons olive oil over medium heat. Sauté any slow-cooking vegetables first until soft, then add any medium-cooking vegetables and lastly any quick-cooking vegetables, and sauté until soft. If using any cooked starchy ingredients, add them now.

3 Heat the oven broiler to the highest setting and place the rack in the top of the oven.

4 Reduce the heat under the skillet to low and pour the beaten egg mixture over the vegetables. Cook on the stove until you can see the egg at the edges beginning to turn opaque. Sprinkle or spoon on any "extra" ingredients, then place the frittata under the broiler, with the handle poking out and the oven door slightly ajar. Cook until puffed and golden.

Gluten Free Don't use pasta for the "starch."

STARCH
(3½ TO 7OZ, SEE
COOKING TIMETABLE ON PAGE 11)

cooked chick peas (garbanzo beans)
cooked cannellini (white kidney) beans
cooked pasta (spaghetti works well)
sliced, parboiled regular or sweet
    potatoes (boil for 5 minutes)
roasted cubed sweet potato
shredded raw sweet potato
cooked brown rice

VEGETABLES
(2 TO 3 HANDFULS)

Quick cooking:
roasted, cubed butternut squash or
    sweet potato
roasted sliced carrot
roasted or steamed florets of broccoli
    or cauliflower
roasted cherry tomatoes
sliced and steamed cabbage
baby spinach
kale (stems removed, leaves chopped),
peas (fresh, shelled or frozen)
corn kernels (fresh, canned or frozen),
green beans (chopped and steamed)

Medium cooking:
diced zucchini
diced eggplant
thinly sliced bell pepper
shredded raw sweet potato
chopped asparagus
sliced leeks
sliced mushrooms

Slow cooking:
sliced onions
diced carrot
diced celery

"CHORIZO" DIP &
RED BELL PEPPER

CAULIFLOWER,
SWEET POTATO
& THYME

PEAS, POTATO
& MOZZARELLA

FRITTATA: CAULIFLOWER, SWEET POTATO & THYME

Serves 2

½ large head of cauliflower, outer leaves removed and cut into medium florets (about 9oz/250g when leaves are removed)
1 medium sweet potato (7 to 10½oz/ 200 to 300g), peeled and cut into 1¼-inch chunks
2 tablespoons olive oil
1 red onion, cut into about 1¼-inch-thick slices
4 sprigs of thyme, leaves picked
6 eggs
salt

My favourite way to use up leftover roasted veg is in a frittata. This recipe is perfect for leftover roasted cauliflower and sweet potato – just skip steps 1 and 2 and continue with the recipe.

1 Preheat the oven to 350°F.

2 On a baking sheet, toss the cauliflower and sweet potato with 1 tablespoon of the oil and a pinch of salt. Roast in the oven for 45 minutes, flipping halfway through, until starting to brown.

3 In a medium, nonstick skillet, heat the remaining oil over medium heat. Add the onion and a pinch of salt and cook, stirring frequently, until the onion is beginning to turn translucent. Reduce the heat to low and add the roasted vegetables and thyme leaves in an even layer.

4 Heat the oven broiler to the highest setting and place the rack in the top of the oven.

5 In a bowl, whisk the eggs with ¼ teaspoon salt, then pour over the vegetables in the skillet. Cook on the stove until the egg at the edges begins to turn opaque. Place the frittata under the broiler, with the handle poking out and the oven door slightly ajar, and cook until puffed and golden.

FRITTATA: PEAS, POTATO & MOZZARELLA

Serves 2

1 medium floury potato (7 to 10½oz/ 200 to 300g), unpeeled and cut into about 1¼-inch-thick slices
1 tablespoon olive oil
⅔ cup/3½oz/100g frozen petite peas or peas
2 garlic cloves, crushed or minced
6 eggs
¼ teaspoon salt
½ ball fresh mozzarella cheese, torn
handful of basil, coarsely chopped

Classic Spanish tortillas are potato and onion heavy. Here, I've layered potatoes with sweet peas and gooey mozzarella.

1 Bring a small saucepan of water to a boil. Add the potato, then reduce the heat and simmer for 10 minutes. Drain and set aside.

2 In a medium, nonstick skillet, heat the oil over medium heat. Add the peas and garlic and cook until the peas have thawed, a minute or so. Reduce the heat to low and arrange the slices of cooked potato in the skillet.

3 Heat the oven broiler to the highest setting and place the rack in the top of the oven.

4 In a medium bowl, whisk the eggs with the salt, then pour over the vegetables in the skillet. Top with the mozzarella and cook on the stove until the egg at the edges begins to turn opaque. Place under the broiler, with the handle poking out and the oven door slightly ajar, and cook until puffed and golden. Sprinkle the basil over before serving.

FRITTATA: "CHORIZO" DIP & RED BELL PEPPER

Serves 2

1 red bell pepper
6 eggs
¼ teaspoon salt
1 tablespoon olive oil or canola oil
2 scallions, finely sliced
½ recipe for "Chorizo" Dip (see page 47)

If you have made the "Chorizo" Dip (see page 47) and are wondering what to do with the rest of it, this is a tasty, unexpected way to use it. Along with the smoky roasted red bell pepper, it's a perfect match of flavors.

1 Either, place the bell pepper directly over a gas flame, turning occasionally until the whole skin of the pepper has been blackened. Or, place the bell pepper on a baking sheet, turn on your oven broiler to the highest setting, and place the rack in the top of the oven. Place the bell pepper under the broiler and turn occasionally until blackened all over.

2 Transfer the hot, cooked pepper to a bowl, cover with a plate, and let steam for 10 minutes. Pierce the pepper with a knife to let any steam escape, then rub the pepper under cold running water to remove the skin. Remove the stem and seeds with your hands and tear the pepper into about 6 strips.

3 Heat the oven broiler to the highest setting and place the rack in the top of the oven.

4 In a medium bowl, whisk the eggs with the salt.

5 In a medium nonstick skillet, heat the oil over medium heat. Once the oil is hot, reduce the heat to low and arrange the torn pepper strips over it. Scatter over the scallions and pour the beaten egg over too. Dot with spoonfuls of the "Chorizo" Dip and cook on the stove until you can see the egg at the edges beginning to turn opaque. Place the frittata under the broiler, with the handle poking out and the oven door slightly ajar, and cook until puffed and golden.

LEFTOVERS: see pp. 228–233

- Cauliflower
- Thyme

- Frozen petite peas or peas
- Mozzarella cheese
- Basil

- Bell pepper
- Scallions

TACO TEMPLATE

Serves as many as you want!

Pick a few different fillings. I usually do 1 starchy, 1 creamy, 2 vegetables, and 1 extra or salsa. Layer them up in a soft or crunchy tortilla and eat!

small tortillas (see page 214) or store-bought, warmed or crunchy corn tortillas, store-bought

STARCHY
(2 TO 3 TABLESPOONS PER TACO, SEE COOKING TIME TABLE ON PAGE 11)
cooked chick peas (garbanzo beans)
cooked cannellini (white kidney) beans
cooked black beans
cooked red kidney beans
cooked green or Puy lentils
cooked brown rice
cooked couscous
cooked quinoa

CREAMY
(1 TABLESPOON PER TACO)
plain yogurt
crème fraîche
ricotta cheese
cooked sweet potato, pureed
cooked butternut squash, pureed
"Chorizo" Dip (see page 47)
Pea Hummus (see page 46)
Pesto (see pages 224–225)
mashed or cubed avocado
Avocado Cream (see page 219)

VEGETABLES
(A SMALL HANDFUL PER TACO)
mixed salad greens, baby spinach, arugula, or pea shoots
finely sliced Little Gem lettuce or Belgian endive
roasted, cubed squash, sweet potato, or regular potato
roasted carrots
roasted or steamed broccoli or cauliflower florets
roasted cherry tomatoes
sliced bell pepper, raw or sautéed in olive oil until soft
balsamic onions (see Lentil & Fennel Ragu on page 150)
fresh corn, cut off the cob, raw or sautéed
raw bean sprouts or grated carrot
steamed Tuscan kale (cavolo nero) or asparagus
thinly sliced cabbage or Brussels sprouts
corn kernels (thawed if frozen, drained if canned)

EXTRAS
(A SPRINKLE, PER TACO)
tortilla chips, crushed, for texture
toasted pumpkin seeds
toasted sesame seeds
coarsely chopped cashews
coarsely chopped walnuts
coarsely chopped almonds
halloumi cheese, dry-fried until golden
firm tofu, baked according to recipe on page 75
cheddar cheese, shredded
feta cheese or Sun Feta (see page 219), crumbled
scallion, finely chopped
Quick Pickled Red Onion (see page 223)
chopped mint, cilantro, or basil
Slaw (see pages 54–55)
thinly sliced radishes

SALSA
(MIX TOGETHER)
3 parts cherry tomatoes, finely chopped
2 parts fruit (peach, mango, pineapple, grape, apple are all good)
1 part red onion, finely chopped
lime or lemon juice, to taste
pinch of salt
pinch of crushed red pepper or a splash of hot sauce
coarsely chopped cilantro, mint, or basil

Vegan Avoid the dairy options in the "creamy' and "extras" sections.

Gluten Free Use certified gluten-free corn tortillas.

GF option

TACOS: HALLOUMI TACOS WITH MANGO SALSA & RICE

Serves 2
(4 small tacos)

scant ½ cup/3oz/80g dry brown rice
   or heaping ¾ cup/5¾oz/160g cooked
4½oz/125g halloumi cheese, cut into
   about ⅛-inch-thick slices
4 soft tortillas, warmed
a few Quick Pickled Red Onions
   (see page 223)
salt

MANGO SALSA
½ ripe mango, cubed
juice of ½ lime
4 cherry tomatoes, finely chopped
handful of cilantro, finely chopped
pinch of crushed red pepper

I usually end up basing tacos around dry-fried halloumi. It's got that "meaty" factor and a heavy salt level to balance with the juicy salsa and sharp, pretty pickled red onions. Brown rice bulks them up with starch, but I also like filling them with crunchy shredded lettuce and sautéed bell peppers if I'm craving a veg-ful taco.

1 If starting with dry rice, put in a medium saucepan, cover well with water, and add a pinch of salt. Bring to a boil, then reduce the heat to a simmer and cook for 20 minutes if using long-grain brown rice or 30 minutes if using short-grain brown rice. Check on the rice as it cooks and add more water as needed to prevent it from drying out and burning. Once cooked, drain and return to the pan, then cover with a lid or plate and let stand for 5 minutes to absorb any excess water.

2 Heat a dry, nonstick skillet over high heat, add the halloumi slices, and cook until they are light golden on the underside, 2 to 4 minutes, then flip over and cook on the other side. Remove from the pan.

3 In a medium bowl, combine all the salsa ingredients and set aside.

4 Divide the rice, salsa, and halloumi among the warmed tortillas. Top with a few strips of Pickled Red Onion.

Gluten Free Use certified gluten-free corn tortillas.

TIPS & SWAPS

Cool and store any extra rice as quickly as possible by rinsing it under cold running water or spreading it out on a plate. Once cooled, store in the refrigerator for 1 day or in a sandwich bag in the freezer for 2 months. When reheating, make sure it is piping hot before serving.

LEFTOVERS: see pp. 228–233

- Mango
- Lime
- Cilantro
- Halloumi cheese
- Brown rice (cooked)
- Cherry tomatoes

V

VG option

TACOS: CRISPY BROCCOLI TACOS WITH "CHORIZO" DIP

Serves 2 (4 small or 2 large tacos)

2 tablespoons olive oil or canola oil
½ head of broccoli, cut into medium florets
about ¾ cup/3½oz/100g all-purpose flour
about ½ cup milk or nondairy milk
about 1⅔ cups/3½oz/100g dry bread crumbs—I like panko here
4 small or 2 large whole-wheat tortillas, store-bought or homemade (see page 214)
½ recipe for "Chorizo" Dip (see page 47)
1 recipe for Avocado Cream (see page 219) or a few tablespoons plain yogurt
handful of mixed salad greens
salt

Coating broccoli in bread crumbs and baking it makes it super-crispy and is a lot less hassle than deep-frying it. With a little smear of "Chorizo" dip, you get a spicy bite, which is delicious with some cooling Avocado Cream.

1 Preheat the oven to 350°C. Grease a baking sheet with half the oil.

2 Add the broccoli to a medium saucepan with a couple of inches of water and bring to a boil. Cover with a lid, reduce the heat to low, and cook for 3 minutes, then drain and set aside.

3 Put the flour, milk, and bread crumbs in 3 separate shallow bowls. Dip the broccoli florets into the flour, turning to coat, followed by the milk, and then in the bread crumbs. Lay the coated florets on the prepared baking sheet, drizzle over the remaining oil, and sprinkle with some salt. Bake in the oven for 20 minutes until golden on the underside, then flip over and cook on the other side for 5 minutes.

4 Warm the tortillas, then spread with some of the "Chorizo" Dip and Avocado Cream. Top with a few salad greens and the crispy baked broccoli.

Vegan Use nondairy milk and Avocado Cream.

LEFTOVERS: see pp. 228–233
- Bread crumbs (panko)

V

GF option

TACOS: SCRAMBLED EGG, PEA, ONION & BASIL

**Serves 2
(4 small tacos)**

1 tablespoon olive oil or canola oil
1 red onion, cut into about
    $\frac{1}{8}$-inch-thick slices
about ¼ cup water
⅔ cup/3½oz/100g frozen petite peas
    or peas
4 eggs
4 small soft tortillas, warmed
a small chunk of cheddar cheese,
    shredded (optional)
handful of basil leaves, torn
salt and freshly ground black pepper

This is a perfect breakfast/brunch taco. Easy and quick to whip up, but also a little more impressive than standard scrambled eggs on toast!

1 In a large skillet, heat half the oil over medium heat. Add the onion with a pinch of salt and cook, stirring frequently, until the onion begins to look translucent. Pour in the water and stir it through, then cook until it has evaporated. Cook the onion until it is completely soft, another 5 to 10 minutes, then transfer to a plate.

2 Return the pan to the heat and add the frozen peas. Cook over medium-high heat, shaking the pan, until they are thawed and warmed through, about 1 minute. Transfer to the plate with the onion and set aside. Rinse out the pan and return to low heat to dry.

3 Meanwhile, crack the eggs into a medium bowl and, using a fork, whisk with a generous pinch of salt and some black pepper.

4 Add the remaining oil to the pan and, once hot, pour in the eggs and cook, stirring frequently, until cooked to the texture you prefer. Remove from the heat and stir through the onion and peas. Divide the mixture among the warmed tortillas and top with the shredded cheddar, if desired, and the torn basil.

Gluten Free Use gluten-free corn tortillas.

LEFTOVERS: see pp228–233

● Frozen petite peas or peas
● Basil

STIR-FRY TEMPLATE

Serves as many as you want!

Use this template like you would one of those supermarket "meal deal" stir-fry mixes. Just remember to get the pan SUPER HOT and prep all the ingredients before cooking.

1 Heat a wok or large skillet over high heat with 1 tablespoon canola oil. If using crumbled tofu as an extra, toss it in a little cornstarch and add to the wok or skillet. Cook, stirring occasionally, until golden, then transfer to a plate. Add another tablespoon of oil to the wok or skillet, if needed.

2 Pick 2 to 4 different vegetables to add to the wok or skillet. Start with the slow-cooking ones and stir-fry until they have softened and are starting to color, then repeat with the medium-cooking ones, and lastly the quick cooking vegetables.

3 If using egg as an extra, make a hole in the center of the vegetables and pour in the whisked egg. Leave for 10 seconds, then stir everything together.

4 Reduce the heat to medium. Mix a sauce and add to the wok or skillet along with the portion(s) of starch. Divide among plates and sprinkle over any toppings.

Vegetarian Use soy sauce or tamari instead of fish sauce.

Gluten Free Use rice noodles, rice, quinoa, or certified gluten-free soba noodles for the "starch." Make sure you use certified gluten-free tamari or soy sauce in the sauces.

TIPS & SWAPS

EXTRAS: Rapeseed oil, for cooking; cubed firm tofu, tossed in cornstarch (3½oz tofu plus ½ teaspoon cornstarch per person); whisked egg (1 per person).

VEGETABLES
(A GOOD HANDFUL PER PERSON):

slow-cooking:
sliced carrots
bell pepper
diced zucchini
diced eggplant
quartered red onion

medium-cooking:
chopped asparagus
chopped bok choy
chopped green beans
chopped or sliced red onion
thinly sliced bell pepper

quick-cooking:
frozen peas
frozen shelled edamame
frozen or canned sweetcorn
bean sprouts
thinly sliced Brussels sprouts or cabbage
spinach, chopped kale, or Tuscan kale
(cavolo nero)
sliced mushrooms
shredded broccoli or cauliflower
finely chopped chiles

require steaming before sautéing
(once steamed are quick-cooking):
broccoli florets
cauliflower florets
sweet potato

SAUCES
(EACH ONE MAKES ENOUGH FOR 2 PEOPLE)

2 tablespoons soy sauce or tamari + 1 teaspoon grated ginger root + 1 crushed garlic clove + 1 teaspoon toasted sesame oil

½ cup orange juice + 2 tablespoons soy sauce or tamari + 2 crushed garlic cloves + 1 teaspoon cornstarch + 2 tablespoons water

2 tablespoons Thai curry paste + ⅓ cup coconut milk + pinch of granulated or brown sugar + juice of 1 lime

juice of 1 lime + 3 tablespoons fish sauce or 3 tablespoons soy sauce or tamari + 2 teaspoons granulated or packed brown sugar, or honey

1 tablespoon sugar or honey + 3 tablespoons mirin + 2 tablespoons soy sauce or tamari + 1 crushed garlic clove + 2 tablespoons rice vinegar or lemon juice + 1 teaspoon cornstarch + 2 tablespoons water

2 tablespoons miso + 2 crushed garlic cloves + 1 teaspoon grated ginger root + 1 tablespoon granulated or packed brown sugar, or honey + 3 tablespoons water

3 tablespoons Date Paste (see page 221) + 2 tablespoons ketchup + ½ teaspoon Chinese five spice + 2 tablespoons rice vinegar + 2 tablespoons soy sauce or tamari + 2 tablespoons water

3 tablespoons apricot jam + 3 tablespoons ketchup + 2 tablespoons soy sauce or tamari + 1 teaspoon grated ginger root + juice of 1 lime + 1 teaspoon cornstarch + 2 tablespoons water

STARCH
(A CUPPED HANDFUL, ABOUT 3½–7OZ, PER PERSON, SEE COOKING TIMETABLE ON PAGE 11)
cooked quinoa
cooked brown rice
cooked udon or soba or rice noodles
cooked pearl barley

TOPPINGS
(A SPRINKLE)
thinly sliced scallion
toasted sesame seeds
chopped cashews, peanuts, or almonds
toasted sunflower seeds
toasted pumpkin seeds
chopped cilantro, basil, Thai basil, or mint
thinly sliced chiles
shredded raw carrot
Quick Pickled Red Onion (see page 223)

STIR-FRY: QUINOA, PEA & BROCCOLI

I never truly like the whole "substitute starches with vegetables" thing... I'm looking at you, "zoodles" and "cauliflower rice." However, these can be used to bulk up whole-grain starches while adding more fiber and some micronutrients. Here I used shredded broccoli to bulk up a dish of simple stir-fried quinoa. It's a good basic stir-fry to know, as you can change the grain (obviously brown rice would be great, but couscous or pearl barley also work) and add other proteins, such as a whisked egg or cooked shrimp, while you fry everything together.

Serves 2

½ cup/3¼oz/90g dry quinoa, rinsed or
⅔ cup/10½oz/300g cooked
1 tablespoon toasted sesame oil
½ head of broccoli, shredded or
pulsed in a food processor
2 teaspoons grated ginger root
2 garlic cloves, crushed or minced
⅔ cup/3½oz/100g frozen petite peas
or peas
2 tablespoons soy sauce or tamari
1 scallion, finely chopped

TO SERVE
mixed salad greens or steamed
vegetables dressed with
Miso Dressing (see page 226)

1 If starting with dry quinoa, put in a small saucepan and cover with water. Bring to a boil, then reduce the heat and simmer for 10 minutes. Drain and return to the pan, cover with a lid or large plate, and let stand for 5 minutes to absorb excess water.

2 In a wok or large skillet, heat the oil over high heat. Add the quinoa, broccoli, and ginger and stir-fry for 30 seconds. Add the garlic and stir-fry for another 30 seconds. Add the frozen peas and soy sauce and stir until the peas are thawed and warmed through. Stir through the scallion.

3 Serve with a simple side of mixed salad greens or steamed vegetables dressed with Miso Dressing.

Gluten Free Make sure that you are using a certified gluten-free tamari or soy sauce.

Omnivores Add cooked, peeled frozen or fresh shrimp with the peas to heat through.

LEFTOVERS: see pp. 228–233

● Frozen petite peas or peas
● Scallions

TIPS & SWAPS

Start by pouring a whisked egg into the sesame oil, then immediately add the quinoa and broccoli on top and continue with the recipe.

Use frozen edamame or corn kernels instead of the peas.

QUINOA, PEA
& BROCCOLI

NOODLES, CRISPY
CRUMBLED TOFU,
BEAN SPROUTS

SPICY COCONUT RICE
WITH BRUSSELS SPROUTS

V **VG**

GF option

STIR-FRY: NOODLES, CRISPY CRUMBLED TOFU, BEAN SPROUTS

Serves 2

4½oz/125g dried soba or udon or rice
    noodles, or about 6oz/175g cooked
7oz/200g firm tofu
5 tablespoons soy sauce or tamari
1 tablespoon granulated sugar
juice of ½ lime
½ teaspoon Chinese five spice
½ cup water
1 tablespoon cornstarch
1 tablespoon toasted sesame oil
1 cup/3½oz/100g bean sprouts
handful of cilantro leaves

I learned about this technique for crumbling firm tofu and stir-frying it with cornstarcj on *Bon Appétit* magazine's web-site. There the author was talking about how this method of cooking tofu kind of makes it seem like ground meat, so is a good intro recipe for tofu haters or meat lovers. I think I still would say this isn't very meatlike, but I prefer tofu in small pieces like this so that it gets nice and saucy.

1 If starting with dry noodles, cook the noodles according to the package directions, then drain and rinse with cold water. Set aside.

2 Press the tofu. Wrap the tofu in a clean kitchen towel and place on a flat surface. Cover with a cutting board and then weigh the cutting board down with something heavy, such as a stack of cookbooks or a saucepan full of water, and let stand for 30 minutes to drain.

3 In a small bowl, mix the soy sauce or tamari, sugar, lime juice, Chinese five spice and water together.

4 Crumble the tofu into another small bowl and toss with the cornstarch.

5 In a wok or large skillet, heat the oil over high heat. Add the tofu and cook, stirring occasionally, until it starts to color. Add the cooked noodles and bean sprouts and stir-fry for 30 seconds. Reduce the heat to medium, pour in the soy sauce mixture, and stir to coat the noodles. Once everything is coated, remove from the heat and serve with the cilantro leaves on top.

Gluten Free Use wide, flat rice noodles instead of the wheat noodles or, use certified gluten-free soba noodles. Make sure that you are using a certified gluten-free tamari or soy sauce.

LEFTOVERS: see pp. 228–233

● Cilantro
● ½ lime
● Firm tofu

STIR-FRY: SPICY COCONUT RICE WITH BRUSSELS SPROUTS

Serves 2 as a side

½ cup/3½oz/100g uncooked brown rice
or 1 cup/2oz/200g cooked
1 tablespoon olive oil or canola oil
1⅓ cups/3½oz/100g thinly sliced
Brussels sprouts
1½ cups/3½oz/100g thinly sliced white
or red cabbage
1 to 3 teaspoons Thai green curry paste
(see page 220 and below)
½ cup coconut milk or 2 tablespoons
creamed coconut mixed with
½ cup water
a pinch of cayenne pepper
(if your curry paste is mild)
juice of ½ lime

The idea here is it's like a slightly better-for-you version of coconut rice that you might order with your take-out. It's bulked up with veggies and uses brown rice to keep you full. I add a little green curry paste too, but not so much to make it taste of a Thai green curry, more to just add heat and a little boost of flavor.

1 If starting with dry rice, put in a medium saucepan and cover with water. Bring to a boil, then reduce the heat to a simmer and cook for 20 minutes if using long-grain brown rice or 30 minutes if using short grain brown rice. Check on the rice as it cooks and add more water as needed to prevent it from drying out and burning. Once cooked, drain and return to the saucepan, then cover with a lid or plate and let stand for 10 minutes to absorb any excess water.

2 In a wok or large skillet, heat the oil over medium heat. Add the Brussels sprouts and cabbage and cook until softened and starting to color. Add the rice and stir-fry for 1 minute.

3 Add the curry paste (start with 1 teaspoon and add more later if you need to) and the coconut milk or creamed coconut and cook until most of the liquid has evaporated. Remove from the heat and stir in the cayenne, if using, and lime juice.

Vegan The recipe for the Thai curry paste is vegan, but if using store-bought paste, then make sure you check the label.

TIPS & SWAPS

Hate Brussels sprouts? Sub in more cabbage or shredded raw cauliflower.

Cool and store any extra rice as quickly as possible by rinsing it under cold running water or spreading it out on a plate. Once cooled, keep in the refrigerator for 1 day or in a sandwich bag in the freezer for 2 months. When reheating, make sure it is piping hot before serving.

LEFTOVERS: see pp. 228–233
- Coconut milk or creamed coconut
- Lime
- Brown rice (cooked)
- Cabbage (red or white)

Cheeky Treats

Gotta love a baked good, eh! I'm a baker at heart, so of course I needed to showcase a selection of sweet treats for you. The great news is that none of the recipes require a stand mixer or electric mixer—they are all pretty much a one-bowl stir-and-bake job. The most complex recipe is probably the Cinnamon Knots, purely because the shaping of them is difficult to explain. However, if you have made bread dough before, it'll be quite simple (and there are pictures to help you with the shaping).

As I'm a bit of a lazy person, I prefer to bake with oil rather than butter most of the time, as butter requires time to soften and is usually more effort to mix into batters and doughs (unless it's melted butter). I do use olive oil in a lot of the baking recipes just because it seems to be the healthiest oil to use. Some people might be horrified by this, but I'm just gonna say that I use refined olive oil (sometimes called "light" olive oil), which has barely any flavor and a high smoke point. I only ever use extra virgin olive oil in my Easy Freezer Chocolate Chip Cookies (see page 204) if I'm in the mood for that deep, savory flavour. If you still are not jamming with the olive oil thing, use an unflavored oil such as canola oil or just melted butter (yum!) instead.

COOKIE DOUGH BALLS

Makes 20 to 24

2 tablespoons olive oil
or 3 tablespoons nut butter
⅓ cup/2¾oz/75g Date Paste (see page 221)*
1 tablespoon packed brown sugar
1 teaspoon vanilla extract
pinch of salt
1 cup/3½oz/100g regular rolled oats
4 tablespoons whole-wheat pastry flour
or Oat Flour (see page 216)
2 tablespoons chopped dark chocolate
(at least 70% cocoa solids) or
mini dark chocolate chips

You know when you're just having a bad day and all you want to do is watch Netflix while eating cookie dough? Yeah, same. I think that's all I need to say to introduce this recipe to you...

1 In a medium bowl, mix together the oil or nut butter, Date Paste, sugar, vanilla, and salt. Stir in the oats, flour, and chocolate until well combined.

2 Roll heaping teaspoons of the dough into balls and place on a plate. Let stand for 30 minutes to dry a little before transferring them to a lidded container. Store in the refrigerator for 3 to 5 days.

Vegan Make sure your chocolate is suitable for vegans.

Gluten Free Use buckwheat flour instead of the whole-wheat flour. If you can tolerate oats, make sure they're certified gluten free. If not, use millet flakes instead.

TIPS & SWAPS

*Make a smaller batch of date paste. Soak ⅓ cup/1¾oz/50g pitted dried dates in boiling water for 15 minutes, then drain. Using a handheld blender in a beaker or a countertop blender, blend with 2 to 3 tablespoons water until smooth. Store in an airtight container in the refrigerator for up to 2 days.

LEFTOVERS: see pp. 228–233

● Nut butter, if using

SINGLE-SERVE CHOCOLATE CHIP COOKIE

Serves 1

1 tablespoon nut butter, such as
   cashew butter or peanut butter
1½ teaspoons honey, or maple syrup
   or golden syrup
pinch of baking soda
splash of vanilla extract
pinch of salt (if nut butter is unsalted)
1½ tablespoons ground almonds
   or Ground Almond Alternative
   (see page 218), or 1 teaspoon
   whole-wheat pastry flour
1 to 2 squares of dark chocolate,
   chopped into chunks

People need to stop with the mug cakes. They are rubbery and weird and, oh, often leak in the microwave. If you're craving a chocolatey dessert just for yourself, try this. It's easier to make (there's no "half an egg" involved) and tastes much better. Eat it warm while it's still soft and melty.

1 Preheat the oven to 350°F.

2 In a small, ovenproof bowl, mug, or ramekin (I use a 2¾-inch one), stir together the nut butter, honey or syrup, baking soda, vanilla, and salt, if using, until well combined. Mix in the ground almonds or alternative and top with the chocolate chunks.

3 Stand the ovenproof bowl, mug, or ramekin on a baking sheet and bake in the oven for 6 to 8 minutes, until set around the edges but still soft in the middle. Eat while warm with a spoon.

Vegan Use maple syrup or golden syrup. Make sure your chocolate is suitable for vegans.

Gluten Free Use ground almonds or Ground Almond Alternative.

TIPS & SWAPS

If your ovenproof container for baking is larger than 2¾ inches, check the cookie after 6 minutes, as it will cook more quickly.

LEFTOVERS: see pp. 228–233

● Nut butter

VG option

INDIVIDUAL APRICOT SUGAR BUNS

Makes 6

PASTE
2 tablespoons whole-wheat flour
⅓ cup water

DOUGH
¼ cup water
2 tablespoons granulated or
    superfine sugar
1 teaspoon instant dry yeast
1½ tablespoons olive oil, plus a little
    extra for greasing
1 cup plus 2 teaspoons/4½oz/130g
    whole-wheat flour, plus extra for
    dusting
¼ teaspoon salt
4 ripe apricots, pitted and
    coarsely chopped

DIP
2 tablespoons unsalted butter
¼ to ⅓ cup superfine sugar
1 teaspoon ground cinnamon

TIPS & SWAPS
Replace the apricots with
5½oz/150g seasonal or frozen
fruit, such as rhubarb (cooked with
2 tablespoons granulated sugar),
blueberries, blackberries,
peaches, or plums.

Did you ever play that game where you had to eat a donut without licking your lips? That's the reason for these donut–bun hybrids. Dipping them in cinnamon–sugar gives that throwback donut flavor.

1   In a small saucepan, combine the paste ingredients and cook over medium-low heat, stirring, until a thickened, smooth paste, 5 to 10 minutes. Remove from the heat and let cool.

2   For the dough, in a medium bowl, mix together the water, half the sugar, and the yeast. Set aside for 5 minutes.

3   Add the slightly warm paste mixture to the bowl with the yeast mixture and stir together. Mix in the oil, then add the flour and salt, and stir until a sticky dough forms. Shape your hand like a claw and use it to beat the dough for about 1 minute. Pour a little oil over the dough and turn it to coat it. Cover with plastic wrap and let rise in a warm place for 1 hour.

4   Meanwhile, in a small saucepan, combine the apricots with 2 tablespoons water and the remaining sugar. Cook for 10 minutes over medium heat, stirring occasionally, until softened and jammy. Let cool.

5   Grease a baking sheet with oil. Punch the dough down, transfer to a work surface, and dust with flour. Divide into 6 equal pieces and roll each piece into a ball. Dust the balls of dough with flour. Take 1 ball of dough and press down in the center of the ball with your thumb to make a 1¼-inch-wide hollow in the dough. Repeat this with the remaining pieces of dough and place on the prepared baking sheet. Fill the indents with the jammy apricots and let the dough balls rise again in a warm place for 30 minutes.

6   Preheat the oven to 350°F.

7   Once the buns have risen, bake them in the oven for 20 minutes until golden.

8   To make the dip, put the butter in a small, heatproof bowl and place in the oven for the final 2 minutes of the bun baking time (this is just so that the butter melts in the bowl). Alternatively, melt the butter in a small saucepan on the stove or in a microwave-safe bowl in the microwave.

9   Brush the baked buns all over with the melted butter. On a plate, mix together the sugar and cinnamon, and roll the buttery buns around in it until they are coated. These are best the day they're made, but will keep for 2 days in a container in the refrigerator. Just warm them up on a baking sheet in an oven preheated to 325°F for a few minutes before eating.

Vegan Swap the butter for melted vegan spread or coconut oil.

CHOCOLATE PEANUT FUDGE CAKE BARS

Makes 8

oil, for greasing
scant ⅔ cup/5¾oz/160g unsalted peanut butter
¼ cup/1¾oz/50g granulated sugar, honey, or maple syrup
1 egg
3 tablespoons unsweetened cocoa, plus extra for dusting
1 teaspoon baking powder
pinch of salt
1 cup/4¼oz/120g shredded carrot

TIPS & SWAPS

*Fold a piece of aluminum foil in half and use it as a divider in a large (2lb/900g) loaf pan.

Replace the carrot with shredded zucchini.

Change the flavor with a different nut butter (hazelnut butter is expensive, but it's amazing in this recipe).

This cake batter will probably seem like the weirdest you have ever made. There's no flour or butter, it's thick, and it may seem that the carrot will make it too "healthy." Just trust me; this will probably be one of the richest, fudgiest chocolate cakes you will ever have. The peanut butter provides the fat and, along with the carrots, brings bulk to the batter. I dust the baked cake with cocoa to balance the richness and, as it doesn't rise too much, cut it into "bars."

1 Preheat the oven to 350°F. Grease and line the bottom and sides of a small (1lb) loaf pan* with nonstick parchment paper.

2 In a medium saucepan, heat the peanut butter over low heat until loosened, then stir in the sugar, honey, or maple syrup. Remove from the heat and let cool until it is only slightly warm. Quickly mix in the egg, then stir in the cocoa, baking powder, and salt. Fold in the carrots.

3 Spread the mixture into the prepared loaf pan and bake in the oven for 30 minutes.

4 Let the loaf cool in the pan, then unmold onto a plate, dust with cocoa, and slice into 8 bars. Store in an airtight container for up to 3 days.

LEFTOVERS: see pp. 228–233

● Nut butter
● Carrots (raw)

VG & GF options

BROWNIES

There are many different types of brownie—cakey, fudgy, gooey—in the world. I'm not one for a cakey brownie, I must say, and this recipe is my current favorite. These are not super-gooey, but dense and fudgy. I love adding chopped hazelnuts or even walnuts to the top for texture and to balance the sweetness, but I know lots of people don't like to add nuts to brownies, so I will leave the addition up to you.

Makes 12 to16

3½oz/100g dark chocolate
   (at least 70% cocoa solids),
   broken into a few large chunks
⅓ cup olive oil or canola oil,
   or melted butter
¼ teaspoon baking powder
1 teaspoon vanilla extract
½ teaspoon salt
⅓ cup/1oz/30g unsweetened cocoa
2 eggs
¾ cup/5½oz/150g granulated sugar
1 cup/4½oz/125g whole-wheat pastry
   flour or Oat Flour (see page 216)
¼ cup/1oz/30g coarsely chopped
   hazelnuts or any other nut or chopped
   dark chocolate (optional)

1 Preheat the oven to 350°F. Line the bottom and sides of an 8-inch square baking pan with nonstick parchment paper.

2 Break the chocolate into small chunks and put in a heatproof bowl set over a saucepan of simmering water over a low heat (make sure the bottom of the bowl doesn't touch the water), until just melted, then remove from the heat. Add the oil, baking powder, vanilla, salt, and cocoa and stir to mix.

3 Crack in the eggs and mix well to combine. Mix in the sugar and stir vigorously for 2 minutes—this helps to dissolve the sugar into the liquids so that you get a nice fudgy brownie. Stir in the flour, then pour the batter into the prepared baking pan and smooth it out into an even layer. Scatter over the chopped hazelnuts, if using, then bake the brownie in the oven for 20 to 25 minutes, until set around the edges but still very soft in the middle.

4 Remove from the oven and let cool slightly before cutting into 12 to 16 brownies. Store in an airtight container at room temperature for up to a week.

Vegan Replace the eggs with 2 tablespoons ground flax seed or chia seeds mixed with 6 tablespoons water or ¼ cup pureed silken tofu. Use olive oil or canola oil. Make sure your chocolate is suitable for vegans.

Gluten Free Use gluten-free oats to make the Oat Flour, or use ¾ cup plus 2 tablespoons buckwheat flour instead (this also works when making the vegan version).

NO-ROLL SCONES

Makes 4

¾ cup plus 1 tablespoon/3oz/80g all-purpose flour

¾ cup plus 1 tablespoon/3oz/80g Oat Flour (see page 216) or whole-wheat pastry flour

2 tablespoons granulated sugar, plus extra for sprinkling

1½ teaspoons baking powder

¼ teaspoon salt

3½ tablespoons unsalted butter, cubed

1 egg

3 tablespoons milk

I'm pretty lazy when it comes to baking. I hate having to drag out a stand mixer or dig through drawers to find cookie cutters. I'm more of a mix, pour, and bake kind of gal than a super-involved baker. That's why these scones are a godsend for me. You don't need to dirty cookie cutters or rolling pins when making them, as you just pat the dough out into a circle and cut it into wedges. Simple as that!

1 Preheat the oven to 350°F. Line a baking sheet with nonstick parchment paper.

2 In a large bowl, combine the flours, sugar, baking powder, and salt. Add the butter and rub it between your fingertips into the dry ingredients until no large chunks of butter remain. Crack in the egg and add the milk, then stir gently until you have a soft, coarse dough.

3 Transfer the dough to the prepared baking sheet and pat out into a circle about ¾-inch thick. Sprinkle over some sugar and cut into quarters. Don't separate the quarters out; keep it as one mega-scone.

4 Bake in the oven for 20 to 22 minutes, until golden and risen. Remove from the oven and cut through the mega-scone where you cut through earlier to separate it into quarters. Store any leftovers in an airtight container for up to 2 days.

Vegan Replace the butter with olive oil or canola oil. Replace the egg with 1 tablespoon ground flax seed mixed with 3 tablespoons water. Use ¼ cup nondairy milk instead of the milk.

ANY-FRUIT FREE-FORM GALETTE

Makes 1 galette

1 recipe for Half-Oat Pie Dough
    (see page 217) or Olive Oil Pie Dough
    (see page 217), or 9oz/250g store-
    bought pie dough
all-purpose flour, for dusting
1lb/450g fresh or frozen fruit, such as
    plums and peaches (see method)
2 to 5 tablespoons granulated sugar
    (depending on sweetness of fruit)

FRANGIPANE

¼ cup/1¾oz/50g granulated sugar or
    Date Paste (see page 221)
3½ tablespoons unsalted butter,
    softened
1 egg
⅔ cup/2¼oz/60g ground almonds or
    Ground Almond Alternative (see page
    218; ¾ cup if using ground coconut)
2 tablespoons all-purpose
    or whole-wheat pastry flour
pinch of salt
1 teaspoon almond or vanilla extract

TO SERVE

plain yogurt, whipped cream, or ice
    cream (optional)

Picture this: it's the weekend, you want to make a tart but you don't have a fancy dish to bake in, and the idea of trying to line a tart pan makes your fists clench in stress. Now, let me tell you about free-form galettes. They are versatile, as you can use any fruit, you don't need any fancy pans (just a regular baking sheet), and, best of all, they are meant to look rustic—the messier it looks, the more... umm... artisanal it is.

1 Preheat the oven to 350°F.

2 Roll the pie dough out on a piece of lightly floured nonstick parchment paper into a large rectangle about ⅛ inch thick and about as big as your baking sheet. Lift the piece of parchment paper up, bringing the dough with it, and lay it down on the baking sheet so that the dough is still on top.

3 To make the frangipane, in a medium bowl, cream the sugar or Date Paste and butter with a spoon until smooth. Mix in the egg, followed by the ground almonds or alternative, flour, salt, and almond or vanilla extract. Spread the mixture over the rolled dough, with a bare border of dough about 1¼ inches wide around the edges.

4 Prepare the fruit(s) you are using. Here are my seasonal suggestions:
SPRING: Rhubarb cut into 1¼-inch lengths with a little grated orange zest.
SUMMER: Peaches, plums, or apricots, pitted and flesh cut into quarters or eighths.
FALL: Pears, cored and cut into eighths mixed with blackberries.
WINTER: Peeled, cored baking or sweet apples tossed in the juice of 1 lemon and cut into eighths.
ALL YEAR: Frozen blueberries, raspberries, and strawberries—no need to thaw, just chuck them in a bowl!

5 Put the fruit in a bowl with 2 tablespoons sugar and stir to coat. Taste and add another 1 to 3 tablespoons sugar, as needed. (Strawberries, blueberries, and peaches will usually need only 2 tablespoons sugar, whereas rhubarb, plums, baking apples, and underripe raspberries may need more.)

6 Lay the fruit over the frangipane and fold over the border of the dough (as shown opposite). Bake in the oven for 40 to 50 minutes, until bubbling with a golden crust. Let cool slightly and serve warm with yogurt, whipped cream, or ice cream, if desired.

Vegan Use Olive Oil Pastry. Use almond or cashew butter or vegan spread instead of butter in the frangipane, and replace the egg with 1 tablespoon ground flax seed mixed with 3 tablespoons water.

LEFTOVERS: see pp. 228–233

● Fresh or frozen fruit
● Pie dough, Half-Oat or Olive Oil

TIPS & SWAPS

If you want to omit the
frangipane, spread a few
tablespoons of your favorite jam over
the pie dough before topping with
the fruit and baking.

Double up on the pie dough and keep
half in the refrigerator or freezer
for another day.

TOP RIGHT: OATY SNACK CAKE
MIDDLE: PEAR & HAZELNUT
BOTTOM: LEMON POPPY SEED

GF option

OATY SNACK CAKE

You may have seen recipes for chick pea blondies or black bean brownies and felt doubtful. I was also a bit unsure about adding beans to desserts, but seriously, if you're still adding fat and sugar, you will end up with an incredibly tasty treat (with no chick pea flavor, I promise). This cake is not overly sweet, is adaptable, and has lots of protein and fiber from the oats and chick peas, so keeps me feeling fuller for longer.

Makes 1 small loaf

⅔ cup/2¼oz/60g old-fashioned rolled oats, or ½ cup Oat Flour (see page 216) or whole-wheat pastry flour

5 tablespoons granulated sugar

2 teaspoons baking powder

¼ teaspoon salt

½ teaspoon ground cinnamon

1½ cups/8½oz/240g cooked chick peas (garbanzo beans), drained and rinsed

2 eggs

¼ cup olive oil or caonla oil

1 Preheat the oven to 350°F. Line the bottom and sides of a small (1lb) loaf pan* or 8-inch round cake pan with nonstick parchment paper.

2 If using a countertop blender or food processor, blend the oats or flour, sugar, baking powder, salt and cinnamon until fine. Transfer to a small bowl and set aside. Blend the chick peas, eggs, and oil until completely smooth. Return the bowl of oat mixture to the blender and blend until smooth.

3 If using a handheld blender, add the chick peas to a large bowl and blitz them up a little. Add the oil and eggs, blitzing again until smooth. Add the oats or flour, sugar, baking powder, salt, and cinnamon. Blitz again until the mixture is as smooth as possible.

4 Pour the batter into the prepared pan, level the surface, and bake in the oven for 30 to 35 minutes in the loaf pan or 20 to 25 minutes in the cake pan. The cake will still look quite pale, but a toothpick inserted into the center should come out clean. Let cool for 20 to 30 minutes before serving. Store in an airtight container for up to 5 days.

TIPS & SWAPS

*Fold a piece of aluminum foil in half and use it as a divider in a large (2lb/900g) loaf pan.

LEMON POPPY SEED VARIATION

Replace the cinnamon with the grated zest of 1 lemon and 1 tablespoon poppy seeds. Once the cake has baked, mix ⅓ cup/1¾oz/50g sifted confectioners' sugar with a little freshly squeezed lemon juice to form a thick liquid and pour over the cake and then sprinkle over the poppy seeds.

PEAR & HAZELNUT VARIATION

Replace the cinnamon with 1 teaspoon vanilla extract. Halve a pear and scoop out its seedy core, then thinly slice it. Pour the batter into the pan, then top with the pear slices and 3 tablespoons coarsely chopped hazelnuts.

Gluten Free If you can tolerate oats, make sure you use certified gluten-free oats in your Oat Flour If not, use an equal weight of ground almonds, chick pea (garbanzo bean) flour, or buckwheat flour instead.

DOUBLE CHOCOLATE COOKIES

Makes 18 to 20

4½oz/125g dark chocolate
(at least 70% cocoa solids),
broken into a few large chunks
5 tablespoons nut butter, such
as cashew, peanut, or almond
1⅓ cups/8½oz/240g can red kidney
beans, drained and rinsed
½ cup/3½oz/100g granulated sugar
½ cup/1¾oz/50g unsweetened cocoa
¾ teaspoon baking powder
¼ teaspoon salt
3 tablespoons finely chopped pistachios,
or any other nut or seed (optional)

I've made black bean cookie recipes before that relied on cocoa for the chocolate flavor and found them quite lacking. By mixing in melted dark chocolate you are adding cocoa along with cocoa butter, which is quite flavorful in itself and, as it's a fat, makes the cookies rich and soft.

1 Preheat the oven to 350°F. Line a baking sheet with nonstick parchment paper.

2 Break the chocolate into small chunks and put in a heatproof bowl set over a saucepan of simmering water over a low heat (make sure the bottom of the bowl doesn't touch the water), until just melted. Remove from the heat and pour about 3 tablespoons of the melted chocolate into a small bowl. Set aside for later.

3 If using a handheld blender, add the nut butter and beans to the saucepan and blitz to a smooth paste. Stir in the remaining ingredients, except the reserved chocolate and pistachios, if using.

4 If using a food processor, pour the melted chocolate into it and add the nut butter and beans. Blend until smooth, scraping down the sides of the bowl as needed. Add the sugar, cocoa, baking powder, and salt and blend again.

5 Place heaping tablespoons of the dough onto the prepared baking sheet—they can be quite close together, as they don't spread much when baking. Wet your hands slightly and flatten the dough with the palm of your hand.

6 Bake the cookies in the oven for 6 to 8 minutes—they should still be soft in the center but set around the edges. Let cool on the baking sheet for 1 minute, then transfer to a wire rack to finish cooling.

7 Put the reserved chocolate in a plastic sandwich bag (you may need to remelt it), cut off the tip of one corner of the bag, and use it like a pastry bag to drizzle the melted chocolate over the cookies. Sprinkle the pistachios, if using, over the cookies while the chocolate is still molten. Let cool and set. Store in an airtight container for up to 3 days.

Vegan Make sure your chocolate is suitable for vegans.

TIPS & SWAPS
Use an equal quantity of black beans instead of red kidney beans.

LEFTOVERS: see pp. 228–233

● Nut butter

BANANA BREAD

If you look in my freezer drawer, you'll always find butter, pesto, peas, and overripe bananas. I'm an overripe banana hoarder, for sure, because I never know when a banana bread craving will hit. This recipe doesn't include eggs because the bananas provide enough moisture to keep the mixture cakey.

Makes 1 loaf

3 large ripe bananas, peeled (about 9oz/250g peeled weight)

scant ½ cup/3¼oz/90g granulated sugar, plus 1 teaspoon for sprinkling

⅓ cup olive oil or canola oil

1 teaspoon vanilla extract

¼ cup milk or nondairy milk

1½ teaspoons baking powder

1 cup/4¼oz/120g whole-wheat pastry flour or 1 cup plus 1 tablespoon/4¼oz/120g chick pea (garbanzo bean) flour

1 scant cup/3¼oz/90g regular rolled oats

½ teaspoon ground cinnamon

1   Preheat the oven to 350°F. Line the bottom and sides of a large (2lb) loaf pan with nonstick parchment paper.

2   Mash the peeled bananas on a plate with a fork. Transfer to a medium bowl and add the sugar, oil, vanilla, and milk and stir well to combine. Add the baking powder, flour, and oats and stir until just combined. Transfer to the prepared loaf pan.

3   In a small bowl, mix the remaining 1 teaspoon of sugar and the ground cinnamon, then sprinkle over the surface of the loaf.

4   Bake in the oven for 50 to 60 minutes, until a toothpick inserted into the center of the loaf comes out clean. Let cool in the pan for 10 minutes, then unmold onto a wire rack to cool completely before slicing.

Vegan   Use nondairy milk.

Gluten Free   Use chick pea (garbanzo bean) flour. If you can tolerate oats, make sure they're certified gluten free. If you can't tolerate oats, use quinoa flakes or millet flakes instead.

TIPS & SWAPS

Use whole or cubed, roasted sweet potato or butternut squash (as long as there are no spices on it) instead of the bananas. Remove any skin and blend the flesh until smooth.

LEFTOVERS: see pp. 228–233

● Bananas

BANANA CHOCOLATE
CHIP BLONDIES

Makes 9 to 12

oil, for greasing

⅓ cup/3oz/85g nut butter, such as cashew or peanut butter

3½ tablespoons unsalted butter

⅔ cup/5½oz/150g firmly packed brown sugar

¼ teaspoon salt (if your nut butter is unsalted)

1 overripe banana, peeled (2¾ to 3½oz/75 to 100g peeled weight) and mashed with a fork

pinch of baking powder

1 teaspoon vanilla extract

½ cup/2¾oz/75g whole-wheat pastry flour

¾ cup/3¼oz/90g Oat Flour (see page 216) or extra whole-wheat pastry flour

⅓ cup/1¾oz/50g coarsely chopped dark chocolate (at least 70% cocoa solids)

A few years ago I was walking around East London with my brother when we stopped by a lovely little bakery called E5 bakehouse. My bro went for a ginger cookie, but my attention was on a fat, squidgy banana blondie, which I then devoured at an incredible speed. This is my homage to that blondie, with a caramel–banana flavor and a fudgy texture. But be warned, they're rich, so you might want to cut them into small pieces!

1 Preheat the oven to 350°F. Lightly grease an 8-inch round cake pan with oil

2 In a small saucepan, melt the nut butter and unsalted butter together over low heat until completely smooth. Remove from the heat and stir in the sugar, salt, banana, baking powder, and vanilla. Add the both flours and stir in until just combined.

3 Transfer the dough to the prepared cake pan. Dampen your hands and use to press the dough out into an even layer, then press the chopped chocolate onto the surface.

4 Bake in the oven for 20 to 25 minutes, until it is set around the edges but still quite soft in the center. Let cool slightly in the pan before slicing into 9 to 12 pieces. Store any leftovers in an airtight container for 3 to 4 days.

Vegan Replace the butter with olive oil or canola oil. Make sure your chocolate is suitable for vegans.

Gluten Free If you can tolerate oats, use certified gluten-free oats to make the Oat Flour and replace the whole-wheat pastry flour with buckwheat flour. If you can't tolerate oats, omit the whole-wheat pastry flour and Oat Flour and use ⅓ cups buckwheat flour instead.

LEFTOVERS: see pp. 228–233

● Bananas
● Nut butter

OLIVE OIL ANY-FRUIT CRUMBLE

I think everyone should know how to make a fruit crumble. They are versatile—you can use frozen fruit or fruit that might otherwise be destined for the garbage, and you can mix up the flavors. My mom always uses oats, which helps the clump-factor of the topping, and I add sunflower seeds for more crunch.

Serves 4 to 6

1 lb/450g mixed fruit (e.g.apples, apricots, blackberries, blueberries, peaches, plums, apricots, nectarines, rhubarb)

2 to 6 tablespoons packed brown or granulated sugar

juice of ½ lemon (optional)

TOPPING

¼ cup olive oil or canola oil

2 tablespoons honey or maple syrup

2 tablespoons packed brown or - granulated sugar

pinch of salt

⅓ cup plus 1 tablespoon/2oz/55g whole-wheat pastry flour or ½ cup/ 2oz/55g Oat Flour (see page 216) or chick pea (garbanzo) flour

1 cup/3½oz/100g regular rolled oats

¼ teaspoon ground cinnamon

3 tablespoons coarsely chopped sunflower seeds (or any nut/seed you desire!)

TO SERVE

plain yogurt, ice cream, or cream (optional)

1 Preheat the oven to 350°F.

2 Prepare the fruit. For apples and pears, peel, core, and cut into ¾-inch chunks. For berries, remove the stems and leaves. For rhubarb, discard the leaves and cut the stalks into ¾-inch lengths. For peaches, plums, apricots, and nectarines, remove the pits and cut the fruit into quarters or eighths. Taste the fruit to gauge its sweetness, then toss with 2 tablespoons sugar and taste again, adding more sugar if needed. If you are using sweet apples, pears, peaches, or nectarines it's nice to add the lemon juice. If you are using baking apples or rhubarb, err on the side of adding more sugar and no lemon juice at all. Add the fruit to a medium casserole dish and cook, uncovered, in the oven for 10 minutes.

3 Meanwhile, make the topping. In a medium bowl, combine the oil, honey or maple syrup, sugar, and salt. Add the flour, oats, cinnamon, and seeds and stir together until clumpy and moist. Scatter the crumble mix over the fruit, cover with aluminum foil, and bake for another 30 minutes. Remove the foil from the dish and return to the oven for a final 10 minutes to brown.

4 Serve hot with yogurt, ice cream, or cream, if desired.

Gluten Free Use chick pea (garbanzo bean) flour. If you can tolerate oats, make sure they're certified gluten free. If not, use millet flakes or quinoa flakes instead.

TIPS & SWAPS

Want a richer crumble? If you can tolerate dairy, rub cubed unsalted butter (instead of olive oil) into the crumble topping.

I love adding a handful of dried fruit to the crumble to intensify the flavor and sweetness. Raisins are an obvious choice, but you could also try chopped, pitted dates or dried blueberries.

LEFTOVERS: see pp. 228–233

- Fresh or frozen fruit
- Lemon

CARAMELIZED APPLE & PECAN BREAD PUDDING

Ⓥ

Serves 6 to 8

14oz to 1lb/400 to 450g peeled and cored apples (3 to 5 apples, depending on size)

6 tablespoons packed brown sugar

½ stick unsalted butter

2 cups milk or nondairy milk

2 eggs

1 teaspoon vanilla extract

¼ cup/1oz/30g whole-wheat pastry flour

⅓ cup/1¼oz/35g coarsely chopped pecans

5 to 6 pieces of (preferably stale) whole-wheat bread, cut into about 1¼-inch squares

salt

Stale bread is a blessing. You can turn it into French toast, bread crumbs, croutons, bread pudding... I like my bread pudding to have a higher ratio of crispy top to gooey middle, so I bake it in a large casserole dish to increase the surface area. The topping of pecan streusel makes it more crunchy.

1 Preheat the oven to 350°F.

2 Chop the peeled, cored apples into ¾-inch chunks. Put in a large skillet with 4 tablespoons of the sugar, 3 tablespoons of the butter, and a pinch of salt. Stir over high heat until the butter has melted, then reduce the heat to low and cook, stirring occasionally, until the apples soften and caramelize, 20 minutes. Remove from the heat.

3 In a bowl, using a fork, whisk together the milk, eggs, vanilla, 1 tablespoon of the sugar, and a pinch of salt.

4 In a small bowl, combine the flour, remaining butter, and the remaining tablespoon of sugar. Using your fingertips, rub together until the mixture is crumbly, then mix in the pecans.

5 In a large casserole dish, layer a third of the caramelized apples, then layer half the bread on top, followed by a third of the apples, the remaining bread, and then the remaining apples. Pour over the milk and egg mixture and sprinkle over the crumbly pecan mixture. Bake in the oven for 30 minutes.

TIPS & SWAPS

If using sweet apples, add a squeeze of lemon juice to the skillet to balance the sweetness.

LEFTOVERS: see pp. 228–233

● Bread, stale
● Apples

CINNAMON KNOTS

Makes 12

STARTING PASTE
⅓ cup water
2 tablespoons all-purpose flour

DOUGH
¼ cup/1¾oz/50g granulated sugar
⅓ cup just-boiled water
½ cup milk or nondairy milk
2¼ teaspoons instant dry yeast
1¼ cups/5½oz/150g all-purpose flour
or 1 cup plus 1½ tablespoons bread
flour, plus extra for dusting
2⅓ cups/10oz/280g whole-wheat
    pastry or whole-wheat flour
⅓ olive oil or rapeseed oil,
    plus extra for greasing
1 teaspoon salt
¼ cup olive or canola oil, or melted
    butter, for brushing over the dough

FILLING
4 teaspoons ground cinnamon
10 green cardamom pods, seeds
    removed and ground in a mortar
    and pestle (optional)
pinch of salt
1 tablespoon all-purpose or
    bread flour
½ cup/4oz/110g firmly packed
    brown sugar

GLAZE (OPTIONAL)
2 tablespoons granulated sugar
2 tablespoons water

These probably aren't the cinnamon buns you are used to —these are made with layered strips of dough twisted into a pretty shape, and are spiked with cardamom. Slather with a cream cheese frosting or sugar glaze for extra sweetness.

1   Line a baking sheet with nonstick parchment paper and set aside. To make the starting paste, in a small saucepan, heat the water and flour over medium heat and stir until thickened. Set aside.

2   For the dough, in a large bowl, mix together the sugar, just-boiled water, and milk. Sprinkle in the yeast and stir, then set aside for 5 minutes. Add the starting paste to the bowl with both flours, the oil, and salt and stir together to form a sticky dough.

3   Transfer the dough to a lightly floured work surface. Dust the dough and your hands with flour and knead it until soft and slightly sticky, adding a little more flour as needed.

4   Pour some oil into the bowl and add the dough. Turn the dough to coat in oil, then cover the bowl with a clean kitchen towel or plastic wrap and let rise in a warm place* for 1 hour.

5   Transfer the risen dough to a lightly floured work surface and dust with flour. Roll it out into a 16 x 24-inch rectangle using a floured rolling pin (or even a wine bottle). Brush the dough with more oil or melted butter.

6   In a bowl, mix together all the filling ingredients, then sprinkle the mixture over the surface of the dough in an even layer. Fold the dough into thirds like a business letter so that you end up with a 16 x 8-inch rectangle. Cut the rectangle in half along the 16-inch edge to make 2 x 8-inch squares. Cut each square into 6 strips. Twist each strip all along its length (it should stretch a bit as you twist it). Coil the strips up like a snail shell, stretching out the last couple of inches over the top of the bun and tucking it in underneath (see picture). Alternatively, simply coil the strips of dough like a snail shell.

7   Place the buns on the baking sheet, spacing them a couple of inches apart, cover with oiled plastic wrap, and let rise in a warm place for 30 minutes.

8   Preheat the oven to 350°F.

9   Once the buns have risen, uncover and bake them in the oven for 20 to 25 minutes, until golden.

10 In a small saucepan, heat the glaze ingredients to dissolve the sugar and brush over the buns with a pastry brush. Let cool slightly before eating. Store extras in an airtight container at room temperature for up to 3 days.

Vegan Use nondairy milk and olive or canola oil.

TIPS & SWAPS

*Create a perfect rising area for your dough—heat the oven to 225°F for 3 minutes, then switch the oven off, place the dough inside, and close the door.

EARL GREY CUPCAKES WITH LEMON GLAZE

Makes 10

¾ cup plus 2 tablespoons strongly brewed Earl Grey tea, cooled
¾ cup/5½oz/150g granulated sugar
⅓ cup plus 1 tablespoon olive oil or canola oil or melted unsalted butter
2 eggs
grated zest and juice of 1 lemon
1 cup minus 1 tablespoon all-purpose flour/4oz/110g
¾ cup plus 2 tablespoons/3½oz/100g whole-wheat pastry flour or more all-purpose flour
1¼ teaspoons baking powder
½ teaspoon baking soda
½ teaspoon salt
1½ cups/5½oz/150g sifted confectioners' sugar

I am an avid Earl Grey tea drinker. I grew up drinking it, so it's probably nostalgia that makes me love it so much. The tea has citrusy notes in it due to the addition of bergamot oil, which comes from the bergamot orange. Given this fact, I think that this tea pairs incredibly well with lemon, especially in cake.

1 Preheat the oven to 350°F. Line a muffin pan with 10 paper liners.

2 In a medium bowl, mix the brewed tea with the sugar, oil, eggs, and grated lemon zest until smooth. Dump both flours, the baking powder, baking soda, and salt on top and stir until just combined. Divide the batter between the paper liners, filling them about three-quarters full.

3 Bake in the oven for 25 to 30 minutes, until a toothpick inserted into the center comes out clean. Let the cakes cool slightly in the pan, then transfer to a wire rack or large platter and let cool completely.

4 In a small bowl, mix the confectioners' sugar with 1 tablespoon of the lemon juice, then gradually add more lemon juice until you have a smooth, spoonable frosting. Spoon over the cooled cupcakes and let set. Store in an airtight container for up to 4 days.

Vegan Use olive or canola oil. Replace the eggs with 2 tablespoons ground flax seed mixed with 6 tablespoons warm water.

TIPS & SWAPS

For the strongly brewed tea, fill a mug with around 1½ cups just-boiled water, add 2 Earl grey teabags, and let infuse for 10 minutes, before measuring out the liquid as needed.

If you are using whole-wheat flour, make sure it's intended for use in cakes and pastries, i.e. whole-wheat pastry flour!

SIMPLE LEMON BISCOTTI

Makes 12

1½ cups minus 1 tablespoon/6oz/170g
   plain whole-wheat pastry flour
1 teaspoon baking powder
5 tablespoons granulated sugar
grated zest of 1 lemon
¼ teaspoon salt
⅓ cup/1¾oz/50g mixed seeds, such
   as sunflower, pumpkin, sesame,
   and flax seed
1 extra-large egg
¼ cup milk or nondairy milk
2 tablespoons olive oil
1 teaspoon vanilla extract
sesame seeds, for sprinkling (optional)

Usually I'm not one to like biscotti (well, cantuccini, as I should call them), as they're often tooth-breakingly dry. I prefer homemade ones, which I bake enough to only slightly dry them out. They're not too sweet and are a great pick-me-up.

1 Preheat the oven to 350°F. Line a baking sheet with nonstick parchment paper.

2 In a medium bowl, combine the flour, baking powder, sugar, lemon zest, salt, and seeds. Make a hollow in the center of the dry ingredients, add the egg, milk, oil, and vanilla, and mix together to form a dough.

3 Transfer the dough to the baking sheet and form into a log about 8 x 3¼ inches. Sprinkle with sesame seeds, if using, then bake for 35 minutes.

4 Remove the log from the oven and let cool for 5 minutes. Slice it into 12 even pieces (a serrated knife is useful for this). Lay the biscotti on the baking sheet. Return to the oven, reduce the temperature to 325°F, and bake for 25 to 30 minutes.

5 Store in a sealed jar for up to 1 month at room temperature. If the biscotti soften up, put them in an oven preheated to 160°F for 10 to 15 minutes to dry them out.

Dairy Free Use nondairy milk.

LEFTOVERS: see pp. 228-233
● Lemon juice

ALMOND COOKIE BAKED PEACHES WITH LEMON YOGURT

Makes 6 peach halves (or serves 3 to 6)

3 ripe peaches, halved and pitted
1½ tablespoons unsalted butter, softened
1½ tablespoons packed brown sugar or 3 tablespoons Date Paste (see page 221)
¼ cup/¾oz/20g ground almonds or Ground Almond Alternative (see page 218)
3 tablespoons whole-wheat pastry flour
pinch of baking powder
pinch of salt
½ teaspoon almond extract or vanilla extract
1 tablespoon milk or nondairy milk
2 tablespoons coarsely chopped almonds or pecans

LEMON YOGURT

large pinch of sugar
grated zest of ½ lemon
6 tablespoons plain yogurt or nondairy yogurt

There's a French pastry recipe called "Bostock" that consists of a slice of day-old brioche, soaked with orange syrup, spread with frangipane, sprinkled with sliced almonds, and baked until caramelized. It's delicious, but I never have brioche around. Frangipane pairs very well with fruit, so I subbed peaches in for the brioche. The peaches soften and sweeten while the almond batter becomes crisp and gooey. The lemon yogurt, which is zingy and zesty, cuts through the sweetness.

1   Preheat the oven to 350°F.

2   Arrange the peach halves on a baking sheet or in an 8-inch round cake pan.

3   In a medium bowl, cream the butter and sugar or Date Syrup until smooth. Mix in the ground almonds or alternative, flour, baking powder, and salt, then stir in the almond or vanilla extract and milk. Spread the mixture over the peach halves and sprinkle with the chopped nuts.

4   Bake in the oven for 25 to 30 minutes, until golden on top.

5   To make the lemon yogurt, in a small bowl, combine the sugar and lemon zest. Using your fingertips, rub together to infuse the sugar with the lemon flavor. Mix in the yogurt.

6   Serve the peaches hot with the lemon yogurt.

Vegan Use vegan spread or cashew or almond butter instead of the butter. Use nondairy milk and yogurt.

LEFTOVERS: see pp. 228–233

● Peaches
● Lemon juice
● Yogurt

TIPS & SWAPS
Use nectarines or ripe plums instead of peaches.

VG option

EASY FREEZER CHOCOLATE CHIP COOKIES

Makes 20 to 24

½ cup extra virgin olive oil, olive oil, or melted unsalted butter

¾ cup/5½oz/150g granulated or firmly packed brown sugar

2 teaspoons miso, any kind, or ½ teaspoon salt

2 teaspoons vanilla extract

1⅔ cups/7oz/200g whole-wheat pastry or whole-wheat flour

¾ teaspoon baking powder

¾ teaspoon baking soda

1 (3½oz/100g) bar dark chocolate (at least 70% cocoa solids), coarsely chopped

1 scant cup/3½oz/100g coarsely chopped pecans or walnuts

1 egg

sea salt flakes, for sprinkling (optional)

Ever wanted to make chocolate chip cookies, but know that you become an incarnation of The Cookie Monster whenever cookies are around (i.e. have no self control)? Look to this recipe to help! The dough is super-easy to make before being shaped into balls and frozen before baking. This improves the texture of the cookie and means you can bake as many as you need, the rest in store for when another cookie craving hits.

1   Line a baking sheet or large plate with nonstick parchment paper.

2   In a medium bowl, combine the oil or melted butter, sugar, miso, and vanilla. Add the flour, baking powder, and baking soda and stir until evenly combined. Add the chocolate and nuts and stir through. Crack in the egg and stir until a slightly crumbly dough forms.

3   Scoop heaping tablespoons of dough into balls, then place on the prepared baking sheet or large plate and flatten the balls slightly. Freeze for 1 hour, then transfer to a labeled and dated sandwich bag and seal. Store in the freezer for up to 3 months.

4   When you are ready to bake, take however many cookie dough balls you want out of the freezer and preheat the oven to 350°F. Line a baking sheet with nonstick parchment paper.

5   Place the cookie dough balls on the prepared baking sheet, spacing them about 1¼ inches apart. Sprinkle with salt flakes, if desired, and bake in the oven for 8 to 10 minutes.

6   Let the cookies cool for a few minutes before eating, as they're fragile when hot. Let the leftovers cool completely, then transfer to an airtight container and store for up to 5 days.

Vegan   Replace the egg with 1 tablespoon ground flax seed mixed with ¼ cup water. Use oil instead of butter. Make sure your chocolate is suitable for vegans.

TIPS & SWAPS

If you are going to bake the cookies right away, only freeze the dough balls for 10 minutes.

If you enjoy the taste of olive oil, opt for extra virgin; use refined olive oil for a neutral taste.

LEFTOVERS: see pp. 228–233

● Miso

V **DF**

GF & VG options

DATE, WALNUT & CHOCOLATE OAT COOKIES

MAKES 20 to 24

⅓ cup plus 2 tablespoons olive oil, canola oil, or melted unsalted butter

¼ cup honey or maple syrup

¼ cup/1¾oz/50g firmly packed brown sugar

1 egg

1⅔ cups/5¾oz/160g old-fashioned rolled oats

½ cup/2¼oz/60g whole-wheat pastry or all-purpose flour

¼ teaspoon baking powder

½ teaspoon ground cinnamon

¼ teaspoon salt

½ cup/1¾oz/50g coarsely chopped walnuts

¼ cup/1¾oz/50g coarsely chopped pitted dried dates

½ (3½oz/100g) bar dark chocolate (at least 70% cocoa solids), coarsely chopped

Oat cookies are often the rejects out of the cookie choices, especially when they contain raisins, but I have a soft spot for them. The chewy oats add texture and the creamy, toasty flavor that I love. In fear of offending too many people by mixing chocolate and raisins together, I opted for dates instead. They bring pops of chewy, caramel sweetness to offset the bitter chocolate and crunchy walnuts.

1 Preheat the oven to 350°C. Line a baking sheet with nonstick parchment paper.

2 In a medium bowl, combine the oil or melted butter, honey or maple syrup, sugar, and egg until smooth. Add the remaining ingredients and stir together until you have a sticky dough.

3 Scoop heaping tablespoons of the dough onto the prepared baking sheet, spacing the balls a couple of inches apart—I usually get about 12 to a sheet. Bake in the oven for 8–12 minutes, until they look dry but are still slightly soft.

4 Let cool on the baking sheet for 1 minute before transferring to a wire rack to cool completely. Repeat with the rest of the dough. Store the cooled cookies in a sealed container for up to 5 days.

Vegan Use olive oil or canola oil instead of the butter, and maple syrup instead of the honey. Make sure your chocolate is suitable for vegans.

Gluten Free If you can tolerate oats, make sure they're certified gluten free. If not, use millet flakes or quinoa flakes instead. Use chick pea (garbanzo bean) flour instead of whole-wheat pastry or all-purpose flour.

LEFTOVERS: see pp. 228–233

● Dates

TIPS & SWAPS

Swap the walnuts for toasted dry unsweetened shredded coconut.

Use raisins instead of dates.

TIPS & SWAPS

Bake the cake in an 8-inch round cake pan if you don't have a bundt tin.

If you are using whole-wheat flour, make sure it's intended for use in cakes and pastries, i.e. whole-wheat pastry flour!

If you have roasted sweet potato (whole or cubed) to hand, use about 7oz of it as long as there are no spices on it. Skip steps 1 and 2 and continue with the recipe.

VG option

ONE-BOWL CHOCOLATE CAKE WITH MAGIC GANACHE

Serves 8 to 10

⅓ cup olive oil or canola oil, plus extra for greasing
⅓ cup/1oz/30g unsweetened cocoa, plus extra for dusting
about 1 medium (5½oz/150g) zucchini, shredded
¾ cup/5½oz/150g granulated sugar
½ teaspoon salt
¾ cup water
1 teaspoon apple cider vinegar, lemon juice, or white wine vinegar
1½ cups/6oz/180g all-purpose or whole-wheat pastry flour
1 teaspoon baking soda

MAGIC CHOCOLATE GANACHE
1 large or 2 small sweet potatoes (about 10½oz/300g)
1 (3½oz/100g) bar dark chocolate (at least 70% cocoa solids), melted (see page 192)
2 tablespoons unsalted butter
1 tablespoon honey or maple syrup
1 teaspoon vanilla extract
pinch of salt
½ to ⅓ cup milk or nondairy milk

TO DECORATE (OPTIONAL)
shaved chocolate
edible flowers

Baked sweet potatoes have such a soft, melty interior and are so tasty in desserts. Mixed with melted dark chocolate and a few other things, you have an A* ganache. You can even chill the ganache, then beat it with a wooden spoon to make more of a buttercream. I like to keep it pourable and drape it over a moist, light chocolate cake. It's so good, no one will ever know you're hiding two types of vegetable in there.

1 Preheat the oven to 350°F. Grease an 8-inch bundt pan well with oil and dust with cocoa, tapping out any excess.

2 Start on the ganache: Prick the sweet potato(es) all over with a knife. Wrap in aluminum foil and bake in the oven for 1 to 1½ hours, until completely tender. Remove and let cool. Keep the oven on for the cake.

3 Once the sweet potato is cool, cut in half and scoop the flesh out into a beaker or deep bowl. Using a handheld blender, blend with the melted chocolate, butter, honey or maple syrup, vanilla, and salt until smooth, then blend in enough milk to make a thick, spreadable ganache. Alternatively, blend the mixture in a countertop blender.

4 For the cake, put the shredded zucchini in a strainer, then hold the strainer over the sink and squeeze the zucchini to remove as much moisture as possible from it. Transfer the squeezed zucchini to a medium bowl. Add the sugar, oil, salt, water, vinegar, and cocoa and stir to combine. Dump the flour and baking soda into the bowl and stir in until just combined.

5 Pour the cake batter into the pan and bake in the oven for 35 to 45 minutes or until a toothpick inserted into the center of the cake comes out clean (the baking time will vary depending on the pan you use).

6 Let the cake cool for 10 minutes in the pan before loosening the edges with a knife and unmolding the cake onto a serving plate. Spread with the ganache and decorate with shaved chocolate and edible flowers, if desired.

Vegan Make sure your chocolate is suitable for vegans. Use 2 tablespoons coconut oil or vegan spread instead of the butter in the ganache. Use maple syrup and nondairy milk.

LEFTOVERS: see pp. 228–233

● Sweet potato (raw or roasted)
● Zucchini

CHOCOLATE CHIP, RASPBERRY & ALMOND CAKE

Serves 6

⅓ cup olive oil, canola oil, or melted unsalted butter, plus extra for greasing

¾ cup plus 1 tablespoon/3oz/80g Oat Flour (see page 216), plus extra for dusting

¾ cup plus 2 tablespoons/3oz/80g ground almonds or Ground Almond Alternative (see page 218; 1 cup if using ground coconut)

⅓ cup/3oz/80g firmly packed brown sugar

¼ teaspoon salt

½ teaspoon baking powder

1 extra-large egg

¼ cup milk or nondairy milk

½ teaspoon almond extract

½ (3½oz/100g) bar dark chocolate (at least 70% cocoa solids), finely chopped

¾ cup (3½oz/100g) frozen or fresh raspberries

TO SERVE (OPTIONAL)
whipped cream or plain yogurt
fresh raspberries

I have never enjoyed making layer cakes that much. There's too much buttercream involved and I reach maximum stress levels when trying to evenly frost the outside. I find it much more satisfying to bake a flavorful single-layer cake. This is one such cake. It's moist and studded with jammy raspberries and deep, dark chocolate chunks. It's the type of cake that you can eat a slice of with a cup of tea at teatime, or with whipped cream and extra raspberries for a special dessert.

1 Preheat the oven to 350°F. Grease a 9-inch round cake pan with oil and dust with flour, tapping out any excess.

2 In a medium bowl, mix the ground almonds or alternative, oil or melted butter, sugar, flour, salt, baking powder, egg, milk, and almond extract until smooth. Pour the batter into the prepared pan. Sprinkle over the chopped chocolate and frozen raspberries, then slightly swirl them into the batter with a spoon.

3 Bake in the oven for 30 to 35 minutes, until the center of the cake springs back when you apply light pressure with your finger.

4 Remove from the oven and let the cake cool in the pan. Once completely cooled, slice and serve as it comes, or with whipped cream or yogurt and fresh raspberries, if desired.

Gluten Free If you can tolerate oats, make sure the oats used to make the flour are certified gluten free. If you can't tolerate oats, use chick pea (garbanzo bean) flour instead.

Dairy Free Use oil not butter in the cake and use nondairy milk. Make sure the chocolate you use is dairy free.

LEFTOVERS: see pp. 228–233

● Raspberries (fresh or frozen)

LEMON, BLUEBERRY & CORN CAKE

Makes 1 loaf cake (Serves 10 to 12)

⅓ cup plus 4 teaspoons olive oil or
  melted butter, plus extra for greasing
1 cup/5¾oz/165g cooked corn kernels
  (I used canned)
2 eggs
grated zest and juice of 1 lemon
½ cup/3½oz/100g granulated sugar,
  plus 1 tablespoon
1½ cups/6½oz/180g whole-wheat
  pastry or all-purpose flour
½ cup/1¾oz/50g Oat Flour
  (see page 216)
1½ teaspoons baking powder
¼ teaspoon salt
1¼ cups/5½oz/150g blueberries, fresh
or frozen

Okay, don't get annoyed with me because I keep putting vegetables into baked goods, but you will love this cake, especially if you're a lemon cake connoisseur like me. The corn here makes the cake taste even more cake-y somehow, while also adding moisture and obviously sweetness. There's lemon zest and blueberries in the batter, plus a strong lemon syrup poured over the cake at the end for that zingy, zesty kick. Go on, I dare you to try it.

1 Preheat the oven to 350°F. Grease and line the bottom and sides of a large (2lb) loaf pan with nonstick parchment paper.

2 Blitz the corn into a paste. This can be done in a beaker or deep bowl using a handheld blender or in a countertop blender.

3 Transfer the blitzed corn to a medium bowl and stir in the oil or melted butter, eggs, lemon zest, and the ½ cup sugar. Add both flours, the baking powder, and salt and stir until just smooth. Fold the blueberries into the batter briefly, then pour the batter into the prepared loaf pan.

4 Bake in the oven for 50 to 60 minutes or until a toothpick inserted into the center of the cake comes out clean (if the toothpick hits a blueberry, test a different spot).

5 Meanwhile, in a small saucepan, heat the lemon juice and remaining tablespoon of sugar just until the sugar dissolves.

6 Once the cake is cooked, let cool in the pan for 10 minutes, then turn out onto a wire rack. Poke it all over with a toothpick and use a spoon to drizzle the sweetened lemon juice all over the cake. Let cool completely before slicing. Store any leftovers in an airtight container for up to 5 days.

Dairy Free Use oil instead of butter.

TIPS & SWAPS

If you don't like corn, omit it and add ½ cup milk or nondairy milk.

Replace the Oat Flour with ground almonds or Ground Almond Alternative (see page 218) for a richer taste.

Use an equal quantity of frozen blackberries or raspberries instead of the blueberries.

LEFTOVERS: see pp. 228–233

● Blueberries (fresh or frozen)

DIY

This is the little section at the back of the book with all the cool, nifty recipes that will boost your pantry and freezer, and make your cooking life easier. All the dressings in the book are listed here so that you don't have to hunt for them if you want to make a specific one. There's also, of course, recipes for things such as pie dough, bread dough, and pesto, which are always better when they are homemade.

TORTILLAS

Makes 12

1½ cups/6oz/180g all-purpose or
  bread flour, plus extra for dusting
1⅔ cups/7oz/200g whole-wheat
  pastry or whole-wheat flour
½ teaspoon salt
¼ teaspoon baking powder
1 cup lukewarm* water
3 tablespoons olive oil

1 In a medium bowl, combine the flours, salt, and baking powder. Make a hollow in the center of the dry ingredients, then pour in the water and oil. Stir until you have a coarse dough. Transfer to a lightly floured work surface and dust with a little more flour. Knead together briefly until smooth. Divide in half and cut each half into 6 pieces. Roll each piece into a ball and let rest for 5 minutes at room temperature.

2 Dust each ball with flour and roll it out into a circle as thinly as possible, dusting with flour as needed.

3 Heat a nonstick skillet over high heat. Once the pan is hot, add a circle of dough to the skillet. It will start to puff up, and once golden spots appear on the underside, flip it over and cook on the other side until speckled.

4 Keep the tortillas warm by wrapping in a clean kitchen towel while you cook the rest of the dough. Store any leftover tortillas in a sandwich bag in the freezer for up to 1 month.

TIPS & SWAPS
Reheat in a skillet with some oil for 2 to 3 minutes; in the oven wrapped in aluminium foil for 10 minutes; or straight over a gas flame for 30 seconds.

VG option

NO-YEAST FLATBREADS

Makes 6 small flatbreads

1¼ cups/5½oz/150g whole-wheat
  pastry or whole-wheat flour, plus
  extra for dusting
½ teaspoon baking powder
¼ teaspoon baking soda
¼ teaspoon salt
4 to 6 tablespoons water
¼ cup plain yogurt
1 tablespoon olive oil, canola oil,
  or melted butter

1 In a medium bowl, combine the flour, baking powder, baking soda, and salt. Make a hollow in the center of the dry ingredients and pour in the wet ingredients. Mix to form a smooth dough, adding more water if needed.

2 Transfer the dough to a lightly floured work surface and knead for a few minutes, then return it to the bowl, cover with a clean kitchen towel, and let rest for 10 minutes.

3 Divide the dough into 6 equal pieces and roll into balls. Using a lightly floured rolling pin, roll them out into circles about ⅛-inch-thick.

4 Heat a dry skillet over the highest heat. Add 1 to 2 circles of dough to the skillet and cook until the bread is browned on the underside. Flip over and cook on the other side until brown. Transfer to a plate and repeat with the remaining dough. Store extra flatbreads in a sandwich bag at room temperature for up to 2 days. When ready to eat, place them in an oven preheated to 350°F for a few minutes.

Vegan Use unsweetened soy yogurt instead of the plain yogurt.

WHOLE-WHEAT PITA
OR STOVETOP FLATBREADS

Makes 6

1 teaspoon instant dry yeast
¾ cup plus 1 tablespoon lukewarm
  water*
1 cup/4½oz/125g all-purpose or bread
  flour, plus extra for dusting
1 cup/4½oz/125g whole-wheat pastry
  or whole-wheat flour
½ teaspoon salt

I like to make this dough on a Sunday and keep it in the refrigerator for quick, weekday flatbreads, which I can either pan-fry or bake each day. Having a freshly made flatbread doesn't sound like anything special, but I find it makes building up a lunch idea much easier!

1 In a large bowl, dissolve the yeast in the lukewarm water and set aside for 5 minutes.

2 Add the flours and salt, and mix to form a coarse dough. Transfer the dough to a lightly floured work surface, sprinkle with flour, and knead for 6 to 10 minutes until smooth. Return the dough to the bowl and cover with a clean kitchen towel or plastic wrap. If baking immediately, let the dough rise in a warm place for 40 minutes. Otherwise, the bowl can be stored in the refrigerator for up to 5 days.

3 Transfer the risen dough to a lightly floured work surface, punch it down, and divide it into 6 equal balls.

4 If making pita breads: Preheat the oven to 475°F. Lightly flour a baking sheet. Roll a ball of dough out into an oval, dusting with flour as needed. The dough should be around ¼ inch thick. Place on the prepared baking sheet and repeat with another ball (depending on the size of your baking sheet). Bake in the oven for 10 to 12 minutes, until puffed and dry.

5 Remove the baked pitas and wrap in a clean kitchen towel to keep them warm and soft. Repeat the rolling and baking with the remaining dough. Store any leftover flatbreads in the freezer for up to 2 months, placing in the toaster to thaw.

6 If making flatbreads, roll out each ball of dough to a circle about 4 inches in diameter. Heat a dry skillet over the highest heat. Once the pan is hot, reduce the heat to medium-high, add a circle of dough to the skillet, and cook until it starts to bubble up and brown on the underside. Flip over and cook on the other side until it is flecked with spots. Transfer to a plate and cook the remaining dough as before.

TIPS & SWAPS
*Make sure the water is only just
slightly warm to the touch.

OAT FLOUR

Oat flour is fabulous to make at home. Oats are inexpensive and oat flour is much better for you than refined, white wheat flour, as it contains more protein and fiber, while also (in my opinion) being tastier than using all whole-wheat flour.

You can use any type of oats as long as "oats" are the only ingredient on the package. You don't want to use flavored oats for this. You also don't want to use steel-cut oats unless you have a high-speed blender.

Blend whatever quantity of oats you need in a blender or food processor until it becomes a coarse flour. Transfer to a labeled, airtight container and store at room temperature for up to a year.

Gluten Free If you can tolerate oats, use gluten-free certified oats.

TIPS & SWAPS

If you can find unflavoured "instant," smooth oatmeal that contains "oat flour" in the ingredients list, you can use that instead of making oat flour. It's more expensive and isn't as fine as oat flour, but if you have it to hand, it usually works.

INSTANT NUT MILK (FOR BAKING)

This is a good one to remember when you're out of milk but want to bake, even if you usually use cow's milk.

Makes ⅔ cup

2 tablespoons smooth unsalted nut butter, any kind (cashew, almond, peanut, creamed coconut…)
⅔ cup hot water

1 In a bowl, stir the nut butter and hot water together until the nut butter has melted and mixed into the liquid. Use in baking recipes where nondairy milk is required.

OLIVE OIL PIE DOUGH

Makes enough for 1 galette or 1 pie top

1 cup/4¼oz/120g all-purpose flour
1 cup/4¼oz/120g whole-wheat
   pastry flour*
½ teaspoon salt
1 tablespoon granulated sugar
   (for sweet recipes)
⅓ cup olive oil
¼ to ⅓ cup cold water

1 In a medium bowl, combine the flours, salt, and sugar, if using. Pour in the oil and stir until evenly mixed into the dry ingredients. Make a well in the center of the dry ingredients and pour in 3 tablespoons of the water. Use your hands to work the water into the dry ingredients, drizzling in more water if it seems too dry.

2 Pat the dough into a circle. You can either use it right away or wrap in plastic wrap and store in the refrigerator for up to 3 days or in the freezer for up to 3 months.

TIPS & SWAPS
*Make sure you are not using regular whole-wheat flour in this recipe.

HALF-OAT PIE DOUGH

Makes enough dough for 1 galette or 1 pie top

7 tablespoons cold unsalted butter,
   cut into ½-inch cubes
¾ cup plus 2 tablespoons/3½oz/100g
   all-purpose flour
1 cup/4¼oz/120g Oat Flour (see page
   216) or whole-wheat pastry flour
¼ teaspoon salt
1 tablespoon granulated sugar
   (for sweet pie dough only)
2 tablespoons plain yogurt,
   crème fraîche, or ricotta cheese
1 to 3 tablespoons cold water

1 In a medium bowl, toss the butter with both flours, the salt, and sugar, if using, and rub the butter into the dry ingredients with your fingertips until you have a coarse, sandy mixture.

2 Make a hollow in the center of the mixture and pour in the yogurt, crème fraîche, or ricotta and 1 tablespoon of the cold water. Mix together gently with your fingertips until it becomes a dough that holds together when pinched. If it's too dry, drizzle in more water as needed.

3 Transfer the coarse dough to a piece of plastic wrap, shape it into a ball, and flatten it into a disk, then wrap in plastic wrap. Chill in the refrigerator for at least 30 minutes before using. The pie dough can be stored in the refrigerator for 3 days or frozen for 3 months.

LEFTOVERS: see pp. 228–233

● Yogurt, crème fraîche, or ricotta

BREAD CRUMBS

1 WITH A FOOD PROCESSOR/BLENDER: Preheat the oven to 275°F. If you have fresh bread, slice it into bite-size chunks and lay the slices on a baking sheet. Bake in the oven for 15 to 25 minutes, until the bread feels dry and crisp. Let cool before using.

Pulse the dried or stale bread in a food processor or blender (you may need to do this in batches) until fine.

TIPS & SWAPS
Sourdough bread doesn't tend to work very well as the crust is too tough.

2 WITH A BOX GRATER: Preheat the oven to 275°F. Slice the bread and shred it against the coarse side of a box grater. Spread the bread crumbs out on a baking sheet and bake in the oven for 10 to 20 minutes until dry. You may need to stir the bread crumbs halfway through their baking time so that they dry out evenly.

3 Store the bread crumbs in a zipper sandwich bag for 1 to 2 weeks at room temperature or in the freezer for up to 3 months.

GROUND ALMOND ALTERNATIVE

sunflower seeds or dry shredded coconut (the unsweetened kind)

This tip is useful for people with allergies or those on a budget. You can grind up pretty much any nut or seed to make a "flour" that can be used for baking. However, sunflower seeds and desiccated coconut seem to be the most inexpensive. Things to be aware of are that sunflower seeds have a mild flavor but sometimes, when baked in combination with baking soda, will turn things green. This doesn't affect the flavor or safety of the baked good, it's just a visual thing. For shredded coconut, it does have a coconut flavor, so may not be useful for all applications, especially if you don't like the flavor.

1 In a food processor or blender, blitz the desired quantity of sunflower seeds or coconut until fine, stopping to scrape down the sides as needed. Don't overblend or you'll start to make sunflower-seed or coconut butter!

2 Store in an airtight container at room temperature for up to 2 months. Use as you would ground almonds in baking recipes.

AVOCADO CREAM

Serves 3 to 4

1 avocado
juice of ½ lime
pinch of salt

This is a cooling, fatty-yet-light sauce to serve with spicy foods. It's a great vegan alternative to sour cream or plain yogurt.

1 Cut the avocado in half and remove the pit. Use a spoon to scoop the avocado flesh out into a beaker or deep bowl if using a handheld blender or blender jar if using a countertop blender. Blitz with the remaining ingredients until smooth. Keep the excess in a lidded container in the refrigerator for up to 3 days.

SUN FETA

Makes about 3½oz

⅔ cup/3½oz/100g sunflower seeds
juice of 1 lemon
½ teaspoon salt
⅓ cup water

I like to sprinkle feta over a simple salad for that salty kick, but when I take a break from dairy (I used to be lactose intolerant and am sensitive of overdoing it on the dairy), I make this. It's affordable to make, and keeps in the refrigerator for a few days.

1 Soak the sunflower seeds in a bowl of water for 8 to 12 hours, then drain and rinse.

2 Preheat the oven to 275°F. Line a baking sheet with nonstick parchment paper.

3 Blend the drained sunflower seeds in a food processor or countertop blender until chunky, then add the lemon juice, salt, and water and blend again until smooth.

4 Pat the mixture into rectangle about ½ inch thick on the prepared baking sheet and bake in the oven for 1½ hours or until firm.

5 Let cool, then slice into cubes. Store in a sealed container in the refrigerator for up to 3 days.

TIPS & SWAPS

For a vegan alternative to sour cream or crème fraîche, cut the salt down to ¼ teaspoon, use the juice of only ½ lemon, and don't bake the mixture. You will be left with a thick, rich, and creamy sauce, which you can use for drizzling on tacos, pizza, and curry or stirring into pasta or risotto. Add 1 tablespoon maple syrup and only use a pinch of salt if you want a sweet cream for serving with berries, cake, oatmeal, or pancakes.

You can also use almonds instead of sunflower seeds here.

NO-COOK PIZZA SAUCE

Makes enough for 4 to 6 pizzas (depending on size)

1 (14½oz) can diced tomatoes
1 tablespoon balsamic vinegar
1 teaspoon mixed dried herbs
1 teaspoon granulated sugar
   or 2 teaspoons Date Paste
   (see page 221)
3 garlic cloves, crushed
generous pinch of salt

1 Blend all the ingredients together, either in a large beaker with a handheld blender or in a countertop blender or food processor.

2 Store any excess pizza sauce in a lidded container in the refrigerator for up to 3 days or freeze for up to 3 months.

TIPS & SWAPS

If I have sauce left over from making pizzas, I usually keep the sauce for the next day, then cook it until thickened to have with pasta.

This sauce is pretty thin because of the fact that it hasn't been cooked down. For this reason, it's best not to use too much on pizzas or things can get soupy, fast! You just need a thin layer on the pizza dough.

PIZZA DOUGH

Makes enough for 2 large or 3 medium pizzas

¾ cup plus 2½ tablespoons water
1 teaspoon instant dry yeast
1 tablespoon olive oil
1¼ cups/5½oz/150g whole-wheat flour
1¼/5½oz/150g cups bread flour or
   all-purpose flour
½ teaspoon salt

1 In a large bowl, combine the water and yeast. Let sit for 2 minutes.

2 Add the oil, both flours, and the salt to the bowl and mix together with a spoon until you get a shaggy dough.

3 Shape your hand like a claw and beat the dough in the bowl—try to stretch it up and then slap it back into the bowl—for about 1 minute. Cover the bowl of dough with plastic wrap or a clean kitchen towel.

If making the pizza soon—let the dough rest at room temperature for 1 hour.

If making the pizza later—let the dough rest in the refrigerator for 2 to 10 hours. Remove from the refrigerator at least 30 minutes before using, to bring to room temperature.

DATE PASTE

Makes about 1 cup

1¼ cups dried dates, pitted
¼ to ⅓ cup hot water

This is a thick, caramellike paste made simply from dates and water. It adds a lovely subtle sweetness to savory dishes and is also delicious on toast or pancakes. It can sometimes be used in baking instead of regular sugar. As it is high in fiber, it is also healthier than using just straight sugar. Due to its high sugar content, date paste keeps very well in the refrigerator in a lidded container.

1 If the dates aren't soft and sticky, let soak in a heatproof bowl of boiling water for 15 minutes, then drain.

2 Blend the pitted dates with the hot water until smooth. This can be done in a large beaker or bowl if using a handheld blender or in a countertop blender.

3 Alternatively, put the dates in a small saucepan and just cover with water. Bring to a boil, then reduce the heat and simmer until the water has mostly evaporated. Add ¼ cup of the water to the pan and keep cooking the dates over low heat, stirring and mashing them with the back of a spoon, until as smooth as possible. Remove from the heat and let cool.

THAI GREEN CURRY PASTE

Makes enough for a curry for 3 to 4 people

½ onion or 2 shallots, coarsely chopped
6 garlic cloves, chopped
1½ tablespoons ground cumin
1½ tablespoons ground coriander
⅔ cup/1oz/30g coarsely chopped cilantro
2 green chiles, finely chopped
3 tablespoons grated or minced ginger root
2 lemon grass stalks, finely chopped
1 tablespoon salt
2 to 3 tablespoons water (optional)

1 Blitz everything together in a beaker with a handheld blender or in a countertop blender until smooth.

2 Store in the refrigerator for up to 3 days. For long-term storage, scoop tablespoons of the paste onto a plate lined with nonstick parchment paper and freeze. Once frozen, transfer the cubes into a labeled and dated sandwich bag, seal, and store in the freezer for up to 3 months.

NO-BLENDER
RED LENTIL HUMMUS

Serves 2 to 3

⅔ cup/4¼oz/120g dry red lentils, rinsed
1 garlic clove, minced or crushed
juice of ½ lemon
¼ cup extra virgin olive oil
pinch of salt

I use this recipe when I either have no access to a blender or I don't have any cooked chick peas to hand. Red lentils are very cheap and quicker to cook than chick peas. They are also more sustainable to grow and make a smoother hummus.

1 Put the lentils in a medium saucepan and pour in enough water to cover. Bring to a boil, then reduce the heat and simmer for 20 minutes until completely soft, adding water if needed to keep the lentils hydrated but not too soupy.

2 After the 20 minutes are up, keep cooking the lentils, stirring frequently, until the remaining water has nearly evaporated and you are left with a thick paste. Remove from the heat and beat in the remaining ingredients until as smooth as possible. Cover and store in the refrigerator for 2 to 3 days.

3 If you have a blender, once the lentils have cooked for 12 minutes, drain them, then either blend with the remaining ingredients using a handheld blender in a large beaker or deep bowl or in a countertop blender or food processor. Cover and store in the refrigerator for 2 to 3 days.

CHICK PEA MAYONNAISE

Makes about ¾ cup

3 tablespoons liquid from a can
    or saucepan of cooked chick peas
    (garbanzo beans)
juice of ½ lemon
pinch of granulated sugar
¼ teaspoon salt
¼ teaspoon Dijon mustard (optional)
⅔ cup olive oil

Ah the magic of chick pea liquid! It's a strange ingredient, also known as "aquafaba," which can act in certain recipes as an egg substitute. Here we utilize the emulsifying properties of the aquafaba to blend oil and lemon juice into a creamy, dreamy mayonnaise substitute, which is completely vegan.

1 Put all the ingredients in a beaker and use a handheld blender to blitz until everything is emulsified. It will be thick and creamy. Pour into a clean jar, seal with the lid, and refrigerate for up to 1 week.

2 To make in a countertop blender, add all the ingredients, except the oil, to the blender, then blitz on medium speed and very, very slowly stream in the oil until emulsified.

LEFTOVERS: see pp. 228–233

● Lemon

QUICK PICKLED RED ONION

Serves 4 to 6

1 red onion, thinly sliced into rings
¼ cup apple cider vinegar
   or rice vinegar
1 tablespoon granulated sugar
½ teaspoon salt
¼ cup water

1 Place the onion rings in a small bowl or a sandwich bag.

2 In a small saucepan, heat the vinegar, sugar, and salt over medium heat, stirring, until the sugar has dissolved. Pour the hot liquid over the onion rings in the bowl or bag, then top up with the water to just cover the onions.

3 Let the onions sit for at least 30 minutes before using.

4 For long-term storage, pour the liquid and the onion rings into a clean jar, seal with the lid, and keep in the refrigerator for a week or so. If you use a sterilized jar (see tips below), they should keep for a few months.

TIPS & SWAPS

To sterilize a jar, wash the jar and lid thoroughly in hot, soapy water. Place on a baking sheet and let dry in an oven preheated to 325°F for 5 to 10 minutes. If your jar has a rubber seal, let this air-dry, as the oven may damage it.

TRIO OF PESTOS

Here we have three different pesto recipes to show off how versatile pesto really is! I always like to make a big batch of pesto to freeze in ice-cube trays—once frozen, I pop the cubes of frozen pesto out into a zipper sandwich bag to store in the freezer. This is much easier to use than if you freeze all the pesto into one large container.

ROASTED EGGPLANT & TOMATO PESTO

Serves 3 to 4

1 large or 2 small eggplants (14oz to 1lb/
    400g to 500g in total)
about 2½ tablespoons sunflower seeds,
    pumpkin seeds, or cashews
1¼ cups/5½oz/150g drained sundried tomatoes in oil
juice of ½ lemon
1 garlic clove, crushed or minced
1 tablespoon olive oil
salt

1 Preheat the oven to 350°F.

2 Pierce the eggplant all over with a knife, then place on a baking sheet and roast in the oven for 1 hour or until soft. Cut the eggplant in half, scoop out the flesh, and discard the skin.

3 If using a handheld blender, finely chop the seeds or nuts, add to a beaker or deep bowl with the eggplant flesh, and blend together. Add the remaining ingredients and blend again. Season with salt to taste.

4 If using a countertop blender or food processor, briefly pulse the seeds or nuts to break them down until coarse. Add the remaining ingredients and blend again, then season with salt to taste.

5 Store in a lidded container in the refrigerator for up to 3 days, or see the introduction.!

TIPS & SWAPS

Turn this pesto into a dip by blitzing in ⅔ cup cooked, or ½ (15oz) can cooked cannellini (white kidney) beans plus 2 tablespoons tahini instead of the olive oil.

You can use 9oz fresh cherry tomatoes instead of sundried tomatoes. Just roast the cherry tomatoes on the same baking sheet as the eggplant for the final 30 minutes of roasting. If you already have roasted cherry tomatoes to hand, you can use 4oz instead of the sundried tomatoes.

LEFTOVERS: see pp. 228–233

● Sundried tomatoes, fresh
    tomatoes, or roasted tomatoes
● Eggplant
● Lemon

BROCCOLI PESTO

Serves 3 to 4

½ medium head of broccoli, cut into florets
small handful of basil (leaves and stems)
2 garlic cloves, crushed or minced
juice of ½ lemon
¼ cup extra virgin olive oil
large pinch of salt

1 Put the broccoli in a saucepan and cover with just-boiled water. Bring to a boil, then reduce the heat and simmer for 10 minutes. Drain, then return the broccoli to the saucepan and mash with a potato masher or the back of a fork.

2 Finely chop the basil and add to the pan with the garlic, lemon juice, oil, and salt, then stir together to combine. Alternatively, use a handheld blender in the pan or a countertop blender to blitz everything together.

3 Store in a lidded container in the refrigerator for up to 3 days, or see the introduction for a long-term storage option!

BASIL & ARUGULA PESTO

Serves 2 to 3

about 2½ tablespoons pumpkin seeds,
    sunflower seeds, or cashews
a few large handfuls of basil,
    coarsely chopped (leaves and stems)
1⅓ cups/1½oz/40g arugula (or use spinach instead)
¼ cup extra virgin olive oil or olive oil
1 garlic clove, crushed
¼ cup water
generous pinch of salt
juice of ½ lemon

1 If using a handheld blender, finely chop the pumpkin seeds and add to a beaker or deep bowl. Coarsely chop the basil and arugula and add them too. Blend a little to start breaking the greens down, then add the remaining ingredients and blitz until as smooth as you can get it.

2 If using a blender or food processor, briefly pulse the seeds to break them down until coarse. Add the remaining ingredients and blend again until smooth.

3 Store in a lidded container in the refrigerator for up to 3 days, or see the introduction for a long-term storage option!

LEFTOVERS: see pp. 228–233

- Basil
- Lemon

LEFTOVERS: see pp. 228–233

- Basil
- Lemon

DRESSINGS

A good salad dressing is the key to turning a pile of drab greens into a bowl of joy. These dressings appear throughout the book, but it's also useful to have them all in one place.

TAHINI DRESSING

Serves 1 to 2

2 tablespoons tahini
1 garlic clove, crushed or minced
pinch of salt
juice of ½ lemon

1   Put all the ingredients in a jar with a screw-on lid, cover with the lid, and shake to emulsify. Store in the refrigerator for up to a week.

PEANUT–GINGER DRESSING

Serves 2

2 tablespoons peanut, almond, or cashew butter, or tahini
1 teaspoon granulated sugar or honey,
    or 1 tablespoon Date Paste (see page 221)
juice of ½ lime
1 tablespoon soy sauce or tamari
1 teaspoon grated ginger root

1   Stir all the dressing ingredients together in a bowl, then add enough water to make a thick, spoonable dressing. Store in the refrigerator for up to a week.

MISO DRESSING

Serves 2 to 3

2 tablespoons miso, any kind
¼ cup olive oil
1 garlic clove, crushed or minced
1 shallot or ¼ red onion, finely diced
2 teaspoons granulated sugar or honey
1 tablespoon lemon juice, or apple cider vinegar or rice vinegar

1   Put all the ingredients in a jar with a screw-on lid, cover with the lid, and shake to emulsify. Store in the refrigerator for up to a week.

CILANTRO–COCONUT DRESSING

Serves 2 to 3

2 handfuls of cilantro leaves
¼oz/10g piece of ginger root, peeled and minced
    or grated
juice of 1 lemon
2 tablespoons soy sauce or tamari
1 tablespoon granulated sugar or honey,
    or 2 tablespoons Date Paste (see page 221)
1 to 2 pinches of crushed red pepper
⅓ cup coconut milk or 2 tablespoons creamed coconut plus
    ¼ cup hot water

1   Blend all the ingredients together until smooth using a handheld blender and beaker or a countertop blender. Store in the refrigerator for up to a week.

HONEY–THYME DRESSING

Serves 2 to 3

2 teaspoons honey
3 tablespoons olive oil
juice of 1 lemon
pinch of salt
¼ red onion, finely chopped
4 sprigs of thyme, leaves picked

1 Put all the ingredients in a jar with a screw-on lid, cover with the lid, and shake to emulsify. Store in the refrigerator for up to a week.

BASIL-AVOCADO DRESSING

Serves 2 to 3

large handful of basil leaves
½ avocado, pitted and peeled
pinch of salt
3 tablespoons water
juice of ½ lime

1 Blend all the ingredients together until smooth, either with a handheld blender and beaker or a countertop blender. Store in the refrigerator for up to a week.

LIME-SOY DRESSING

Serves 2 to 4

1 tablespoon soy sauce or tamari
2 teaspoons honey, or maple syrup or golden syrup
juice of 1 lime
1 tablespoon toasted sesame oil

1 Put all the ingredients in a jar with a screw-on lid, cover with the lid, and shake to emulsify. Store in the refrigerator for up to a week.

GINGER-LIME DRESSING

Serves 3 to 4

2 teaspoons minced or grated ginger root
juice of ½ lemon or lime
1 teaspoon honey or maple syrup
2 tablespoons soy sauce or tamari
1 scallion, finely sliced
2 tablespoons olive oil or canola oil

1 Put all the ingredients in a jar with a screw-on lid, cover with the lid, and shake to emulsify. Store in the refrigerator for up to a week

APPLE YOGURT DRESSING

Serves 3 to 4

1 apple, shredded
1 tablespoon honey
generous pinch of salt
⅓ cup olive oil
6 tablespoons plain yogurt or crème fraîche
2 tablespoons apple cider vinegar

1 In a small skillet, cook the apple and honey over low heat until softened. Let cool, then transfer to a beaker, add the salt, olive oil, and yogurt or crème fraiche, and blend using a handheld blender until smooth. Alternatively, chuck it all into a countertop blender and blend until smooth.

2 Stir in the vinegar and thin out with enough water to make a pourable dressing. Store in the refrigerator for up to a week.

Gluten Free Make sure that you are using certified gluten-free tamari or soy sauce, when using.

MAKEOVERS WITH LEFTOVERS

FRUIT & VEG

Apples
Any-fruit Galette (p. 188)
Apple Cinnamon Scuffins (p. 39)
Broccoli Apple Yogurt Slaw (p. 55)
Cannellini Bean & Apple Salad (p. 87)
Caramelized Apple & Pecan Bread Pudding (p. 197)
Chick Pea "Tuna" Salad (p. 69)
Olive Oil Any-fruit Crumble (p. 196
Overnight Oats (p. 18)

Avocado
Avocado Cream (p. 219)
Corn, Peach & Pearl Barley Salad (p. 81)
Crispy Tortilla Strips with Corn & Quinoa (p. 125)

Bananas
Banana Bread (p. 194)
Banana Bread Oatmeal (p. 28)
Banana Chocolate Chip Blondies (p. 195)
Banoffee Peanut Bites (p. 40)
Coconut–Banana Granola Bars (p. 45)
Smoothie Boxes (p. 38)

Beets
Beet, Hazelnut & Crispy Sage Salad (p. 72)
Beet Flatbread (p. 59)
Roasted Beet, Cumin & Crispy Chick Peas (p. 65)

Bell Peppers
Frittata (p. 162)
Lentil & Yogurt Pita Dip (p. 106)
Orange, Fennel, Olive & Pearl Barley Stew (p. 154)
Paprika Bean Stew (p. 134)
Pizza (p. 158)
Potato, Halloumi & Zucchini Bake (p. 105)
Shakshouka (p. 131)
Stir-Fry (p. 174)
Taco (p. 166)

Blackberries (fresh or frozen)
Any-fruit Galette (p. 188)
Olive Oil Any-fruit Crumble (p. 196)
Smoothie Boxes (p. 38)

Blueberries (fresh or frozen)
Any-fruit Galette (p. 188)
Lemon, Blueberry & Corn Cake (p. 211)
Microwave Blueberry "Muffin" (p. 26)
Olive Oil Any-fruit Crumble (p. 196)
Smoothie Boxes (p. 38)

Butternut Squash (raw)
Orzo with Squash, Chile, Lemon & Peas (p. 126)
Roasted Squash with Brown Rice & Halloumi (p. 92)
Squash & Cinnamon Dip (p. 47)
Squash, Cauliflower & Roasted Garlic Gratin (p. 109)
Squash, Potato & Chile Cakes (p. 76)
Taco (p. 166)

Butternut Squash (roasted)
Frittata (p. 162)
Pizza (p. 158)
Taco (p. 166)

Cabbage (red or white)
Frittata (p162)
Miso Mango Slaw (p55)
One-pan Creamy Pasta with Asparagus, Lemon & Basil (p145)
Stir Fry (p174)
Taco (p166)

Carrots (raw)
Cannellini Bean & Apple Salad (p. 87)
Carrot Breakfast Bread (p. 23)
Carrot Cake Overnight Oats (p.18)
Carrot Ribbon, Cinnamon & Halloumi Salad (p. 83)
Cauliflower, Leek & Sage Pie (p. 133)
Chick Pea Stew 3 Ways (p. 129)
Chick Pea "Tuna" Salad (p. 69)
Chocolate Peanut Fudge Cake Bars (p. 185)
Frittata (p. 162)
Paprika Bean Stew (p. 134)
Roasted Carrots with Couscous & Pickled Onion (p. 67)
Roasted Tomatoes & Carrots with Black Beans & Tahini (p. 80)
Smoothie Boxes (p38)
Stir-Fry (p. 174)
Taco (p. 166)
Tahini Carrot Slaw (p. 54)
Zingy Carrot & Rice Noodle Salad (p. 155)

Carrots (roasted)
Frittata (p. 162)
Pizza (p. 158)
Stir-Fry (p. 174)
Taco (p. 166)

Cauliflower
Frittata (p. 162)
Pizza (p. 158)
Squash, Cauliflower & Roasted Garlic Gratin (p. 109)
Warm Roasted Cauliflower & Chick Pea Salad (p. 84)

Celery
Cauliflower, Leek & Sage Pie (p. 133)
Chick Pea Stew 3 Ways (p. 129)
Chick Pea "Tuna" Salad (p. 69)
Frittata (p. 162)
Paprika Bean Stew (p. 134)

Dates
Banana Bread Oatmeal (p. 28)
Chick Pea, Date & Ginger Tagine (p. 94)
Coconut & Cocoa Bites (p. 41)
Cookie Dough Balls (p. 182)
Date, Walnut & Chocolate Oat Cookies (p. 205)
French Toast with Miso–Date Butter (p. 34)
Ginger-pickled Mushrooms with Date Rice (p. 66)
Olive Oil Any-fruit Crumble (p. 196)
Roasted Tomatoes & Carrots with Black Beans & Tahini (p. 80)
Squash & Cinnamon Dip (p. 47)

Eggplants
Chick Pea, Date & Ginger Tagine (p. 94)
Easy Summer Pasta (p. 149)
Eggplant, Pomegranate & Chick Pea Salad (p. 68)
Eggplant, Red Lentil & Coconut Curry (p. 95)
Frittata (p. 162)

MAKEOVERS WITH LEFTOVERS

Plums
Any-fruit Galette (p. 188)
Olive Oil Any-fruit Crumble (p. 196)

Pomegranate
Eggplant, Pomegranate & Chick Pea Salad (p. 68)
Fattoush Dip (p. 51)
Roasted Squash with Brown Rice & Halloumi (p. 92)

Potatoes (raw)
Chile Roasted Potatoes with Granola & Lime–Soy Dressing (p. 60)
Frittata (p. 162)
Lazy Potato Hash (p. 114)
Potato, Caramelized Onion & Thyme Pizza (p. 160)
Potato, Halloumi & Zucchini Bake (p. 105)
Roasted Potato 3 Ways (p. 96)
Squash, Potato & Chile Cakes (p. 76)

Raspberries (fresh or frozen)
Any-fruit Galette (p. 188)
Chocolate Chip, Raspberry & Almond Cake (p. 208)
Donut Oatmeal (p. 29)
Olive Oil Any-fruit Crumble (p. 196)
Peach & Raspberry Crunch Overnight Oats (p. 18)
Smoothie Boxes (p. 38)

Red Onions
Carrot Ribbon, Cinnamon & Halloumi Salad (p. 83)
Chick Pea "Tuna" Salad (p69)
Corn, Peach & Pearl Barley Salad (p. 81)
Eggplant, Red Lentil & Coconut Curry (p. 95)
Frittata (p. 162)
Lime–Chile Corn & Crispy Onions (p. 63)
Quick Pickled Red Onion (p. 223)
Pear, Ricotta & Endive Salad (p. 88)
Potato, Caramelized Onino & Thyme Pizza (p. 160)
Roasted Squash with Brown Rice & Halloumi (p. 92)
Stir-Fry (p.174)
Taco (p. 166)
Warm Roasted Cauliflower & Chick Pea Salad (p. 84)

Rhubarb (fresh or frozen)
Any-fruit Galette (p. 188)
Olive Oil Any-fruit Crumble (p. 196)

Spinach (baby, fresh)
Carrot Ribbon, Cinnamon & Halloumi Salad (p. 83)
Corn, Peach & Pearl Barley Salad (p. 81)
Egg, Spinach & Cherry Tomato Pizza (p. 161)
Frittata (p. 162)
Ginger-pickled Mushrooms with Date Rice (p. 66)
Minestrone (p. 130)
Miso–Garlic–Chile Broccoli with Pasta & Tomato (p. 121)
Pesto, Spinach & Sweet Potato Galette (p. 101)
Roasted Potato 3 Ways (p. 99)
Roasted Squash with Brown Rice & Halloumi (p. 92)
Smoothie Boxes (p. 38)
Spanakopita Quesadillas (p. 78)
Spinach & Feta Balls with Spaghetti (p. 122)
Stir-Fry (p. 174)
Sweet Miso Eggplant & Walnut Salad (p. 62)
Thai Green Curry Pea Soup (p. 143)

Strawberries (fresh or frozen)
Any-fruit Galette (p. 188)
Oat Squares with Stawberry Compote & Coconut (p. 21)
Olive Oil Any-fruit Crumble (p. 196)
Smoothie Boxes (p. 38)

Sweet Potatoes (raw)
Chile Roasted Potatoes with Granola & Lime–Soy Dressing (p. 60)
Fritatta (p. 162)
One-Bowl Chocolate Cake (p. 207)
Pesto, Spinach & Sweet Potato Galette (p. 101)
Roasted Potato 3 Ways (p. 96)
Smoothie Boxes (p. 38)
Spiced Sweet Potato Fries with Smoky Dip (p. 52)
Spiced Sweet Potatoes with Raw Beet & Miso Dressing (p. 53)
Taco (p. 166)

Sweet Potatoes (roasted)
Frittata (p. 162)
Pizza (p. 158)
Taco (p. 166)

Tomatoes (raw)
Cannellini Beans with Balsamic Onions (p. 71)
Chick Pea Stew 3 Ways (p. 129)
Easy Summer Pasta (p. 149)
Fattoush Dip (p. 51)
Halloumi Tacos with Mango Salsa & Rice (p. 169)
Miso–Garlic–Chile Broccoli with Pasta, Tomatoes & Spinach (p. 121)
Pizza (p. 158)
Roasted Potato 3 Ways (p99)
Roasted Tomatoes & Carrots with Black Beans & Tahini (p. 80)
Scrambled Chick Pea Tacos with Peach Salsa (p. 31)
Taco (p. 166)

Tomatoes (sundried)
"Chorizo" Dip (p. 47)
Crispy Tortilla Strips with Corn & Quinoa (p. 125)
Pizza (p. 161)
Roasted Eggplant & Tomato Pesto (p. 225)

Tomatoes (canned, chopped)
Chick Pea, Date & Ginger Tagine (p. 94)
Chick Pea Stew 3 Ways (p. 129)
Curried Tomato–Coconut Soup (p.144)
Lentil & Fennel Ragu (p. 150)

Tomatoes (roasted)
Taco (p.166)

Tuscan kale (cavolo nero)
Creamy Tuscan Kale, Leek & Pea Pasta (p. 147)
Lazy Potato Hash (p. 114)
Minestrone (p. 130)
Pizza (p. 158)
Rice Bowl with Greens & Cilantro–Coconut Dressing (p. 117)
Roasted Potato 3 Ways (p. 98)
Spanakopita Quesadilla (p. 78)
Stir-Fry (p. 174)
Taco (p. 166)

MAKEOVERS WITH LEFTOVERS

Nut Butter
Banana Bread Oatmeal (p. 28)
Banana Chocolate Chip Blondies (p. 195)
Banoffee Peanut Bites (p. 40)
Charred Lettuce with Baked Tofu & Peanut Dressing (p. 75)
Chocolate Peanut Fudge Cake Bars (p. 185)
Cookie Dough Balls (p. 182)
Double Chocolate Cookies (p. 192)
Microwave Blueberry Oat "Muffin" (p. 26)
Single Serve Chocolate Chip Cookies (p. 183)
Smoothie Boxes (p. 38)

Pesto
Lazy Potato Hash (p. 114)
Pesto, Spinach & Sweet Potato Galette (p. 101)
Pizza (p. 158)
Ricotta Gnocchi with Pesto & Zuccchini (p. 138)
Roasted Carrots with Couscous & Pickled Onion (p. 67)

Tahini
Charred Lettuce with Baked Tofu & Peanut Dressing (p. 75)
Crispy Broccoli & Barley Bowl with Tahini Dressing (p. 113)
Eggplant, Pomegranate & Chick Pea Salad (p. 68)
Lentil & Yogurt Pita Dip (p. 106)
Pea Hummus (p. 46)
Roasted Squash with Brown Rice & Halloumi (p. 92)
Roasted Tomatoes & Carrots with Black Beans & Tahini (p. 80)
Smoothie Boxes (p. 38)
Spiced Sweet Potato Fries with Smoky Dip (p. 52)
Tahini Carrot Slaw (p. 54)

Thai Green Curry Paste
Stir-Fry (p. 174)
Thai Green Curry Pea Soup (p. 143)

HERBS & AROMATICS

Basil
Basil & Arugula Pesto (p. 224)
Cannellini Beans with Balsamic Onions (p. 71)
Corn, Peach & Pearl Barley Salad (p. 81)
Halloumi & Mango Noodle Salad (p. 153)
Miso–Garlic–Chile Broccoli with Pasta, Tomatoes & Spinach (p. 121)
One-Pan Creamy Pasta with Asparagus, Lemon & Basil (p. 145)
Orange, Fennel, Olive & Pearl Barley Stew (p. 154)
Peas, Potato & Mozzarella Frittata (p. 164)
Pesto Crumb Zucchini with Weeknight Focaccia (p. 110)
Pizza (p. 161)
Potato, Halloumi & Zucchini Bake (p. 105)
Ricotta Gnocchi with Pesto & Zuccchini (p. 138)
Roasted Potato 3 Ways (p. 99)
Scrambled Egg, Pea, Onion & Basil Tacos (p. 173)
Stir-Fry (p. 174)
Zuccchini & Garlic Quesadilla (p. 78)

Chile
Charred Lettuce with Firm Tofu & Peanut Dressing (p. 75)
Chile Roasted Potatoes with Granola & Lime–Soy Dressing (p. 60)
Eggplant, Pomegranate & Chick Pea Salad (p. 68)
Lime–Chile Corn & Crispy Onions (p. 63)
Miso–Garlic–Chile Broccoli (p. 118)
Paprika Bean Stew (p. 134)
Pizza (p. 161)
Squash, Potato & Chile Cakes (p. 76)
Stir-Fry (p. 174)
Zingy Carrot & Rice Noodle Salad (p. 155)

Cilantro
Blitzed Corn, Cilantro & Scallion Pizza (p.160)
Carrot Ribbon, Cinnamon & Halloumi Salad (p. 83)
Chick Pea "Tuna" Salad (p. 69)
Crispy Broccoli & Barley Bowl with Tahini Dressing (p. 113)
Curried Tomato–Coconut Soup (p. 144)

Falafel Smash (p. 56)
Fattoush Dip (p. 51)
Halloumi & Mango Noodle Salad (p. 153)
Miso–Garic–Chile Broccoli with Onion, Cumin & Beans (p. 121)
Miso Mango Slaw (p. 55)
Rice Bowl with Greens & Cilantro–Coconut Dressing (p. 117)
Roasted Potato 3 Ways (p. 99)
Roasted Squash with Brown Rice & Halloumi (p. 92)
Roasted Tomatoes & Carrots with Black Beans & Tahini (p. 80)
Shakshouka (p. 131)
Stir-Fry (p. 174)
Taco (p. 166)
Tahini Carrot Slaw (p. 54)
Thai Green Curry Paste (p. 221)
Thai Green Curry Pea Soup (p. 143)
Zingy Carrot & Rice Noodle Salad (p. 155)

Mint
Eggplant, Pomegranate & Chick Pea Salad (p. 68)
Fattoush Dip (p. 51)
Lentil & Yogurt Pita Dip (p. 106)
Roasted Beet, Cumin & Crispy Chick Peas (p. 65)
Roasted Tomatoes & Carrots with Black Beans & Tahini (p. 80)
Stir-Fry (p. 174)
Taco (p. 166)

Sage
Beet, Hazelnut & Sage Salad (p. 72)
Cauliflower, Leek & Sage Pie (p. 133)
Pasta with Mushrooms, Crispy Sage & Garlic Bread Crumbs (p. 141)
Pizza (p. 161)

Scallions
Eggplant, Red Lentil & Coconut Curry (p. 95)
Cannellini Bean & Apple Salad (p. 87)
Charred Lettuce with Baked Tofu & Peanut Dressing (p. 75)
Chile Roasted Potatoes with Granola & Lime–Soy Dressing (p. 60)
"Chorizo" Dip & Red Bell Pepper Frittata (p. 165)

MENU PLANS

For 2 people

Here is an example of a menu plan and shopping list based on recipes from this book. It shows how you can prepare ingredients on the weekend to use throughout the week. It also shows how to double up on ingredients when you cook them during the week so that you can use them in other meals (which is especially useful when it comes to prepping lunchboxes). If you have a well-stocked pantry, it shouldn't be too much hassle to buy the fresh ingredients needed for a weekly shop and use the same ingredient a few times without getting bored!

SHOPPING LIST

FRESH INGREDIENTS

large bag of carrots
1 head of celery
pot of plain yogurt
2 oranges
bag of lemons
small bag of pea shoots
10 apples
2 large bunches of cilantro
6 small sweet potatoes
8oz chunk of feta cheese
small bag of mixed salad
    greens
2 heads of broccoli
8 eggs
small bag of frozen petite
    peas or peas

milk
unsalted butter
    (if making the Miso–Date
    Butter for the French toast)
chile (if not using crushed
    red pepper)
bunch of scallions
7oz cherry tomatoes
small bunch of mint
1 bell pepper
bunch of Tuscan kale
    (cavolo nero)
small bunch of basil
small Parmesan wedge

PANTRY INGREDIENTS

SPICES
Ground cinnamon, ginger, cumin, coriander, and turmeric, smoked paprika, crushed red pepper, green cardamom, fennel seeds, mixed dried herbs, salt

GRAINS/LEGUMES/STARCH
Dried chick peas (garbanzo beans) or 3 x (15oz) cans chick peas, dried Puy or green lentils, brown rice, whole-wheat flour, all-purpose flour, oats, pasta (orzo or another small pasta shape)

AROMATICS
Red onions, garlic, ginger root

NUTS & NUT BUTTERS
Tahini, nut butter, creamed coconut (or coconut milk), sesame seeds, dry unsweetened shredded coconut

"BAKING" INGREDIENTS
Instant dry yeast, raisins, dates, sugar, honey

OTHER
Soy sauce, Worcestershire sauce (optional), vegetable bouillon cubes, apple cider vinegar, balsamic vinegar, 1 (14½oz) can diced tomatoes

Weekend

Roast 6 small sweet potatoes, peeled and cubed, in 2 tablespoons olive oil and a pinch of salt, in an oven preheated to 350°F for 30 to 40 minutes. Flip halfway through.

Soak 1½ cups dried chick peas (garbanzo beans), then drain and cook (see cooking table on page 11)—you need 4⅓ cups chick peas. Or buy 3 (15oz) cans of chick peas.

Cook green or Puy lentils—use 2 cups dried lentils (you should get 4½ cups cooked lentils). See cooking table on page 11.

Make a double batch of Quick Pickled Red Onion (see page 223)

Mix up a batch of whole-wheat pita or flatbread dough (see page 215) and bake. Store at room temperature in an airtight container or freeze; thaw in the toaster as needed. Alternatively, buy 6 whole-wheat pita breads.

Prep a double batch of Carrot Cake Overnight Oats (see page 18).

Prep lunch for tomorrow.

Monday

BREAKFAST Carrot Cake Overnight Oats (see page 18).

LUNCH 2 baked pitas (see page 215) + 1 recipe for Chick Pea "Tuna" Salad (see page 69).

DINNER Make Paprika Bean Stew (see page 134). Replace the beans with the precooked chick peas (garbanzo beans) + 2 pita breads. Prep lunch for tomorrow. Make extra Tahini Dressing (see page 226) so that you have enough for lunch and dinner.

Tuesday

BREAKFAST Carrot Cake Overnight Oats (see page 18).

LUNCH 1½ cups cooked lentils + 2 carrots, peeled into ribbons + 1 recipe for Tahini Dressing (see page 226) + 1 tablespoon sesame seeds + handful of chopped cilantro + 1 diced apple.

DINNER Roasted Squash with Brown Rice, Halloumi & Tahini Dressing (see page 92). Replace the squash with roasted sweet potato and use raisins instead of pomegranate. Use pea shoots and mixed salad greens instead of spinach and use feta cheese instead of halloumi. Bake Carrot Breakfast Bread (see page 23).

Prep lunch for tomorrow.

Wednesday

BREAKFAST Carrot Breakfast Bread (see page 23) with nut butter + an apple each.

LUNCH 2 baked pita breads (see page 215) + recipe for Falafel Smash (see page 56).

DINNER Rice bowl with Greens & Cilantro–Coconut Dressing (see page 117). Cook extra broccoli and peas and make extra dressing for lunch tomorrow. Prep lunch for tomorrow.

Thursday

BREAKFAST Carrot Breakfast Bread (see page 23) with nut butter + an apple each.

LUNCH 1½ cups cooked lentils + 1 recipe for Cilantro–Coconut Dressing (see page 117) + some Quick Pickled Red Onion (see page 223) + handful of mixed salad greens + the extra cooked peas and broccoli from dinner.

DINNER Orzo with Squash, Chile, Lemon & Peas (see page 126). Replace the squash with roasted sweet potato.

Friday

BREAKFAST Carrot Breakfast Bread (see page 23) with nut butter + an apple each.

LUNCH 1½ cups cooked lentils + ⅓ cup crumbled feta + handful of pea shoots + 2 small roasted, cubed sweet potatoes + 1 recipe for Tahini Dressing (see page 226) + handful of raisins.

DINNER Frittata template (see page 162)—use up leftover ingredients.

Saturday

BREAKFAST Use the remaining Carrot Breakfast Bread to make French toast with Miso–Date Butter (see page 34).

LUNCH Roasted Tomatoes & Carrots with Black Beans & Tahini (see page 80). Use chick peas (garbanzo beans) instead of black beans.

DINNER Lentil & Fennel Ragu (see page 150). Use celery instead of fennel and omit the walnuts. Eat with the rest of the dried pasta (the orzo or small pasta shapes) instead of tagliatelle.

INDEX

ACKNOWLEDGMENTS

READERS! Over the years of following my food journey along on my blog and Instagram, you have been my biggest drive and source of creative ideas. It's an honor to have you reading and making my recipes, and it makes me so happy to have your encouragement.

MOM, DAD, JASPER As per usual, thank you for providing me with endless inspiration, support, and love. It's cliché to say, but I know I wouldn't have been able to make this cookbook without you all there.

ROBERT I think you really are my number one fan and I honestly couldn't be more glad. You have always egged me on and kept me going throughout my whole career.

ANDY I couldn't have asked for a kinder, more supportive human being to know. Thank you for not getting sick of me forcing food upon you and thanks for all the help with the washing the dishes!

MARTINE (AND MIMI) Without you ladies to guide me through this, there wouldn't have been a book. Thank you for all the hard work you put in to helping me bring my initial ideas to a fully formed concept.

ALISON, ELLA, JULIETTE Your belief in my vision for the book made this whole process so lovely! I'm so pleased with how it all came together and, with your help, became an actual real-life book.

CAS, SAM, HAMISH, ALEX, ANNA, JAKE, ISAAC You all know that in some way you inspired some of the recipes in this book! Especially you, Anna, I'm already missing our chef/sous-chef days.

BEA, RHIANNON, SARAH You're always there for me. You always make me laugh and fill my life with happiness. Oh, and you're always willing to be force-fed whatever food I've been testing!

MAX, ELLIE AND PORTIA You ladies kept me motivated to keep on cooking and photographing for a whole month, even on days when I was seriously lacking motivation. You were all awesome and I can't thank you enough for all the help!

RECIPE TESTERS My lovely, lovely recipe testers! I'm so pleased you were able to get involved with the book-writing process and give me honest recipe feedback. Thanks for your generosity in helping this gal out! Shout out to Clare Robinson, Sarah Duignan, Ela , Shirl, Myrsini, Maggie Kolasky, Susan Barrie, Maggie McKune, Christine Monaghan, Jessica Chan, Kelsey Blodgett, Shoshana Snider, Jasmine Delves, Melissa Golubski, Alexandra Inchenko, Sarah Lundqvist, Katja Haudenhuyse, Alyssa Vratsanos, Lisa Maxwell, Maureen Bilyeu, Winnie Reeves, Kate Loannou, Lauren O'Sullivan, Lizzie Henderson, Indira Shinn Rees, Rebecca Webber, Zara Britton-Purhonen, Samira Zippel, Sian Poulton, Caroline Hunt, Emilia Luis, Daisy Nutting, Sarah Cutter, Injy Rawlings, Jennifer Buggica, Martino Mandelli, Dana Gerard, Danielle Deskins, Katie Wesolek, Kelsey Tenney, Isa Ouwehand, Rachel Chen, Louise Hadley, Lucia Hua, Jaqui Tuthill, Sarah Nelson, Eva Donlon, Anne-Katherine Schirlitz, Elise Akin, Marie-Eve, Marie Nyberg, Ubavi Nesta, Brady Johnson, Tjitske Boersma, Lucie Costes, Katrin Erb, Laura Valli, Beth Kerr, Yvonne Barber, Emily Jelassi, Cori Moen, Aislinn Hyde, Linnea Sansqvist, Carina Mancione, and Hanna Hoskins.

IZY HOSSACK is a 21-year-old blogger and Instagram sensation, and her hit blog izyhossack.com is the go-to place for delicious sweet and savory recipes on both sides of the Atlantic. She has an impressive fan base, with more than 220,000 followers on Instagram.

Much of Izy's food is inspired by her Italian-American heritage. Many of her recipes are gluten free and/or vegan. Izy collaborates with many different publications and brands including JamieOliver.com, IKEA, Cuisinart UK, Green & Black's, Romeo Gelato, theKitchn.com, Food52.com, Miss Vogue, and SORTED to name a few. Izy has appeared on Channel 4's 'Daily Brunch' and has made videos for Waitrose TV, Endemol Shine's new channel Wild Dish, and for Tesco Real Food. *The London Times Magazine* recently named Izy as one of the world's most followed foodies and she has been featured in British *Vogue*.

Her first cookbook *Top With Cinnamon* was published by Hardie Grant in the UK and Rizzoli in the US in Autumn 2014, and reissued in paperback in spring 2016 as *Everyday Delicious*. As well as being a food writer, Izy is a photographer and food stylist, and styled and photographed all the food for her books herself. Izy is studying Food Science and Nutrition at Leeds University in England.